Praise for

*La Bella Lingua*

"*La Bella Lingua* will keep you turning pages, nodding along in agreement, laughing, even learning ... And Dianne's writing? A sheer pleasure. Truly. *La Bella Lingua* is a must for any lover of the Italian language."  —Michele Fabio, www.bleedingespresso.com

"To say Dianne's journey and her book were captivating would be an understatement. The uniqueness of her story, the vibrant prose contained within this non-fiction book, and her tales of some of her mishaps as she learned to speak Italian, kept me turning the pages, eager to learn more. Her book honors Italy and Italians everywhere. A highly recommended read—but beware—it will make you want to vacation there yourself. Brava, Dianne! Encore!"
  —Mirella Patzer, www.bestofitaly.blogspot.com

"*La Bella Lingua* is the kind of book you want to savor slowly, like a small piece of fine chocolate melting on your tongue ... In Dianne's expert hands a grammar lesson becomes an ambrosial experience, and by drawing on the riches of Italian art, history, cooking, literature, film, customs, and romance (as well as countless anecdotes from her travels and research), Hales tempts us to fall as madly and deeply in love with Italian as she has."
  —Michelle Ward, the Sweet Life blog at www.lolalina.com

"Hales' unrestrained joy of all things Italian jumps off each and every page as the author traces the history of modern Italian from its multiple origins in the dialects of the country. As we follow the historical journey of Italy's linguistic twists and turns throughout the centuries, Hales interjects humorous anecdotes and folk tales. Around each ccorner of her narrative lies another surprising jewel of a discovery ... A wonderful journey of all things Italian rolled up in an enjoyable history lesson. Don't be a *brutta figura!* Go now and buy it!"  —*ComUNICO,* the national UNICO newsletter

"Every Italian family should own *La Bella Lingua*."
—Vito Finizio, president, Amici della Lingua Italiana

"A praiseworthy feature of *La Bella Lingua* is the way Hales peppers her narrative with hundreds of Italian words, idioms, and figures of speech—all chosen with gusto and brio and clearly translated into English—to introduce readers to the sonic and semantic seraglio that is the Italian language. A separate chapter on 'Irreverent Italian' highlights *la parolaccia,* the earthy lexicon of invective and jocular sensuality that contemporary Italians imbibe with their mother's milk but foreign students of Italian rarely get to savor."
—Peter D'Epiro and Mary Desmond Pinkowish, authors of *Sprezzatura: 50 Ways Italian Genius Shaped the World*

"An impassioned student, Dianne Hales takes us along on her delightful pilgrimage to the speaking heart of Italy. The rhythmic beat she comes to feel and love teaches her how to live, in beautiful and idiomatic Italian, 'a language as rich in flavors and varieties as Italian cooking.' The reading pilgrim's reward is this delicious feast of a book, a strong mix of cultural and spoken treasure."
—Susan Cahill, author of *Desiring Italy* and *The Smiles of Rome*

"Dianne Hales is just about pitch perfect as she weaves the engaging story of her *innamoramento* with Italian, hitting the high notes of Italian culture . . . a lovely, touching tribute to the many fine civilizing gifts that Italy has shared with the world. Any smart traveler to Italy would want to read *La Bella Lingua.* It's not only readable and engaging but informative about things not easily found in guidebooks and common tourist materials."
—Julia Conaway Bondanella and Peter Bondanella, authors and editors of *The Italian Renaissance Reader,* *Italian Cinema,* and the *Cassell Dictionary of Italian Literature*

"*l'ho letta 'tutta d'un fiato,'* degustandola come un ottimo bicchiere di Chianti! Ho colto in ogni parola, espressione, frase, riferimento, traduzione, interpretazione ... il suo grandissimo 'innamoramento' e 'amore' per la lingua italiana." (I read it all in one breath, savoring it like an excellent glass of Chianti! I grasped in every word, expression, phrase, reference, tradition, interpretation ... your very great infatuation and love for the Italian language.)

—*Professor Pasquale Fantasia, Ufficio Scuola Consolato d'Italia, Detroit*

"Ms. Hales captures the real essence of not only the language, but the culture of 'il bel paese' ... She stuffs her pages with the history of the language and its people. She explores the very foundations of modern Western culture through the contributions of great Italians and their culture throughout history ... Ms. Hales' style is never preachy, never overtly reverent. She is an experienced journalist who takes the reader on a voyage of discovery and along the way she shares her admiration, occasional frustration, and always her humor. I highly recommend this book. It is a great summer read and would even be useful in the classroom. I think teachers of the language and anyone who shares the author's love of Italian will enjoy this book."

—Alfred J. Valentini, adjunct professor of Italian at Utica College, vice president/treasurer of Italian Teachers of Central New York

La Bella Lingua

*Broadway Books*

New York

# La Bella Lingua

MY LOVE AFFAIR WITH
ITALIAN, THE WORLD'S
MOST ENCHANTING LANGUAGE

Dianne Hales

BROADWAY

Copyright © 2009 by Dianne Hales

Published in the United States by Broadway Books, an imprint of
the Crown Publishing Group, a division of Random House, Inc., New York.
www.crownpublishing.com

BROADWAY BOOKS and the Broadway Books colophon are trademarks of
Random House, Inc.

Originally published in hardcover in the United States by Broadway Books,
a division of Random House, Inc., New York, in 2009.

Quotations from the Web edition of Dante's *Divine Comedy* from
www.italianstudies.org/comedy/index.htm. Used by permission of Mario
Mignone, director, Center for Italian Studies, State University of New York at
Stony Brook.

*The Penguin Book of Italian Verse*, edited by George R. Kay (Penguin Books 1958,
revised edition 1965) copyright © George Kay, 1958, 1965. Used by permission of
Penguin Group (UK).

From *Sprezzatura: 50 Ways Italian Genius Shaped the World* by Peter D'Epiro and
Mary Desmond Pinkowish, copyright © 2001 by Peter D'Epiro and Mary
Desmond Pinkowish. Used by permission of Anchor Books, a division of
Random House, Inc.

The author also wishes to acknowledge and thank Susan Rhoads for making
many out-of-print Italian works, including Francesco Redi's poem "Bacchus in
Tuscany," available online at www.elfinspell.com.

Library of Congress Cataloging-in-Publication Data
Hales, Dianne
La Bella Lingua : my love affair with Italian, the world's most enchanting
language / Dianne Hales.
Includes bibliographical references.
1. Italian language—Social aspects 2. Language and culture—Italy. I. Title.
PC1074.75.H35 2009
450—dc22
2008023006

ISBN 978-0-7679-2770-3

Design by Maria Carella
Title page illustration by Rayne Beaudoin

PRINTED IN THE UNITED STATES OF AMERICA

10 9 8 7 6 5 4 3 2 1

First Paperback Edition

*A tutti gli italiani che hanno condiviso la loro lingua—*
*e la loro vita—con me*

To all the Italians who have shared their
language—and their life—with me

*Il cor di tutte*
*Cose alfin sente sazietà, del sonno,*
*Della danza, del canto e dell'amore,*
*Piacer più cari che il parlar di lingua,*
*Ma sazietà di lingua il cor non sente.*

Of all things, the heart grows sated—
Of sleep, of love, of sweet song, and merry
  dance—
Things which give more pleasure than the
  tongue does in speech,
And yet of the tongue the heart is never sated.

GIACOMO LEOPARDI, *1798–1837*
Italian poet, essayist, and philosopher

# Contents

# Acknowledgments

*Grazie. Grazie tanto. Grazie mille. Vi ringrazio.*

I wish there were more ways to say thank you to the many, many people who helped me with *La Bella Lingua*.

I am most grateful to my collaborator, tutor, and coach, Alessandra Cattani, *proprio un tesoro*. I wouldn't have been able to pull off this *bella sfida* (lovely challenge) without her creativity, vast knowledge, endless patience, and good humor. Our mutual friend Francesca Gaspari, director of San Francisco's ItaLingua Institute, first ignited my passion for Italian with her vivacious zest for her native tongue. I send *un abbraccio forte* to Cristina Romanelli of the Società Dante Alighieri in Florence, who brought the history of Italian to life for me.

Many distinguished champions of the language were extremely generous with their knowledge and time. I was honored to meet and interview Francesco Sabatini of L'Accademia della Crusca, Ambassador Bruno Bottai of the Società Dante Alighieri (La Dante), and Luca Serianni of La Sapienza in Rome. I became a fan of Valeria della Valle and Giuseppe Patota after reading their lucid books on Italian's history and usage, but my admiration has soared since meeting them. I truly consider myself their humble *allieva* (pupil), and I thank Valeria for the very special gift of her friendship. I am particularly indebted to the amiable Lucilla Pizzolli of La Dante, who provided books, contacts, explanations, and enthusiasm. I also want to thank Alessandro Masi and Raffaella Fiorani of La Dante and Delia Ragionieri and Paolo Belardinelli of La Crusca.

Many others served as my "faculty" in Florence, including Contessa Maria Vittoria Rimbotti, Enrico Paoletti of the local Società Dante Alighieri, Professors Ernestina Pellegrina and Massimo Fanfani of the University of Florence, Philip Taylor of Polimoda Institute, Pamela Pucci of the Florence tourism office, and Ignazio Leone of Libri d'Arte. A heartfelt *grazie* to Rita, Antonella, Annalisa, Daniel, and the entire staff at Palazzo Magnani Feroni, who made me feel *a mio agio* in Florence.

I am thankful to Ludovica Sebregondi and Maestro Mario Ruffini for everything they taught me about art and opera, but most of all for the delight of their company and the joy of their friendship. The same holds true for Maestro Maurizio Barbacini and his wife, Antonella. In San Francisco, Kip Cranna of the San Francisco Opera and Luciano Chessa further enhanced my musical education.

I learned to appreciate the language of Italian cinema with the help of Gianfranco Angelucci, Sergio Raffaeli, Maurizio di Rienzo, Tullio Kezich, and the helpful staff at Rome's Casa del Cinema. I owe much of my knowledge of Italian cuisine to Guido Tommasi of Guido Tommasi Editore; Gabriella Ganugi of Apicius, the Culinary Institute of Florence; Luca and Francesco Bracali of the fabulous Ristorante Bracali in Ghirlanda Massa Marittima; poet and food historian Luigi Ballerini; and Leonardo Fasulo of Osteria Fasulo in Davis,

California, whose food makes us feel that we're eating in Italy. I am grateful to several women, among them Giulia Pirovano of the Camera Nazionale della Moda Italiana, Anna Fendi, and Elisa Roggiolani, and to David Mohammadi of San Francisco's Emporio Armani for all they've taught me about Italian style.

Beppe Severgnini's wit and insight deepened my appreciation of Italian and its speakers. The effervescent actor and *dantista* Roberto Benigni opened my eyes to an entirely new way of appreciating Dante. Vito Tartamella taught me more than I ever thought I'd want to know about Italian's *parolaccia* or bad language. Alberta Campitelli of Rome's office of Beni Culturali provided an enchanting insider's view of the city's historic villas. Aldo Colonetti of the Istituto Europeo di Design greatly broadened my understanding of Italian design. I thank Raffaele Simone for the gift of his book and his perspective and Maurizio Borghi for introducing me to the works of Niccolò Tommaseo. I add *un bacio* to Crescenzo, Andrea, and Simone D'Ambrosio, whose much-missed father taught me some of my earliest Italian phrases.

My research in the United States began at the Istituto Italiano di Cultura di San Francisco, where I was fortunate to find Annamaria Lelli, Valeria Rumori, and the aptly named Robin Treasure. Elisabetta Nelsen of San Francisco State University was a rich source of ideas and insights. Carol Field, both through our talks and her books, provided a wealth of information on Italian cooking and cooks.

I also thank Stefania Scotti, my conversation and literature teacher for several years, for preparing me for my first research trip to Italy and her husband, Federico Rampini, for helping me identify sources. My thanks also go to my other Italian teachers, including Lorenza Graziosi, Valeria Furino, and Tony Sottile. Among others in the Bay Area who contributed to my research are Carla Falaschi; Lido Cantarutti of the Marin Italian Film Festival; Caterina Feucht, Armando di Carlo, and Steven Botterill of the University of California, Berkeley; Carla Melchior; Paola Sensi-Isolani of St. Mary's College; chef Daniel Scherotter of Palio d'Asti restaurant in San Francisco; and Sandow Birk and Marcus Sanders, coauthors of an illustrated contemporary version of the *Divine Comedy. Grazie,* also, to Judith Greber and the wonderful women of her writing group, who encouraged me to think—and write—outside the box.

The books and translations of Julia Conaway Bondanella and Peter Bondanella of the University of Indiana were invaluable resources, and I was even more appreciative of the mini-tutorial they gave me in Italian literature, history, and cinema. I also am grateful for the assistance of Peter D'Epiro and Mary Desmond Pinkowish, authors of *Sprezzatura*; Beverly Kahn and Aldo Belardo of Pace University; Valerie Steele of the Museum of the Fashion Institute of Technology; Paul Salerni of Lehigh University; and Traci Timmons of the Seattle Art Museum.

Italian translates "friendship" as *amicizia*, but I learned its true meaning from Roberto and Carla Serafini, who served as my first Italian instructors and taught me so much about language, food, history, and their beloved Rome. Other dear friends, Andrea Fasola Bologna and his son, Lorenzo, modern reincarnations of true Renaissance men, welcomed my family into their magnificent home and their lives. I send *baci e abbracci* (kisses and hugs) to *la mia cara amica* Cinzia Fanciulli, another of my guides into Italian culture, and her ever-charming husband, Riccardo Mazurek. I am grateful to another Italian friend, Narriman Shahrokh, for her careful reading of the final manuscript.

I wrote the proposal and first draft of *La Bella Lingua* in a very special place called L'Ercolana. We thank the most gracious Alain and Cristina Camu for sharing their home with us. I add an affectionate *grazie* to Giustina, Maria-Augusta, and Ubaldo, our extended family in Porto Ercole, and to Ferruccio and Erasmo of F-Marine, delightful companions on land and sea.

*La Bella Lingua* might have forever remained a dream if not for the encouragement and expertise of another *tesoro*, my wonderful agent and friend, Joy Harris. It was pleasure indeed to work again with my *gentilissima* editor Jennifer Josephy, who shares my enthusiasm for all things Italian and who was absolutely critical in helping me find the voice for *La Bella Lingua.* I thank Annie Chagnot for all her help and send *complimenti* to copyeditor Alison Miller, designer Maria Carella, and production editor Ada Yonenaka.

My deepest appreciation, as always, goes to my *carissimi*, my dearest Bob and Julia, who never expected to end up with an Italian wife and mother. Sharing this adventure with *Roberto e Giulia* has made it all the more fulfilling and fun.

*A tutti, grazie di cuore.*

☀

**A note on publication of the paperback edition**: Since publication of *La Bella Lingua*, many *sostenitori* (supporters) have contributed to its success. I am profoundly grateful to former ambassador Giovanni Castellaneta, Consul General Fabrizio Marcelli, Consul General Francesco Talò, Marco Salardi, Silvia Bascelli, Alfio Rossa, Luigi de Sanctis, Pasquale Fantasia, Amelia Carpenito Antonucci, Berardo Paradiso, Ilaria Costa, Martin Stiglio, and Adriana Frisenna.

I owe a special thanks to Vito Finizio, Bill Cerruti, John Price,

Franca Riccardi, Cathy Vignale, Phyllis Pizzolato, Paul Ferrari, Louis Napoli, Kathleen Strozza, Beverly Mele Occulto, Michele Fabio, Gina Chinchilla, Gerardo Rodriguez, Paola Bagnatori, and Kathy McCabe. I'd like to express my appreciation to the independent bookstores that have hosted readings of *La Bella Lingua*, including Book Passage in Corte Madera, Mrs. Dalloway's in Berkeley, and the Gallery Bookshop in Mendocino.

I would also like to thank the LBL "team" at Broadway Books, who adopted my orphaned book and championed it as their own. To Charles Conrad, Jennifer Robbins, Ellen Folan, and Jenna Ciongoli, *grazie mille!*

## AUTHOR'S NOTE

I am neither a linguist nor a scholar, but throughout *La Bella Lingua*, I have tried to use the most widely accepted forms of Italian spelling and punctuation. If I have committed any *strafalcioni*, the Italian word for blatant linguistic blunders, I apologize. The fault is entirely mine. *La colpa è solo mia.*

*La Bella Lingua*

# Introduction: My Italian Brain and How It Grew

"LEARNING A NEW LANGUAGE IS LIKE GROWING a new head," a European friend told me long ago. "You see with new eyes, hear with new ears, speak with a new tongue." Neuroimaging has proved her right: the mental gymnastics of groping for even the simplest words in a different language ignites brand-new clusters of neurons and synapses. And so I, lacking a single drop of Italian blood, can nonetheless claim something utterly, wholly, irrevocably Italian as my own: the language hot spots that have been growing steadily deep within my brain for more than a quarter-century.

Never did I—a sensible woman of sturdy Polish peasant stock—expect to become madly, gladly, giddily besotted with the world's most luscious language. But when I traveled through

Italy on a mostly mute maiden voyage, Italians had talked constantly to, at, and around me. Yearning for a few words to offer in return, I decided to study their language.

My first teacher was an intense young woman from the Abruzzi who had recently moved with her new American husband to San Francisco. She insisted that I repeat an Italian sentence that translated into "I am going into the corridor to smoke a cigarette."

"But I don't smoke," I objected.

"Italians smoke," she countered. *"Signora, questa frase è importante."*

"It's not important to me," I persisted. "I am never, ever going into a corridor in Italy to smoke."

She sighed. I changed the subject and asked her what she missed most about Italy. *"La piazza,"* she said as wistfully as if it were the name of a loved one left behind. After a few seconds, she added, *"La domenica."*

"Sundays?"

"When you go to Mamma's." She began to sob. Shortly thereafter she packed up and returned to Italy.

My next teacher, an aspiring actress who taught Italian to local children, displayed picture books of baby ducks and puppies. When I balked at learning *ninnananne* (lullabies), she handed me off to her father, who taught Italian at the local community college. Tony, a trim Neapolitan who biked over the hills to my home, would break into arias, dropping to one knee to serenade me with *"E lucevan le stelle"* and *"Che gelida manina."* One day, arriving in a fierce rainstorm, he shook himself dry on the doormat and unforgettably taught me a new word by proclaiming himself *inzuppato*—literally, "dunked in the soup."

Soon I was a goner, inebriated with Italian's sounds, lovesick for its phrases. My next classroom was a Sausalito bungalow festooned with so many cherubs and hearts that I thought of its voluptuous owner as *la mia Valentina*. A *Romana* (and professional chef) of indeterminate age with henna hair and a full figure Italians might describe as *abbondante*, she served me delectable *merende* (snacks) and juicy tales of long-ago lovers.

"*Aspetta!*" ("Wait!"), Valentina would prompt as she eased the cork from a bottle of *prosecco* and then sighed at the sound of its pop. "*Viene!*" ("She comes!") From her I learned my first smattering of *parolacce*, or naughty words, as well as slang for various anatomical parts. I have never looked at a fig in the same way since.

At the ItaLingua Institute, a warm and welcoming *pezzo d'Italia* (piece of Italy) in the Bay Area, I took seminars on opera, art, manners, poetry, architecture, wine, and cinema. In grammar workshops with its native-born teachers, I paddled through Italian's treacherous tenses, trying to navigate the confounding conditional and the slippery subjunctive. With even greater effort I struggled to corral its impish pronouns, which flit from the front to the back of sentences, disappear entirely, or latch on to verbs like fleas to a cat's ear.

Crossing the line from tourist to scholar, I decided I was ready to study in Italy. However, the first teacher I had arranged to study with developed a leg cramp while swimming off the Amalfi coast. A Sicilian prince sailing nearby swept her onto his private yacht—and then into a *castello* by the sea. She never again gave lessons—or, for all I know, decamped from her royal digs. I had better luck at a private school in a Renaissance villa in Assisi, where a distinguished professor, Angelo Chiuchiù, headed a faculty of striking young women (who did indeed excuse themselves to smoke cigarettes in the corridor).

Although my basic grammar skills earned an encouraging "*Complimenti!,*" *il professore* grimaced at my accent. "*Non è bello,*" he said, recounting an anecdote about Richard Strauss, who told an orchestra that they were playing all the right notes yet not making music. I must have looked crestfallen, for he hastened to assure me that this was "*un problemino,*" a teeny-tiny problem. All that I had to do was talk with more Italians.

Returning to Italy every year since then, I improved my Italian in the most tried-and-true way: by tripping over my tongue and learning from my mistakes. At Camponeschi, our favorite restaurant in Rome, the waiters giggled when they overheard me describe the wonderful view from our apartment terrace of the roofs of Rome. Instead of the masculine *tetti* (roofs, pronounced tet-tee), I had used the feminine slang *tette* (tits, pronounced tet-tay).

After other embarrassing slips, I learned to hold double consonants for three beats to avoid saying "*ano*" (anus—and its cruder forms) instead of "*anno*" (year). On a boat we chartered to Sardinia I invited our co-captains Ferruccio and Erasmo (an Italian George Clooney look-alike) to accompany us to dinner in Porto Rotondo because after so much time together I feared that my husband was getting bored—except I said that he was getting boring. (It made for an interesting three days at sea.)

Somewhere en route to fluency, I turned into *Diana*, pronounced Dee-ahn-aah, and entered a parallel universe where I wear my heels higher and my necklines lower, dance barefoot under the Tuscan moon, and swim in island coves so blue that the Italians say the color twice: *azzurro-azzurro*. Best of all, I have realized how right the British author E. M. Forster was when he urged visitors to drop "that awful tourist idea that Italy's only a museum of antiquities and art." "Love and understand the Italians," he urged, "for the people are more marvelous than the land." Indeed they are—and I have had the good fortune both to love and understand some of them and to be loved and understood in return.

In our stays at historic Monte Vibiano Vecchio, which produces outstanding Umbrian wines and olive oil, Lina, our adopted *nonna* (grandmother), showed me and my daughter, Julia, whom she dubbed her *coccolona* (cuddly one), how to *impastare* our hands with dough and roll *pici*, the local pasta, to cook on the cantankerous old stove she calls *la bestia*. Its gracious owners, Andrea and Lorenzo Fasola Bologna, taught us not just the names but the tastes of wines made with Sangiovese, Syrah, Sagrantino, Merlot, and Montepulciano grapes.

My friend Carla Nutti, a va-va-voom gorgeous blonde, instructed me in how to bargain with vendors at the Sunday flea market on the Tiber and how to negotiate Rome's slippery cobblestones in heels (you shift your weight to the ball of the foot as if tiptoeing). On shimmering Sunday afternoons, she and I would sit on a shady terrace as she read me poems by Giacomo Leopardi, a brooding nineteenth-century intellectual whose words seemed to dance in the breeze.

Being married to a psychiatrist turned out to be an even greater advantage in Italy than it is in the United States. Although many Italians might never go (or admit going) to a *psichiatra*, they relish the opportunity to tell their stories to one. Long before my husband, Bob, could *capisce un' acca* (understand an *h*) in their language, Italians would pour out their souls to me to translate for him. Bob, an accomplished nodder, listened empathically. *"Mi dica"* ("Tell me"), he'd say. *"Ho capito."* ("I understand.") When my Italian wasn't nimble enough to translate his advice, I'd offer my own—for better or worse.

This, I came to learn, is in itself *italianissimo* (very, very, very Italian). At grand rounds at the medical school of the University of Pisa, Galileo's alma mater, *Dottor* Giovanni Cassano stepped to the lectern to introduce Bob as the day's speaker. Deeply tanned, with spiky silver hair and gleaming white teeth, Italy's best-known psychiatrist exuded the same charisma as the celebrities who have flocked to his care. Although they had met before, he had obviously never read Bob's curriculum vitae.

*"Dottor* Hales," he began in Italian, "graduated from West Point, the United States Military Academy, in 1970." He paused and reflected, "at the time of the Vietnam War." He then observed that my husband had trained as a *paracadutista* (parachutist). As he skimmed ahead, his face suddenly lit up.

*"Dottor* Hales," he announced dramatically, "parachuted

into Vietnam and won the highest military honors and many medals for his bravery."

*"Che eroe!"* a young doctor behind me murmured in admiration. Not comprehending a word, my husband, whose only assignment outside the continental United States had been in Hawaii, nodded, as if in modest recognition. Struggling not to laugh, I applauded the Italian knack for reassembling mere facts into a far more intriguing fiction.

The madly ambitious idea of a book about a language other than my own grew out of a fiction-writing group I belonged to for several years. I wrote a rather dreadful novel called "Becoming Italian" about the adventures of a group of students, interspersed with notes on the language. Character, plot, and dialogue didn't much interest me; writing about Italian was the most fun I'd ever had with a word-processing program.

Although my Italian could keep me afloat in friendly conversations, I realized I would need much more intensive study to manage interviews and research. And so I arranged private lessons in Florence, the cradle of the language. Some American friends joked that the entire undertaking seemed a ruse to spend more time in Italy, especially when I mentioned *il mio palazzo*—not really mine, of course, but the Palazzo Magnani Feroni, a boutique hotel in a sixteenth-century palace in the charming neighborhood of San Frediano. I arrived in a cold, rainy March, and the managers—all beautiful, dynamic young women—upgraded me from a studio to a suite named Beatrice (for Dante's muse), with lavishly decorated ceilings, Venetian chandeliers, and handmade soaps presented like jewels in a velvet-lined case so each guest could choose a favored scent.

Best of all, I could climb a sixty-step staircase to the terrace of a medieval tower with a 360-degree view of Florence's spectacular skyline and distant hills. Last year Bob and I celebrated our thirtieth wedding anniversary on this magical perch with a romantic dinner for two, a cake with our names entwined with hearts, and an exquisite bouquet that was a special gift from the lovely ladies who have been my cheerleaders from the very beginning of this project.

I found another cheerleader and coconspirator in San Francisco, Alessandra Cattani, the diction tutor for the San Francisco Opera. A *Romana* who migrated to the United States years ago, she taught me Italian the way Italians learn the language— through fairy tales, comic books, epic poems, classic novels, operas, folk songs, movies, newspapers, and hours and hours of chatting (*chiacchierare*) in Italian.

I began each session with a mantra: *"Sono italiana, sono italiana, sono italiana"* ("I am Italian, I am Italian, I am Italian"). I must see with Italian eyes, Alessandra would remind me, hear with Italian ears, speak with Italian rhythms.

"How would you say, 'Give me a kiss'?" Alessandra asked one day.

*"Dammi un bacio,"* I replied, somewhat taken aback by the query.

*"No, no, no,"* she chastised gently, explaining that the combination of *n* and *b* strikes an Italian ear as *molto brutta,* so I must run them together into an *m.*

*"Dammi umbacio!"* I dutifully repeated, although this phrase

seemed even less likely to enter my conversations in Italy than the one that would excuse me to smoke in the hallway.

I was wrong. One of the many Italians who coached me in their language asked for a kiss (and, yes, he said *umbacio*) the first time we met. When I pulled away, he added the irresistible kicker, "But I'm eighty-seven!" Born into the Sicilian aristocracy, Ignazio Leone fled as a boy with his family to Florence during World War II. By listening to the state-sponsored radio, he taught himself perfectly enunciated Italian. In conversations with him at *Libri d'Arte*, his antique shop near the Ponte Vecchio, I learned the words for, and the stories behind, his heirloom jewelry, rare books, archaeological oddities, antique dolls, and other treasures.

Rather than contacting perfect strangers and asking them questions (as I have done routinely as a journalist in the United States), I had to find sources the Italian way—by building a network, conversation by conversation, person by person, friend by friend. I doubted if I'd ever hear back from a real VIP (Italians pronounce this abbreviation veep). But one evening as Bob and I were taking our usual *passeggiata* through Rome's tranquil Borghese gardens, I heard the *squillo*, or ring, of my tiny Italian *telefonino* in his trouser pocket.

"Your pants are ringing!" I said, taking the phone from him to talk to our friend Roberto, whose call I was expecting.

"*Ciao, Roberto!*" I said merrily.

"*Ma, Diana, sei proprio brava! Come sai il mio nome?*" ("But Diana, you are really great. How did you know my name?")

It wasn't our friend Roberto, but the voice sounded oddly familiar. As I struggled to keep up with his rapid-fire Italian, I realized that the caller was the actor Roberto Benigni, a friend of a friend of a friend's. "If you love my language," he declared, "I love you."

When I began interviewing linguists, historians, and scholars at Italy's leading language institutions, such as L'Accademia della Crusca and the Società Dante Alighieri, Lucilla Pizzolli, a young collaborator, gasped that I was being *"un po' audace"*—a bit daring. I agreed and spent days preparing for each interview. As extra insurance, I wore great shoes (always Italian) and wrapped myself in an elegant black shawl (which I came to think of as my magic cape) so I could, at the least, *fare bella figura* (make a good impression).

In time all of Italy became my schoolhouse, and virtually every Italian I met—from the ebullient Contessa Maria-Vittoria Rimbotti, who advised me to stop thinking about the language and just live in it, to a comic cast of cabbies—became a tutor. In Verona, at the home of Maestro Maurizio Barbacini, his beautiful wife, Antonella, a soprano who has performed opera's leading roles, soared into an aria to illustrate how lyrics and music blend together. Clutching a candle in the Colosseum on Good Friday, I listened to one of the most moving lessons I've ever had in any language: dramatic interpretations by professional actors of the gospel descriptions of Christ's suffering on the *via crucis* (the way of the cross)—a phrase Italians use, ironically and not, for any difficult path.

My greatest resources turned out to be the Italians themselves, their deep pride in their native tongue, and their infinite patience with those who try to learn it. In contrast to the French, who praise an impeccable speaker for having *une langue châtiée*, which literally means "a punished tongue," an Italian friend gave me the highest of compliments when he said that my Italian had progressed from being *involto* (rolled tight, like cannelloni) to *disinvolto*, as loose and easy, in his words, as a lasagna noodle. Then he taught me a delightful Italian tongue twister (*scioglilingua*):

> *Al pozzo dei pazzi c'era una pazza*
> *che lavava una pezza mangiando una pizza.*
> *Arriva un pazzo e butta la pazza, la pezza,*
> *E la pizza nel pozzo dei pazzi.*

> At the well of the crazies, there was a crazy woman
> Who was washing a rag eating pizza.
> A crazy man arrives and throws the crazy woman, the rag, and the pizza into the well of the crazies.

Italians say that someone who acquires a new language "possesses" it. In my case, Italian possesses me. With Italian racing like blood through my veins, I do indeed see with different eyes, hear with different ears, and drink in the world with all my senses—an experience Italian encapsulates in the word *sentire*.

"*Sei proprio italiana*" ("You really are Italian"), Roberto Scio, the owner of Il Pellicano, the seaside hotel we've returned to annually for twenty years, assures me—not because of the language, he notes, but of what I've learned from it: *come far sorridere l'anima* (how to make the soul smile).

In *La Bella Lingua*—a true *opera amorosa*, a labor of love—I invite you to come along on my idiosyncratic journey through what I consider the world's most loved and lovable language. I have cherry-picked the liveliest parts of Italian's history and the golden eras of its literature, art, music, movies, and culture. In these pages, you will meet the people, visit the places, read the words, behold the paintings, hear the music, taste the meals, watch the movies, and discover the secrets that bring joy to my soul—and, I hope, to yours.

*Cominciamo!* Let's get started!

# Confessions of an Innamorata

When I arrived in Italy for the first time in 1983 I knew only one Italian sentence: *"Mi dispiace, ma non parlo italiano"* ("I'm sorry, but I don't speak Italian"). In my first minutes in the country, I repeated it half a dozen times, with ever-mounting panic in my voice, interspersed with pleas of "Stop this train!" Other passengers responded with concerned looks and torrents of incomprehensible Italian. Only the weary conductor followed my gaze as I pointed to my forlorn black suitcase, which the porter had left behind on the platform in Domodossola.

*"La sua valigia?"* ("Your suitcase?")

*"Sì."* I nodded, frantic that I would never be reunited with it again.

*"Non c'è problema,"* he announced loudly. *"Domani mattina a Milano."*

The faces encircling me smiled in relief. "*Domani mattina,*" they repeated reassuringly. "*Domani mattina.*"

Settling into my seat, I rolled the melodious syllables around my mouth. Yes, as soon as I arrived in Milan, I would find Signor Domani Mattina, and he would somehow retrieve my bag. In the colossal bleakness of the Milan station, I threaded my way down massive stone staircases. Late on a Sunday afternoon, everything was closed. I rushed to a man in a blue custodial uniform and entreated, "*Signor Domani Mattina?*"

"*No, signorina,*" he said, looking confused. I whipped out my pocket English-Italian dictionary to find the Italian word for "where," which I mispronounced as if it were the English name of a gentle white bird: "*Dove?*"

"*Doh-VAY!*" he boomed before breaking into laughter. "No, *signorina,* the day after today. *Domani mattina.*"

My quest for the quixotic "Mr. Tomorrow Morning" launched my journey into the Italian language. Throughout that first semisilent excursion in Italy, I delighted in the beauty of what I saw, but I craved comprehension of what I heard. I wanted to understand the waiter's quip when he set down my cappuccino, the *barzelletta* (funny story) the shopkeeper told with a wink, the verbal embraces couples exchanged as they strolled at twilight. And so, unlike Italophiles who trek through frescoed churches or restore rustic farmhouses, I chose to inhabit the language, as bawdy as it is beautiful, as zesty a linguistic stew as the peppery *puttanesca* sauce named for Italy's notorious ladies of the night.

Over the last quarter-century, I have devoted countless hours and effort—enough, if applied to more practical pursuits, for the down payment on a villa in Umbria—to the wiliest of Western tongues. I have studied Italian in every way I could find—from Berlitz to books, with CDs and podcasts, in private tutorials and conversation groups, and during what some might deem unconscionable amounts of time in Italy.

I've come to think of Italian as a *briccone*—a lovable rascal, a clever, twinkle-eyed scamp that you can't resist even when it plays you for the fool. *Croce e delizia*, torment and delight, Verdi's Violetta sang of love. The same holds true for the language his operas carried on golden wings. Yet, to an extent I never dreamed possible, Italian has become not just a passion and a pleasure but a passport into Italy's *storia*—a word that means both "history" and "story."

As a country Italy makes no sense. Think of it: a spiny peninsula stretching from snowcapped Alps to sunbaked islands, spattered with stone villages bound by ancient allegiances, a mosaic of dialects, cuisines, and cultures united into a nation barely a century and a half ago. Metternich dismissed it as a "geographic expression." Too long to be a nation, sniffed Napoleon. Possible to govern, growled Mussolini, but useless to try. The real Italy resides somewhere beyond blood or borders in what former President Carlo Azeglio Ciampi has called *"la nostra prima patria"* ("our first fatherland")—its language.

And what a language it is! Italian, handcrafted by poets and wordsmiths, embodies its native speakers' greatest genius: the ability to transform anything—from marble to melody, from the humble noodle to life itself—into a joyous art. English, like a big black felt-nosed Magic Marker, declares itself in bold statements and blunt talk. Italian's sleek, fine-pointed quill twirls into delicate curlicues and dramatic flourishes. While other tongues do little more than speak, this lyrical language thrills the ear, beguiles the mind, captivates the heart, enraptures the soul, and comes closer than any other idiom to expressing the essence of what it means to be human.

Centuries before there was an Italy, there was Italian. Its roots date back nearly three millennia. According to legend, in 753 B.C., Romulus, son of the god Mars and a vestal virgin, after killing his twin brother, Remus, founded a settlement for his band of itinerant shepherds and farmers on the hills above the Tiber. Their utterances evolved into the *volgare* (from the Latin *sermo vulgaris*, for the people's common speech), the rough-and-ready spoken vernacular. Scrappy street Latin, not the classical, cadenced rhetoric of Caesar and Cicero, gave rise to all the Romance languages, including Italian, French, Spanish, Portuguese, and Romanian.

The first miracle of Italian is its survival. No government mandated its use. No mighty empire promoted it as an official language. No conquering armies or armadas trumpeted it to distant lands. Brutally divided, invaded, and conquered, the Mediterranean peninsula remained a patchwork of dialects, often as different from one another as French from Spanish or English from Italian. Sailors from Genoa couldn't understand—or be understood by—merchants from Venice or farmers from Friuli. Florentines living in *il centro*, the heart of the city, couldn't speak the dialect of San Frediano, my favorite neighborhood, on the other side of the Arno.

Italian as we know it was created, not born. With the same thunderbolt genius that would transform art in the Renaissance, writers of fourteenth-century Florence—Dante first and foremost—crafted the effervescent Tuscan vernacular into a language rich and powerful enough to sweep down from heaven and up from hell. This priceless living legacy, no less than Petrarch's poetry, Michelangelo's sculptures, Verdi's operas, Fellini's movies, or Valentino's dresses, is an artistic masterwork.

Through centuries of often brutal foreign domination, words remained all that Italy's people could claim as their own. "When a people has lost homeland and liberty, their language takes the place of a nation and of everything," observed Luigi Settembrini, a nineteenth-century Neapolitan "professor of eloquence" who dedicated his life to the language that came to define Western civilization. "Italians" gave the name "America" (a tribute to the Florentine navigator Amerigo Vespucci) to Americans; created the first universities, law and medical schools, banks, and public libraries; taught diplomacy and manners to Europe; showed the French how to eat with a fork; mapped the moon (in the 1600s); split the atom; produced the first modern histories, satires, sonnets, and travelogues; invented the battery, barometer, radio, and thermometer; and bestowed on the world the eternal gift of music.

Yet as a national spoken tongue, Italian, practically born yesterday, is *nuovissimo* (very, very new), says the noted linguist Giuseppe Patota in an interview in his apartment in Rome. Rallying for one nation united by one language, Italians won their country's independence in 1861, almost a century later than the United States. At the time four in five of its citizens were illiterate. Fewer than 10 percent spoke Italian exclusively or with greater ease than a local dialect. Not until 1996—135 years after unification—did more than half of Italians report using *italiano standard* (the national language) rather than dialect outside their homes. Word by word, generation by generation, village by village, the people of the peninsula became Italian speakers.

Ever-growing numbers of people around the world are trying to do the same. English may be the language everyone *needs* to know, but Italian is the language people *want* to learn. With only an estimated 60 to 63 million native speakers (compared to a whopping 1.8 billion who claim at least a little English), Italian barely eclipses Urdu, Pakistan's official language, for nineteenth place as a spoken tongue. Yet Italian ranks fourth among the world's most studied languages—after English, Spanish, and French. In the United States, Italian has become the fastest-growing language taught in colleges and universities. So popular is the "new French," as the *New York Times* dubbed it, that parents—and not just those of Italian descent—are sending toddlers to *piccole scuole* (little schools) to learn it.

This trend mystifies many. When I mentioned my Italian studies to a venture capitalist in San Francisco, he asked if I could have chosen a less practical language. I might have cited Urdu, but I saw his point. My husband can unfurl his college French (or at least a few tattered remnants of it) everywhere from Paris to Polynesia, and Spanish unlocks the keys to an entire atlas of nations. Only four countries other than Italy— Switzerland, Croatia, San Marino, and Slovenia, along with the Vatican—recognize Italian as an official language. No scientific society, multinational trade association, or global enterprise, even if based in Italy, requires Italian as its lingua franca. And certainly tourists can get by with a smile and a *ciao* in a country that has been serving, seducing, and satisfying foreigners for centuries.

So why do so many people want to study Italian? "I suspect it is because Italy and the Italian language are perceived as beautiful, fun, and sexy," observed Stephen Brockman, a professor at Carnegie Mellon University, in a recent essay called "A Defense of European Languages," adding, "And why not? I can't see anything wrong with that." The Italian newspaper *La Repubblica*, reporting on the boom in Italian courses at American universities, cited the soaring popularity of Italian food, fashion, art, architecture, music, and culture and noted that Americans see Italian *"come una lingua polisensoriale capace di aprire le porte al bello"* ("as a multisensory language able to open the gates to beauty").

I bring the question of Italian's eternal appeal to the language's oldest and most prestigious champion: the Società Dante Alighieri, founded in 1889, with some five hundred branches spanning the globe, from Australia to Argentina to Nepal to Croatia. Its offices in Rome's Palazzo Medici, once the ornate home of the Florentine ambassador, are a shrine to the language, with shelves of leather-bound volumes lining the walls of the high-ceilinged rooms, and busts of Dante and other literary giants mounted on pedestals.

In these hallowed halls, Luca Serianni, a renowned professor of the history of the Italian language at Rome's La Sapienza University and one of the Società's *consiglieri*, tells me that the foreigners thronging to Italian classes around the globe are seeking more than vocabulary and grammar. "You cannot separate our language from our culture," he explains. "When you learn

Italian, you enter our history, our art, our music, our traditions."

In fact, you enter the Italian soul. Acclaimed as the most musical of tongues, Italian is also the most emotionally expressive. Its primal sounds—virtually identical to those that once roared through Roman amphitheaters and forums—strike a chord in our universal linguistic DNA.

"*Pronto!*" ("Ready!"), Italians say when they answer the telephone. And ready they are—to talk, laugh, curse, debate, woo, sing, lament. Their native tongue conveys a sense of something coming alive. Its sinewy verbs flex like *muscoli* (muscles), from a Latin word for "little mice," scampering under the skin. In Italy the ubiquitous @ in e-mail addresses mischievously curls into a *chiocciola*, or snail, just as a spiral staircase spins into a *scala a chiocciola*. Rome's local dialect describes a tightwad as someone with pockets in the shape of a snail.

Even ordinary things—such as a towel (*asciugamano*) or handkerchief (*fazzoletto*)—sound better in Italian. The reasons start with its vigorous *vocali*, or vowels, which look like their English counterparts but sound quite different. In my first formal class in Italian, the teacher had us look in a mirror as we mouthed a-e-i-o-u in the flat English manner and then in the more emphatic Italian style, with the vowels puffing our cheeks, tugging at our lips, and loosening our jaws.

An Italian *a* slides up from the throat into an ecstatic "aaaah." Its *e* (pronounced like a hard English *a*) cheers like the hearty "ay" at the end of *hip-hip-hooray*. The *i* (which sounds like an English *e*) glides with the glee of the double *e* in *bee*. The *o* (an English *o* on steroids) is as perfectly round as the red circle

Giotto painted in a single stroke for a pope demanding a sample of his work. The macho *u* (deeper, stronger, and longer than its English counterpart) lunges into the air like a penalty kick from Italy's world-champion soccer team, the Azzurri (the Blues).

Sounds of all sorts take on different accents in Italian. Rather than with a sloppy "ah-choo," an Italian sneezes with a daintier *"eccì."* Italian distinuishes between the sound of swallowing water (*glu glu glu*) and chewing food (*gnam gnam gnam*). Bells ring *din don dan*. Trains *ciuff-ciuff*. Motors *vrum-vrum*. Clocks *tic-tac*. Guns fire with a *pim pum pam*. A telephone's busy signal stutters *tuu tuu tuu*. Over the years I've been awakened by little birds that *cip cip cip*, dogs that *abbaiano*, roosters that go *chic-chirichì*, and crickets that *cri-cri-cri*. In the morning, Bambola, the mangy stray cat who has become my pet at the villa we rent every summer, curls onto my lap and *fa le fusa* (purrs).

A color becomes more than a hue in Italian. A *giallo* (yellow) refers to a mystery—in life, literature, or movies—because thrillers traditionally had yellow covers. A Telefono Azzurro (blue telephone) is a hotline for abused children; a *settimana bianca* (white week), a ski holiday in winter; and a *matrimonio in bianco* (white wedding), an unconsummated and ostensibly unhappy marriage. While Americans who overspend their budgets wind up in the red, Italians go to the green (*al verde*), an expression that dates back to the time when the base of a candle was painted green. When the flame burned down to the green, people, presumably out of money to buy another, ran out of light as well. According to another etymological explanation, *al verde* refers to the hapless state of a gambler who has lost everything—

*il proprio gruzzoletto*, his hard-earned life savings—and sees only the bare playing table, traditionally green, in front of him.

Prince Charming always appears as *Principe azzurro* (the blue prince). *Viola* (purple) triggers so much apprehension that the wife of the Italian consul in San Francisco stopped our interview to ask me to switch to a different pen. Italians, she explained, associate purple with Lent, when drapes of that color shroud church statues. For many centuries, theaters closed during this penitential season so actors and singers lost their jobs and incomes. Because of their misfortune, unlucky purple became a color to avoid.

Italian's basic word chest, as tallied in a recent dictionary, totals a measly 200,000, compared to English's 600,000 (not counting technical terms). But with a prefix here and a suffix there, Italian words multiply like fruit flies. *Fischiare* (whistle) sounds merry enough, but *fischiettare* means "whistling with joy." No one wants to be *vecchio* (old), but *invecchiare* (to become old) loses its sting—and, according to an Italian proverb, no one does so *al tavolo* (at table). Sooner or later we all may end up in a *garbuglio*, or muddle, but stumbling through the syllables of *ingarbugliarsi* is sure "to get (you) muddled." A sign outside a rustic *osteria* (a tavern serving simple food) summarized its entire menu in three variations on a single word: *pranzo* (lunch)—fifteen euro; *pranzetto* (lighter lunch)—ten euro; *pranzettino* (bite to eat)—five euro.

I might never have appreciated such linguistic finesse if not for Niccolò Tommaseo, a nineteenth-century essayist and iconoclast (arrested and exiled for his political views) whose passions included women and words. He demonstrated his devotion to the latter by compiling the *Dizonario dei sinonimi*, an encyclopedic narrative dictionary of Italian synonyms, published in 1830, and unmatched in any other language and literature. Italian alone, he contended—and in particular the Tuscan dialect that shaped the language—captures life's *sfumature* (nuances), the same word Italian uses for Leonardo's subtle brushstrokes.

"It is worth learning Italian just for the pleasure of reading Tommaseo's dictionary," Maurizio Borghi, a visiting professor from Milan, tells me during an interview at the University of California, Berkeley. Rather than compiling a straightforward list of words, Tommaseo played with Italian's treasure chest of metaphors and diminutives in a mammoth collection of 3,579 synonyms, from *abbacare* (to daydream) to *zuppa* (soup). As soon as I read a sampling, I pegged him as a kindred soul, as captivated as I by the ability of Italian words to take flight, soar, spin, dip, and pirouette with incomparable flair.

Take, for instance, Tommaseo's entry on Italy's national pastime (past and present): flirting, which translates into *fare la civetta*, or "make like an owl." Only Italian distinguishes between a *civettino*, a precocious boy flattering a pretty woman; a *civettone*, a boorish lout doing the same; a *civettina*, an innocent coquette; and a *civettuola*, a brazen hussy. A *giovanotto di prima barba* (a boy who starts flirting even before growing a beard) may turn out to be a *damerino* (dandy), a *zerbino* (doormat), a *zerbinetto* (lady-killer), or a *zerbinotto* (a fop too old for such foolishness). If he becomes a *cicisbeo*, he joins a long line of Italian men who flagrantly courted married women.

I've met every one of these varieties over the years. On my first trip to Florence, I was craning out the window of a taxi to take in the Duomo's multistriped magnificence when I felt a hand sliding up my skirt.

"What are you doing?" I snapped at the young driver.

"Just looking," he responded in English, although that's not what he was doing. (Italians picked up this phrase, I later learned, from the standard American reply to a shopkeeper's offer of help.) For the most part, Italian flirts keep their hands to themselves and rely on their looks—and their lines. Most have complimented my eyes, a quite ordinary green that passes unnoticed in the United States but grabs attention on the streets of Florence. A few years ago at a festive reception in that city, two men behind me—never thinking I might understand Italian—began debating whether my eyes were the color of *giada* (jade) or *smeraldo* (emerald). When one seemed to imply that I had an artificial eye, I couldn't stay silent any longer.

"*No, no, no, signora,*" the speaker protested, explaining that to him my eyes seemed made of porcelain, created by an artist greater even than those of his native city. "*Bellini*" ("little beauties"), he added, using one of the ubiquitous diminutives that sweeten the language like the heaps of sugar Italians add to a thimbleful of espresso.

*Vento* (wind) melts into *venticello* (a nice little breeze); *caldo* (hot) snuggles into *calduccio* (nice and warm). When an Italian stuffs cash in appreciation or anticipation of a favor into an envelope, a *busta* becomes a welcome *bustarella*. A tiny tail at the end of the word transforms the coarse *culo* into *culetto* (a sweet little baby bottom) or *culoni* (big butts), a popular nickname for Americans. The Italian physicist Enrico Fermi (1901–1954) added the term *neutrino* (little neutral one) for a particle even smaller than the neutron, to the scientific lexicon. In music *prestissimo* means a little faster than *presto* (fast) and *andantino* not as slow as *andante* (slow).

Although endings such as *-ino*, *-otto*, or *-ello* are generally endearing, my Italian friends warn me to beware of anyone asking for a little anything, whether it's a tiny little moment of your time (*attimino*), a peck of a kiss (*bacino*), or a bit of help (*aiutino*). Bigger (indicated with *-one* as in *torrione* for big tower) isn't necessarily better. Italians mistrust a *parolone* (a big meaningless word) in the mouths of politicians and scoff at *sporcaccioni* (dirty old men). Suffixes such as *-astro*, *-ucolo*, or *-accio* also spell trouble. No one wants to hire an *avvocatuccio* (small-time lawyer), read the works of a *poetucolo* (untalented poet), wear a *cappellaccio* (ugly hat), or drive on a *stradaccia* (bad road).

Just about everything that can be said has been said in Italian—then rephrased, edited, modified, synthesized, and polished to a verbal gleam. It's no wonder that a single Italian word can reveal more than an entire English paragraph. A headline in Rome captures the misadventures of Britney Spears with a nickname: *la scandalosa*. A historian's description of Machiavelli as a *mangiapreti* (priest-eater) neatly sums up the master strategist's religious views. An Italian friend winces and blames *"il colpo della strega"* (the strike of a witch, a fitting term for a back spasm). *Barcollare*—to move like a boat—perfectly conveys the swaying stride of a drunken sailor. Although I have yet to use it in a sentence, the very existence of *colombeggiare*, which means "to kiss one another like doves," makes me smile.

Italians' irrepressible wit sparkles in words like *trucco* (trick) for makeup and *bugiardino* (little liar), the term doctors use for the patient information insert for a prescription drug. Friends encapsulate the fourteen-inch height discrepancy between my husband and me by describing us as an *il*—the combination of a short *i* and a tall *l* that translates into "the." Neapolitans' invention of a word for a man who painted the eyes of day-old fish in markets so they appeared fresh crystallized the ingenious survival skills of the locals. Would-be buyers of Tuscan villas might take heed of a new meaning for the word *falsificatore* to refer to a craftsman who makes new furniture look antique and sells it at exorbitant ·prices to gullible foreigners. "To trust is good," says an old Italian proverb my friends like to quote. "Not to trust is better."

A very good person, someone we might praise in English as the salt of the earth, becomes *un pezzo di pane* (a piece of bread) in Italian. Rather than having heart or guts, a brave Italian has *fegato* (liver), while a man *in gamba* (literally "on a leg") is on top of his· game. In Italian, it's a compliment to be praised for your nose (*naso*), for intuition; hand (*mano*), for artistry; or testicles (*coglioni*), for being, well, ballsy.

One night, dressed *di tutto punto* (to the nines) at an informal wine-tasting with friends on the roof of Rome's Hassler Hotel, we found ourselves in a linguistic barnyard, with the waiters chiming in with examples of bestial metaphors. Italians, although quite foxy, have no word to say so. Yet Italian corrals animals of every sort to describe a person who eats like an ox (*bue*), sings like a nightingale (*usignolo*), cries like a calf (*vitello*), fights like a lion (*leone*), hops like a cricket (*grillo*), or sleeps like a dormouse (*ghiro*). As in English, a *testa dura* (hard head) can be as stubborn as a mule (*mulo*), but an Italian also may be as silent as a fish (*pesce*), crazy as a horse (*cavallo*), or mischievous as a monkey (*scimmia*). And without clothes, an Italian is—proudly, I would venture—*nudo come un verme* (naked as a worm). *"In bocca al lupo!"* "In the mouth of the wolf!," Italians say to wish someone luck (*"buona fortuna"* is considered unlucky). The correct response: *"Crepi il lupo!"* ("Let the wolf die!")

Just as in Italy's cars, clothes, and countryside, there is nothing happenstance about the language. English speakers blurt, spitting out words without a moment's thought. Italians, skilled in the art of *sistemarsi* (organizing a life), assemble a sentence as meticulously as they construct tiramisu. *"Tutto a posto e niente in ordine,"* my friend Cinzia Fanciulli, manager of the Borgo San Felice resort in Chianti, likes to say as she surveys her gleaming realm, every flower bed manicured, every tabletop shining. "Everything is in order, and nothing is disorganized." Romans, scanning the city even they describe as *caotica* (chaotic), prefer to joke, *"Niente a posto, e tutto in disordine"* ("Nothing is in order, and everything is disorganized").

Italian devotes an entire tense, the elusive *congiuntivo*, similar to English's little-used subjunctive mood, to desires, doubts, wishes, dreams, and opinions. My friend and teacher Francesca Gaspari considers it the sexiest of verb forms because of its ambiguities; for this very reason, I never use it without trepidation. Thankfully, you can often dodge this tricky tense by prefacing a subjective comment with *"secondo me,"* "according to me," and using the just-the-facts declarative.

Italy's long past requires four tenses (not counting the subjunctive's past forms): *passato prossimo*, *trapassato prossimo*, *passato remoto*, and the *imperfetto*, or imperfect—"the most Italian of tenses," one of my teachers contends—for unfinished business. Business can remain unfinished a long time in Italy. A researcher tells of requesting a book from the catalog of the Vatican Library only to receive a notice stating, "Missing since 1530."

Northern Italians relegate the musty *passato remoto* to historical events such as Dante's birth. Southern Italians, with a telescoped sense of time, use it to recount what they had for breakfast. In literary Italian (though not daily conversation) memories of times past can be summoned up in three words and ways—*rammentare* (with the mind, for facts), *ricordare* (with the heart, for feelings), and *rimembrare* (with the body, for physical sensations).

What Italian doesn't say also is revealing. Italian has no words that precisely translate *lonely* (unthinkable for its gregarious speakers), *privacy* (equally unthinkable in an Italian family), *spelling* (since words generally look as they sound—to Italians, that is), or *dating* (although it begins before puberty). Yet some of the most tantalizing Italian words, such as *garbo*, a pitch-perfect combination of style and grace, and *agio*, a sense of comfort and ease, don't translate into English.

Even when foreigners learn Italian words, they often miss their hidden meanings. Only after years of visiting Italy did I realize that that Italians admire rather than disdain a *furbo*, someone cunning enough to pull off a clever deception. A young *furbetto* shifts the blame for a childish prank to his little brother. A shrewd *furbacchione* obtains a coveted building permit for a rectangular, cement-lined hole in his backyard by describing it not as a swimming pool (prohibited by law) but as a storage vat for water that local firefighters might need to douse a blaze. A more deceitful *furbastro* somehow manages to make money in the process, while a wheeler-dealer *furbone* reaps big profits by negotiating permits for an entire village.

My husband, transformed from Bob to Roberto in Italy, cannot resist a little linguistic *furbizia*. When he casually drops well-rehearsed Italian witticisms into conversations as if he were fluent, Italians invariably applaud his facility with their language. Giustina, who looks after the villa we rent in Tuscany, praises Professor Roberto for improving his pronunciation every year while dismissing my Italian as *un po' arrugginito* (a little rusty). However, a bit of *furbizia* also lurks in my soul. The very first aphorism I taught Bob—and encouraged him to say on every occasion—was *Mia moglie ha sempre ragione.* (My wife is always right.)

I snatched other sage sayings from hand-painted ceramic ashtrays, the sort you find at kitschy souvenir stores next to aprons decorated with pasta shapes or the chubby cherubs with mischievous grins that decorated Renaissance ceilings. Several years ago, during Bob's academic sabbatical in Italy, we rented the thousand-year-old *castello* at Monte Vibiano Vecchio in Umbria, with a stone watchtower dating back yet another millennium, a Renaissance maze, an amphitheater, a chapel, and a peacock that strutted majestically around the grounds. Adjacent to its grand formal rooms, with fireplaces so big that we posed for photographs standing inside them, there was a smallish alcove for cards and other games. Hundreds of hand-painted ceramic ashtrays, each with a different saying, covered the walls with pithy words of wisdom.

The whimsical wall treatment inspired me to select a few

choice phrases to teach Bob on our daily hikes through the postcard-perfect countryside. *"Il padrone sono io,"* he would repeat, and repeat, and repeat (rapid language acquisition is not one of Bob's many natural gifts), *"ma chi comanda è mia moglie."* "I'm the head of the house but the one in charge is my wife."

I cribbed the words from another ashtray for a *brindisi*, or toast—one thing I do better in Italian than English—for a final dinner with the *castello*'s owners, with whom we'd become friends. *"Chi trova un amico trova un tesoro"* ("Whoever finds a friend finds a treasure"), I said. *"E qui, in questa bella casa antica, abbiamo davvero trovato un tesoro."* ("And here in this beautiful ancient home, we have found treasure indeed.")

An Italian expressing such sentiments would have inserted a word or two in dialect that would have brought other Italians to tears or laughter. For foreigners, dialect words simply add to the dizzying complexity of the language. Depending on where you are in Italy, you might sit on a *sedia, seggiola*, or *seggia*; blow your nose into a *fazzoletto, pezzuolo*, or *moccichino*; and wear *calzini, calzette, calze, calzettoni, calzettini*, or *pedalini* with your shoes. A thousand years ago Italian Jews fashioned a dialect of their own mixed with Hebrew, now called Italkian, which is still spoken by about four thousand natives. A Venetian translated Shakespeare's plays into his dialect because he felt that Italian was insufficient to transmit their emotional complexity.

Even metaphors vary by region. Florentines call a blowsy lady an "unmade bed" and an aging cavalier a "tired horse." The long-impoverished Calabrians lament their plight with sayings like "Dogs only bite the poor." When bored, Romans complain that they are "dying of pinches." A *Romano de Roma* (dialect for a Roman whose family has lived in the city for several generations) describes a local politician as "the best cat in the Colosseum" (which is overrun by feral felines), the figure who comes off best in a difficult situation.

"To remain like Father Falcuccio," another Romanesco idiom, refers to a hypothetical priest who, having lost his clothes, had to cover his naked private parts with "one hand in front and another one behind." A Roman ends up in this hapless predicament when, for instance, he wrecks his car before paying off the loan or his wife finds him with his mistress and both women dump him.

Death too takes different forms in dialects. Romans call it "the skinny woman." When Italians in other regions die, they "go to the pointed trees" (cypresses, often found in Tuscan cemeteries), "make soil for chick peas" (a common vegetable), "stretch their legs," "wear the other trousers" (the good ones saved for special occasions), or, oddly, "pull the robin's dick."

"We have *campanilismo* in everything," says my tutor Alessandra Cattani, referring to Italian's allegiance to all that lies within view of the local bell tower. This attitude treats even folks on the next hilltop as out-of-towners to be viewed with a certain amount of suspicion—and sometimes derision. Northerners scoff at southerners as *terroni* (peasants who work the land). Southerners snipe at northerners as *polentoni* (big eaters of polenta, once standard fare for the *popolo magro*—the skinny or poor people). *"Non fare il genovese"* ("Don't act like someone from Genoa!"), I've heard one friend chide another—in other words, don't be cheap. *"Fare alla romana"* translates into going Dutch. And every time we've headed for Pisa, someone has intoned,

*"Meglio un morto in casa che un pisano all'uscio"* ("Better a corpse in the house than a Pisan at the door!"). The Pisans' response: *"Che dio t'accon tenti!"* (May God grant your wish!)

Perhaps because of this Babel of dialects, Italians cultivated an alternative language: gestures. In Italy, the shrug of a shoulder, the flip of a wrist, or the lift of an eyebrow says more than a *sacco di parole* (sack of words). A clenched fist signifies rage, irritation, anger, or threat; fingers bunched together indicate complexity or confusion. A tug at the corner of an eye means "Watch out!" A tap on the head indicates comprehension, intuition, or idiocy.

After a few hours of careful observation in a piazza, anyone can become fluent in this wordless variant of Italian. Need a favor? Clasp your palms together with fingers extended as if in prayer and press them in front of your chest. Don't give a damn? Slide your fingers upward from your neck past the tip of your chin. Was the dinner or day absolute perfection? Draw a straight horizontal line in the air. A Neapolitan waiter showed us how he signals the best-tasting dishes on the menu—by corkscrewing an index finger into his cheek, a gesture Italian men repeat on the street when a tasty-looking girl walks by.

Such silent entertainment is one of the pleasures of Italy that come, as Luigi Barzini observed in *The Italians*, from living in a world "made by man, for man, to the measure of man." The pleasure of Italian's man-made language, he noted, comes from teaching "that things don't have to be exactly what they look like, reality does not have to be dull and ugly."

With words alone, Italians have developed simple, life-affirming ways to transform dreary days into delightful ones and mundane chores into memorable events. Bob and I have entered wineshops looking only for a nice bottle to drink with dinner and emerged hours later after having toured a subterranean vault, sampled several vintages, and listened to a tutorial on the differences between Sangiovese, the pride of Tuscany, and Nebbiolo, the Piedmont wine with a name (little fog) that describes the region's typical weather.

In the process, we invariably acquire a new word or two. Any connoisseur may appreciate a fine wine, we've learned, but Italians prefer to *approfondire* (go deeper) and *assaporare*—surrender themselves to the slow discovery of its fullness. The very last drop from a bottle of wine (*la scolatura*) always goes to the *belli di natura*—to the greatest natural beauties, male or female. Italians so appreciate the final sips of wine that the Roman dialect poet Giuseppe Gioacchino Belli once celebrated the delights of *sgoccetto*, savoring these last drops, in verse.

Like the pleasure of such terms, words for pleasure take tantalizing forms. A nation of inspired cooks and enthusiastic eaters has, of course, coined a specific word for a lust for a food—*goloso* (from *gola* for "throat"), which goes beyond mere appetite, craving, or hunger. Friends readily, even proudly confess to being *golosi* for *cioccolata*, *sfogliatelle* (stuffed pastries), or *supplì* (melt-in-your-mouth rice and cheese balls).

One evening I regaled a conversation group with a tale about an article called "Twenty-four Hours in the Life of a Medical Student" that I had written as a young reporter. "I had no idea that I was spending the night with the future surgeon general," I said in Italian, "and I enjoyed it." The teacher, a worldly sophisticate who speaks four languages, leaned close to whisper that the term I had used referred only to sex.

An Italian *amante* (lover) may be *amoroso* (amorous), *amabile* (lovable), *amato* (beloved), or all three. Many an Italian man is an *amatore* (a lover of, say, wine, women, or song). An Italian woman may be an *amatrice* (a lover, perhaps, of the fine things in life). There is no English word that quite captures the sensation of *innamoramento*, crazy head-over-heels love, deeper than infatuation, way beyond bewitched, bothered, and bewildered. But that's what I am—an *innamorata*, enchanted by Italian, fascinated by its story and its stories, tantalized by its adventures, addicted to its sound, and ever eager to spend more time in its company.

# *The Unlikely Rise of a Vulgar Tongue*

"WHERE DID THEY COME FROM?" I ASK OUR balding, paunchy guide in Pompeii's notorious brothel. He looks at me quizzically. "The prostitutes," I say, adding *povere donne*—poor women.

"*No, signora,*" he bristles, insisting that Pompeii's ladies of the night were anything but poor. In fact, they were well fed and well dressed—and lucky to have Roman soldiers, the finest men on earth, as their lovers. When I object that the women were nonetheless selling their bodies, the guide dismisses my protest with a toss of his hand.

"They would have paid for the privilege." I raise an eyebrow.

"It still happens," he insists. Rustling through his wallet, he retrieves a dog-eared identification photo of himself at twenty, so *bello* that women offered money to sleep with him. To distract him, I point to the graffiti scrawled on the walls, clearly not the Latin I studied in high school.

"Of course not," he says. "It's the *volgare*." As he translates with undisguised relish the crude testimonials to Myrtis's skills at fellatio and to the services Drauca delivers for a *denaro*, "vulgar" also applies.

Not all of Pompeii's graffiti was so graphic. In a simple red script with letters about six inches high, signs along the town's narrow streets endorsed political candidates; denounced deadbeats; declared that the next gladiatorial show in the amphitheater would be the biggest, finest, most spectacular Pompeii had ever seen (it was certainly its last); and issued no-nonsense directives, such as "If you must lean against a wall, lean against someone else's." A notice in the dining room of a fashionable home asked visitors to refrain from casting lascivious looks at the serving women or making passes at the wives of other guests and, above all, to keep the conversation clean. "If you can't," the blunt last line exhorted, "please go home."

Pompeii, buried by an eruption of Vesuvius in A.D. 79, seems to have been the Las Vegas of its day. No evidence exists that Christianity ever breached its walls. In this thoroughly pagan place, pleasures—of the bedroom, the table, the theater, and the sports arena—were the true religion. Yet we owe a debt to Pompeii's freewheeling citizens and their incorrigible urge to write on walls. The sheer zest of their words testifies to the potency of the upstart language created by and for the people of the Roman Empire—and provides a fitting start to the saga of how Italian became Italian.

Latin, both formal and informal, evolved from the dialect of the tribes of Lazio, the region around Rome. In other parts of the peninsula locals spoke various languages—Etruscan in Etruria (the area in central Italy that includes Tuscany), more Greek-influenced tongues to the south, and distinctively different dialects to the north, east, and west. When Roman troops conquered the Italian peninsula and then marched to the ends of the known world, classical Latin became the official language of government, commerce, and learning. Its imprint remains on everything from coins to monuments, temples, and tombs. The manhole covers of Rome are still emblazoned with S.P.Q.R., the Latin abbreviation for the *Senatus Populusque Romanus*, the senate and people of Rome. (Italians joke that it really stands for *Sono pazzi questi romani*—These Romans are crazy.)

The ephemeral vernacular lived in the air—in the shouts of the amphitheater, the banter of the marketplace, the jokes at bawdy street shows. No one knows what the *volgare* sounded like in the mouths of the earthy citizens of Pompeii, but I have a hunch. It came to me at Il San Pietro di Positano, a hotel just down the spectacularly scenic Amalfi coast.

One entire wall of our room, built into the side of a cliff, was made of black rock. But what grabbed my eye as we entered was the size of the bed. "It must have been made for orgies," I whispered to Bob. As soon as I peeked in the bathroom, I knew I was right. There, towering over a sunken tiled tub big enough for a half dozen well-lathered bodies stood a marble hermaphrodite with a knowing grin, a gleaming bosom, and a huge erect phallus, adorned with several strings of gemstones, that doubled as a spigot.

Bathing in that tub felt wanton, if not downright decadent—
exactly as I imagine speaking the region's *volgare* once did. Then
as now an unabashed earthiness permeates both Italy's language
and culture. To ward off bad luck or *malocchio* (the evil eye), for
instance, men long ago developed the habit of touching their
genitals when, say, discussing a serious illness or passing a
cemetery. The phrase *"Io mi tocco"* ("I touch myself") remains as
common as "Knock on wood" in English, but the actual act,
committed in public by a forty-two-year-old man from Como,
recently led the Italian supreme court to ban such "potentially
offensive" behavior. The judges advised superstitious men to
delay reaching for their crotches until within the privacy of
their homes.

The ancient Romans didn't have to worry about breaking
any rules when they spoke the vernacular; there weren't any.
Neither did the *volgare* impose any class or social distinctions.
Because classical Latin was essentially a literary language, citizens of every stripe and status had to speak some form of the
vernacular in everyday life, certainly in their beds and baths.

Educated Romans probably used a somewhat more refined
idiom than the masses in the markets. However, the letters that
the supreme stylist Cicero (106–43 B.C.) wrote to family and
friends were so pocked with slang and sloppy grammatical mistakes (along the lines of "he did good") that they horrified Renaissance translators. And consider the immortal words that a
distinguished physician left behind, as recorded by Luca Canali
and Guglielmo Cavallo in *Graffiti latini: Scrivere sui muri a Roma antica.* (Latin Graffitti: Writings on the Walls of Ancient Rome):
*"Apollinare, medico di Tito imperatore, in questo sito egregiamente cagò"*

("Apollinare, the doctor of the emperor Tito, on this site shat splendidly").

The good doctor's last word, *cagò* (defecate), has passed unchanged into contemporary Italian slang—as I learned from a little boy in Orbetello, a lively Tuscan village suspended between two lagoons that one enters through a still impressive Roman arch.

"*La signora è americana*," his grandmother explained to the lad as she and I discussed the ripeness of a watermelon (*cocomero* in the south, *anguria* in the north—and an insulting way to say "blockhead" throughout Italy).

"*Da Chi-cago?*" ("From Chicago?"), he asked with a mischievous grin, and began giggling.

"No," I replied to the unexpected question as his blushing *nonna* hustled him away. The amused vendor explained that the name of America's windy city sounds like "*ci* (pronunced chee) *cago*" ("I poop here").

Roman power and influence peaked in A.D. 117, when the empire stretched to Carthage, Egypt, Syria, Macedonia, Corsica, Gaul, the Iberian Peninsula, the British Isles, and east to what is now Iraq. With the gradual erosion of Roman might, classical Latin began to lose its status. In the far-flung territories, the Latin *volgare* evolved into local vernaculars. Eventually the dialect of the most powerful cities—Paris in France, Madrid in Spain, Lisbon in Portugal—elbowed aside other regional variations to become the national language. In Italy's hodgepodge of warring city-states, the gap between the ways people wrote and spoke widened into a chasm. Classical Latin calcified into the lifeless language of church rituals and government documents, "a beautiful mummy," as the linguist Ernst Pulgram describes it in *The Tongues of Italy*.

To find out how the rapscallion vernacular, long relegated to the walls of brothels and bathrooms, somehow managed to usurp regal Latin, I arranged for a tutorial on the history of Italian at the Società Dante Alighieri in Florence. On a brisk spring day I made my way to the converted fifteenth-century cloister that now houses the school. My ebullient teacher, Cristina Romanelli, had served as a docent for a recent Uffizi exhibition on Italian's history, *"Dove Il Sì Suona"* ("Where the *Sì* Doth Sound," from Dante's description of his "fair land" in the *Divine Comedy*). The moment I saw the stack of books and illustrations she'd prepared, I knew I had come to the right person at the right place—except that I'd secretly been hoping that Cristina would speak just a little English. She didn't.

Maybe that's why Cristina provided so many visual aids to help me see the gradual transformation of a spoken tongue into a written language. Exhibit A was a page in the appendix of a grammar book from about A.D. 300. Unearthed from the ruins of a school near Rome's Colosseum, it reveals the frustration of a teacher named Probus. With almost palpable irritation, he identifies 227 mistakes his pupils consistently made by substituting street words for the correct Latin terms. *Calida*, not *calda* (hot), he reprimanded his charges, *aqua*, not *acqua* (water), *tabula*, not *tabla* (table).

*"Povero!"* Cristina sighs as we pore over a copy of the tattered *Appendix Probi*. The earnest instructor had fought a losing battle. The schoolboys' slipshod errors, not his meticulous corrections, found a place in the evolving language. So did many

others. *Testa*—slang for "pot" and an ancient insult—replaced the reputable Latin *caput* for "head." *Caballus*, the vernacular for "nag," upstaged the Latin *equus* and morphed into the modern Italian *cavallo* for "horse," the root of "cavalry" and "cavalier."

About the same time, another revolutionary force, Christianity, was transforming the lives and language of Romans. Initially the church's official tongue was Greek, but it switched to Latin about the year 350. However, long before then, novel religious concepts and forms of worship demanded new words, such as *battesimo* (baptism) and *eucaristia* (eucharist or Holy Communion), in the vernacular.

Many existing Latin words took on new meanings in the Christian era. *Massa*, for instance, meant nothing more than a lump of dough until St. Paul used it to refer to a group of people. Italian's words for "word," *parola*, and for "speaking," *parlare*, derive from the Greek *parabole* (a comparison) and the intermediate Latin term *parabola* (for "parable," a story with a moral lesson). When Christianity became the official religion of the Roman Empire under Theodosius in 380, the prestige of the people's tongue, spoken by the faithful of all classes, also rose.

Neither words nor religion could protect Rome from the waves of barbarians who, beginning in the fifth century, swept over the peninsula and plunged the largest, strongest, and proudest of empires into darkness and silence. The Romans, who described their orderly style of warfare as *bellum*, couldn't withstand the disorderly tactics of the Germans, whose *werra* (war) became the Italian *guerra* and the root of the English "guerrilla."

One of my college history professors used to refer to the bleak period that followed as "a thousand years without a bath."

In this dark and mirthless time, the only lights of intellectual enterprise burned in monasteries and abbeys, where men of God preserved early Western civilization by copying its classic works. The *volgare* had to fend for itself. Yet despite overwhelming odds, this orphan tongue not only survived but triumphed.

The invaders' Germanic dialects had little significant impact on the vernacular, beyond a motley assortment of words, including *scherzare* (to joke), *ricco* (rich), and *russare* (to snore). Some imports reflect the miseries the barbarians inflicted—*gramo* for "wretched," *scherno* for "scorn," *smacco* for "shame." Others reveal the Romans' contempt. Italian uses *zanna*, "tooth" in German, for an animal's fang and *stalla*, German for "house," for a horse stall or a pigsty. But one Gothic import remains ubiquitous. As we were tooling around Lago Maggiore many years ago, Bob asked me, "Who is this guy Albergo and why is his name on so many buildings?" I gently told him that *albergo*—from the Gothic *haribergo* for "military lodging"—means "hotel."

Cristina produced another piece of evidence of the still scruffy vernacular's encroachment into respectable territory: a template for confessing sins, an early form of the modern "Bless me, Father, for I have sinned." Even though priests conducted religious services in Latin, she explained, they had to understand and be understood by their largely unschooled congregations. For this reason in 813 Charlemagne ordered prelates throughout Christendom to preach their sermons in the local idiom.

To elevate their parishioners' souls, some priests decided to add music to their services and composed religious lyrics with vernacular words set to the melodies of popular folk songs and dance tunes. Their congregations sang along zestfully—usually substituting the familiar, often raunchy words they already knew. The practice continued until the 1500s, when an outraged Council of Trent threatened to ban music entirely from Catholic liturgy.

The task of convincing the reformers otherwise fell to Giovanni Pierluigi da Palestrina (c.1515–1594), who as a boy sang so sweetly on the streets of Rome while selling produce from his parents' farm that a choirmaster from the church of Santa Maria Maggiore provided for his musical education. His polyphonic Missa Papae Marcelli (Mass of Pope Marcellus) convinced the ecclesiastical reformers of the edifying value of church music—and helped create Italian classical composition in the process.

Clerics weren't the only ones to acquire at least some functional knowledge of Latin in the Dark Ages. A new breed of professional scribes called *notai* served indispensable roles in preparing and copying official documents with what came to be known as the prized "fine Italian hand." (*Notai*, not to be dismissed as glorified American-style notaries, remain crucial for almost any legal transaction in Italy today.) These shrewd men of business and law have long known a thing or two about treachery. To foil unscrupulous schemers who might add a codicil in a margin to alter a deed's intent or terms, they filled the white space of official documents with elaborate doodles, whimsical verses, or brain-teasing puzzles—all in the homespun *volgare*. Some vented their rage with scorching colloquial invectives that still simmer on faded parchment. One, aimed at a Signore Caprotesta (Mr. Goathead), beseeched the devil to damn the miserable cuckold and his whore of a wife to hell.

Cristina warns me that the most famous marginal musing may also strike me as a little bit crude. *L' indovinello di Verona*, the riddle of Verona, was written some time in the 700s or 800s but only discovered in a liturgical book in 1924. Atop one of the pages, the author penned an enigmatic description of two oxen sowing black seed as they pull a plow forward over a white field. Rearranged in verse, the lines translate as:

> Leading oxen in front of him
> White fields he plowed
> A white plow he held
> A black seed he sowed.

What did these curious, vaguely suggestive words mean? Were they part of a farmer's song or some sort of agricultural treatise? The riddle was unraveled in 1925—thanks not to a linguistic archaeologist but to an Italian grandmother. During a lecture at the University of Bologna, a student, Liana Calza, announced that she recognized this verse as one of the nursery rhymes her grandmother had taught her as a little girl. The dumbfounded professor listened with amazement as the young woman explained that the humped beasts were the knuckles of a writer's hand holding a white quill pen that "sowed" a stream of black ink across a "field" of white paper.

Cristina provided other "sightings" of the feisty vernacular—in battle accounts, business ledgers, crusaders' letters, and an occasional serious musing on science or philosophy. But the great monument of early Italian, the first official document to include the *volgare*, didn't appear until 960—Italian's designated birth year. A court judgment called the *Placito di Capua* settled a property dispute between the monks of the famed Benedictine monastery at Monte Cassino in central Italy and a neighbor who had filed a claim for a plot of adjacent land.

After the official Latin summary of the case, the three judges repeated the verdict, granting the land to the monks on the basis of prior possession. Once Italian students memorized the historic words each judge scrawled in his own hand in a language that was no longer Latin but not yet Italian: *"Sao ko kelle terre, per kelle fini qui ki contene, trenta anni le possette parte Sancti Benedicti."* "I know," each judge wrote, "that the abbey of St. Benedict possessed these lands, within the borders to which this refers, for thirty years."

*"Ero molto emozionata!"* ("I was very excited"), Cristina tells me, recalling that tears flooded her eyes the first time she saw the original manuscript, which the abbey lent to the Uffizi for its exhibit on the Italian language. As she unfurls a copy of the oversize document before me, I can understand why. In the crude lettering and crooked lines of the three judges, you can sense a linguistic embryo stirring to life.

The *Placito di Capua* marked a sea change for Italian. For the first time the people of the peninsula clearly realized they were speaking a language distinct from Latin. This vernacular came to be known as *lingua materna*, the mother tongue, while Latin, which students had to go to school to learn, was called *la grammatica*. Although Latin retained its monopoly on scholarship, law, medicine, and religious studies, higher education itself inspired Italian words, such as *università* (first defined as a corporation, then as a body of students), *facoltà* (faculty), and *lettura* (lecture).

The number of recognized words in the mother tongue roughly tripled between the years 950 to 1300, from a mere

5,000 to an estimated 10,000 to 15,000. Their scribes snatched syllables out of thin air, writing what they heard exactly as the word sounded. Although the inhabitants of Bologna, Genoa, Venice, Salerno, Palermo, and other places contributed some widely used words, the resourceful Tuscans proved the most creative in inventing names for whatever new concepts, techniques, materials, and diversions the volatile times demanded.

Of course, Italians first had to name themselves. Ancient Romans, such as Gaius Julius Caesar and Marcus Tullius Cicero, bore three names: a basic first name, a clan name, and also a family name that was handed down. By medieval times, the latter two names disappeared and people were known by only one name, which became confusing as the population grew and the Marios and Marias multiplied. And so Italians began adding a second distinguishing label or surname (called a patronymic) to their names, sometimes with the prefix *di* to mean "son of" or *da* for a town of origin, as in Leonardo da Vinci.

Occupations inspired names such as Tagliabue for "ox-cutter" or "butcher" and Botticelli for "barrel maker" (the nickname later given to the artist Alessandro di Mariano di Vanni Filipepi, better known as Sandro Botticelli, whose brother made barrels). Others acquired names inspired by their appearance (Basso for "short," Rosso for "redhead"), or personality (Benamato for "well loved"; Bentaccordi for "congenial"; Benedetto for "blessed"; Bonmarito for "good husband"). Orphans, abandoned anonymously on church or convent steps, were given names such as Esposito, meaning "exposed" from the Latin for "placed outside," Poverelli for "poor little ones," Trovatelli for "little foundlings," or Orfanelli for "little orphans."

The bearer of the sinister name Guido Bevisangue (Drink-blood) came by this moniker in a particularly horrific way. The story starts with a guy named Guido, who married the pretty, virtuous daughter of the Duke of Ravenna. Their son, setting himself up as Ravenna's lord, debauched the wives of the town's leading families. The local men rose up and massacred the licentious ruler and his entire family, except for an infant named Guido, who was away with a wet nurse. When he reached manhood, Guido wreaked such fierce revenge on the people of Ravenna that he became known as Bevisangue for his repulsive habit of licking the blood of his many victims from his sword.

A string of grandsons, all called Guidoguerra, fought staunchly in a seemingly endless series of bloody conflicts. One of these skillful warriors became political counselor to Matilda, the *gran contessa* of Tuscany (1048–1115), an armor-wearing, horse-riding regent who ruled over a vast state in central Italy. Her castle at Canossa earned a place in the history of the Italian language in 1077. After years of conflict with Pope Gregory VII, the German king Henry IV crossed the Alps in winter to appear outside its gates as a barefoot penitent seeking absolution from Matilda's papal guest. Gregory kept the emperor waiting three days below the snow-swept castle before agreeing to see him. To this day, the phrase *andare a Canossa* (to go to Canossa) means to humble oneself in a dispute.

The vernacular might have retained its second-class linguistic status if not for the inspiration of the romantic songs of the Provençal troubadours. While Italy was still finding its tongue, these roving entertainers were traveling from court to court in southern France, serenading the ladies of the castles (many with husbands away on crusades) with lilting odes to their beauty and grace.

The troubadours of Provence inspired the earliest composition in Italian that can be called literary—the *ritmo laurenziano*, twenty rhyming lines scrawled on the last page of a manuscript now in Florence's Biblioteca Medicea Laurenziana, the glorious Medici Library. Writing in a script typical of the late-twelfth or early-thirteenth century, a minstrel heaped praise on the archbishop of Pisa, lauding him as worthy of elevation to the papacy. His ulterior motive was persuading the prelate to give him a horse. The minstrel promised that if he did so he would show it to the bishop of nearby Volterra—although whether to impress or irritate isn't clear.

Growing up in a Catholic family, I learned about the value of currying a bishop's favor. However, I found the colorful stories of the saints far more appealing. The children's favorite was St. Francis of Assisi (1181–1226), if only because we could bring our pets to church for a blessing on his feast day. Yet this beloved saint, renowned for his rapport with all God's creatures, didn't start out on a godly path.

When his French-born wife gave birth to a son who was christened Giovanni, Pietro di Bernardone, a wool merchant in Assisi, renamed him Francesco as a tribute to her and to the country he most admired. A sickly but charming child, Francesco became the ringleader of a group of fun-loving, hard-drinking, spoiled young men. According to his first biographer, he had the distinction of acting "even more stupidly than the rest." Among the young playboy's delights were the charming chansons of Provence, which had migrated to Italy.

Hungry for adventure, Francesco joined Assisi's military to fight neighboring Perugia. After being captured by enemy troops, he spent nearly a year in prison before his father ransomed him. This traumatic experience, followed by a serious illness, changed Francesco. Over a period of several years, he pulled away from his rowdy gang to meditate in the mountains and pray in the dilapidated chapel of San Damiano in Assisi. One day Francesco heard the figure of Christ on the crucifix above the altar instruct him, "Repair my house, which you see is in ruins."

Francesco sold his horse and his father's finest cloth and tried to give the proceeds to the pastor. His incensed father charged him with theft. At a public hearing before the bishop of Assisi, Francesco returned the money to his father—along with every stitch of clothing he was wearing. As the naked youth explained to the bishop, he now had only a heavenly father.

Devoted to "his bride," Lady Poverty, Francesco renounced all earthly possessions and formed a religious order of "begging brothers." They built simple huts around the chapel, known as the *Porziuncola*, for little portion of land. A grand church now rises above this tiny structure, which remains one of the most sacred places I've ever visited.

Wearing the crude brown robes of the poorest Umbrian beggars, the Lord's troubadours wandered the countryside chanting God's praises in songs called *laudes* that Francesco wrote in the Umbrian dialect. Even animals responded to his heartfelt words. When a gargantuan wolf terrorized the town of Gubbio, the friar approached the beast. The wolf lunged at him, but Francesco stood his ground and entreated him not to eat "Brother Ass" (as he referred to his body). The wolf, curling up at his feet, promised not to attack the townspeople, who provided food for the animal at the gates of their city for the rest of its life. In the town of Greccio near Assisi, Francesco brought a real ox and donkey into the church at Christmastime to create the first live crèche or Nativity scene.

Despite chronic health problems, including an eye infection that eventually blinded him, Francesco delighted in being a child of the universe. His *Canticle of the Creatures*—which one translator describes as "the first real knock-your-socks-off masterpiece of Italian poetry"—celebrates with innocent wonder Master Sun, Sister Moon, Brother Wind, Sister Water, Brother Fire, and Mother Earth. Although it was probably meant to be sung, the tune was lost. However, lines like these capture its melodic spirit:

> Be praised, my Lord, for Sister Moon and stars
> in heaven you formed them—lovely, precious, clear.
> Be praised, my Lord, for Brother Wind and air,
> and every kind of weather, cloudy and fair,
> by which you give your creatures what they need.
> Be praised, my Lord, be praised for Sister Water—
> she is so useful, precious, chaste, and humble.

(D'Epiro and Pinkowish, *Sprezzatura*, p. 76)

With this verse—comprehensible in its original language to contemporary Italians—the humblest of saints raised the humble vernacular to a heavenly height. Francesco remains almost a living presence in the hill town of Assisi, where I returned twice to study Italian—once before the 1997 earthquake damaged the cycle of twenty-eight frescoes, painted by Giotto and his followers, in the Basilica di San Francesco and once a few years later. In a Holy Week concert beneath the lovingly restored works, I smiled at a little girl who commented—rather astutely, I thought—that it seemed as if the angels and saints on the ceiling were actually singing.

If Francesco was medieval Italy's most famous saint, Federico II (1194–1250), head of the Holy Roman Empire and the kingdom of Sicily, who doubted the existence of an afterlife and dared to defy a string of popes, was its most infamous sinner. As a flame-haired boy of three, Federico inherited the kingdom of Sicily. Eventually he expanded his territory to the north, east, and west, and declared himself Holy Roman Emperor despite the pope's threat of excommunication. His peripatetic Magna Curia (Great Court) traveled throughout Sicily and southern Italy, always with a caravan of mules toting the emperor's beloved books.

Hailed as Stupor Mundi, or wonder of the world, Federico reportedly spoke more than half a dozen languages. The works of the French troubadours' rhymes so impressed the monarch that he launched a literary revolution. Renouncing Latin's assumed supremacy, Federico established the first formal school for vernacular poetry at his court. This cutting-edge salon concocted a new language, a blend of many southern dialects. The brightest of its stars, Giacomo da Lentini, developed the first sonnet (*sonetto*, from the Provençal *"sonet,"* or "little poem"), one of the most enduring and endearing literary forms. His best-known poem began with the delectable word *meravellosamente* (*meravigliosamente* in modern Italian, for "wonderfully"), which is how love seized him.

According to *Il novellino*, a late-thirteenth-century collection of anecdotes, Federico was a generous patron whose court attracted "all sorts of people"—judges, politicians, learned men, musicians, eloquent speakers, artists, jousters, swordsmen, and exotic dancers from Middle Eastern states. Curious about everything, Federico posed questions such as "How does God sit on his throne?" and "What do the angels and saints do in his presence?" Considered the father of ornithology, he wrote *The Art of Hunting with Birds*, a treatise still read and admired by falconers; founded the first state-funded library at Naples; supported the medical schools at Palermo and Salerno; and maintained a lavish menagerie for studies in animal breeding.

In *De vulgari eloquentia*, his treatise on language, Dante exalted the "nobility and righteousness" of Federico and his son Manfredo. "In their time," he wrote, "whatever the best Italians attempted, first appeared at the court of these mighty sovereigns." Nonetheless, in canto 10 of the *Inferno*, Dante damns Federico to a fiery tomb with other heretics who denied the existence of life after death.

A self-styled scientist as well as poet, Federico conducted one of the earliest—and cruelest—experiments in language acquisition. Curious about which tongue infants would speak if they were exposed to none, the emperor ordered complete silence among those caring for several newborns. The babies, starved of human sound, all died. In another ghoulish experiment, Federico reportedly had a man suffocated in a sealed barrel to see whether his soul could be observed leaving the container.

Federico clashed repeatedly with a string of popes, who excommunicated, deposed, denounced, and allegedly tried to poison him. The fierce ongoing power struggle between his imperial party, the Ghibellines, and the papal faction, the Guelfs, triggered the bloody conflicts that convulsed Italy's city-states for decades. Federico died of dysentery in southern Italy in 1250. When Pope Innocent IV announced his death, he declared, "Let us rejoice and be glad!" The congregation shouted, "Down to hell he went!" According to Sicilian legend, devils carried Federico's soul through Mount Etna into the inferno.

Taking a different direction, the freshly minted language of Federico's court drifted north to Florence, the Latin name of which means "flourish." It was about to do just that. In the thirteenth century, this thriving boomtown blossomed into the economic and cultural center of the medieval world, the greatest money market in Europe, second only to Paris in population and prominence. The citizens of this cultural hothouse would invent the Renaissance, which, as Mary McCarthy observed, "is the same as saying that they invented the modern world."

For centuries Florentines, prickly by nature, had fought their fiercest battles among themselves. Pugnacious clans routinely slaughtered each other on street corners and razed each other's houses and fortified towers. Prosperity, which demanded an end to such carnage, forced Florentines—described by a historian of the times as *colti* (educated), *benestanti* (well off), and *litigiosi* (quarrelsome)—to channel their hostility into less bruising forms of dispute such as public debates and private litigation. A twelfth-century census recorded ten times as many lawyers and *notai* as doctors and surgeons.

From dawn into darkness Florence's narrow streets echoed with words. Heralds on horseback proclaimed decrees and death sentences. Vendors hawked their wares, criers called out for wet nurses and laborers, minstrels sang, and friars chanted praises to

God. The quick-witted townspeople turned daily dialogues into verbal jousts, while aggrieved citizens aired their complaints at the "harangue site" in front of Palazzo Vecchio, the town hall.

Traders transporting silks, spices, salt, and other prized commodities from the Middle East brought currencies to exchange in Florence. As their businesses grew, local money changers expanded from tables to counters called *banchi*, the origins of the word "bank." In 1250 the city coin, the florin, nicknamed Messer Fiorino, with the image of its patron saint, John the Baptist, on one side, became the currency of Europe. The founding families of the Florentine banks, which loaned millions of florins to popes, kings, and princes, turned into medieval Midases.

Florence's craftsmen, organized into guilds called *arti*, set new standards for innovation and workmanship. Its wool and silk businesses dressed and draped the courts of Europe. The best catalog of the city's prospering trades comes from its streets, named for the makers of the pointy-toed footwear seen in Renaissance paintings (Calzaioli), wool carders (Cardatori), the vats of cloth dyers (Caldaie), metalworkers who produced silver thread for sumptuous fabrics (Ariento), tanneries (Conçe), and buckle makers (Fibbiai). Woodworkers may have earned Via Chiucchiurlaia its appellation as Noisy Street—although many others probably qualified.

To this day *fiorentinità* signifies taste, quality, and the world's finest leather goods and items, such as the handcrafted boxes of inlaid wood, metal, and stone that I collect. I purchased my latest acquisition, a hinged box of yellow Siena marble with inlays of *pietra dura* (hard stone) and various minerals, at the Galleria Romanelli, which has been in business since 1860. The grandfather of the current owner, the sculptor Folco Romanelli, carved the bust of the sculptor Benvenuto Cellini that sits on the Ponte Vecchio, where my daughter, Julia, and I would pause to listen to impromptu concerts on summer evenings.

After starting our conversation in Italian, the salesclerk and I switched to our native English (mine American, hers British). When I told her about my book project, she compared the local language to Tuscan bread—simple and unsalted, so it soaked up all sorts of rich and pungent sauces. As I left, she added that I should have seen Florence fifty years ago, when she first arrived and "all the interesting people were still alive."

I wondered about her lamented acquaintances' current location when I crossed the river to the intersection of Via dell'Inferno and Via del Purgatorio. Neither was named for their place in Dante's *Divine Comedy* but for competing wineshops or inns, one a hell and the other a purgatory. The condemned men en route to these otherworldly destinations walked along the Via dei Malcontenti (Street of the Discontented) accompanied by hooded members of the Compagnia dei Neri (Company of the Blacks), through the Porta alla Giustizia (Gate of Justice) to the scaffold.

One of Florence's oldest streets, Via Burella, dates back to Roman times, when its underground chambers housed both prisoners and wild animals, all of whom would fight in the local amphitheater. Dante used *burella* in his *Divine Comedy* to describe a dark cell, "ill-floored and scant of light." In medieval times, cheap wine cellars and brothels lined Via Burella. More upscale pleasure-seekers strolled to the Via delle Belle Donne (Street of the Pretty Women), where amorous beauties displayed their charms.

Not surprisingly, a city with such sonorous street names

boasted the highest literacy rate in Europe. About 30 percent of Florentine men could read and write Latin. Yet the city's brash young writers preferred playing with their vibrant vernacular. Inspired by the Sicilians' lyrical verses, which had been "Tuscanized" by scribes as they made their way north, the Florentines perfected a sweet new style (*dolce stil nuovo*) for love poetry. The sole woman among them, known as Compiuta Donzella (almost certainly a pen name), left behind a single sad poem about being forced to marry a man she did not love.

> For my father has wronged me . . .
> he wishes to give me a husband against my will.
> And I have no wish or desire for that
> And spend every hour in great torment
> So that no joy comes to me from either flower or leaf.
>
> (Kay, *The Penguin Book of Italian Verse*, p. 52)

Although the sweet new stylists mainly explored the spiritual and psychological nature of love, the red-blooded Tuscan men couldn't resist coarser themes, as in these lines:

> When you find yourself alone with her
> Take her in your arms confidently,
> Showing then how strong and hard you are,
> Then shove the peg in.
>
> (Usher, "Origins and Duecento," p. 7)

Some speculate that the author of this bawdy lyric was none other than the young Dante Alighieri, who could wield a pen as aggressively as a sword. In the medieval equivalent of modern online "flaming," his quick-witted contemporaries exchanged barbs and taunts grievous enough to provoke long feuds. After actual battles, they circulated insulting verses about their defeated foes—and sometimes acted them out. When they won the battle of Campaldino, in which Dante fought, the Florentines threw thirty dead jackasses with bishop's miters (representing Arezzo's fighting prelate) over the town walls.

Dante, who would be driven at midlife from friends, family, and Florence, abandoned rambunctious versifying for a far more ambitious mission. He consciously set out to craft an "illustrious" language, illuminated and illuminating, that would be worthy of a great court and government—if any was ever to emerge in his battered peninsula. In his *Divine Comedy*, Dante achieved his goal. This linguistic alchemist spun Italy's lusty, lively, long-maligned vulgar tongue into literary gold: a gleaming new language second to none in its power and profundity.

But the medieval poet with whom I feel the most personal bond is Cecco Angiolieri of Siena (1260–1312), who accomplished a feat that had frustrated many of my earlier tutors: teaching me the tricky two-tense combination required for an Italian "hypothetical." Although Cristina originally introduced me to his poetry for purely historical reasons, she mentioned that one verse in particular could serve as a how-to for hypotheticals. It begins with the memorable line *"Se i' fosse foco, arderei il mondo"* and translates as,

If I were fire, I'd burn up the world.
If I were wind, I'd storm it.

If I were water, I'd drown it.
If I were God, I'd send it into the abyss.

After venting more rage in this string of if-onlys, the volatile
Angiolieri concludes with a twist:

If I were Cecco, as I am and was,
I would take all the women who are young and gay
And leave the old and ugly to other men.

(Kay, *The Penguin Book of Italian Verse*, p. 70)

As a tribute to Cecco's feisty spirit, I taught my husband,
Bob, a seemingly straightforward hypothetical phrase that actually requires some fancy grammatical footwork: "If I were to
study Italian more, I would speak it better." *"Se io studiassi di più
l'italiano, lo parlerei meglio."* Every time this intricate phrase slides
smoothly off his tongue, Italians practically give him a standing
ovation. I silently take a bow and think of Cecco, burning up
the world with his words.

# To Hell and Back with Dante Alighieri

IT WAS DISLIKE AT FIRST SIGHT. EVERYTHING about Dante Alighieri put me off. As artists traditionally portrayed him, the medieval poet seemed a ferocious grump with a big beak, jutted chin, petulant sneer, and hooded eyes. His brooding face glowered at me everywhere I turned in Italy—in classrooms, museums, civic halls, even on a tapestry in the parlor of the cozy apartment that I rent in Rome and a pedestal in a suite named for his muse Beatrice in the palazzo in Florence where I stay. Although writers like William Blake learned Italian just to read Dante, I resisted. The *Divine Comedy* seemed too daunting, too distant, too terribly fourteenth century.

Then Paola Sensi-Isolani, a Florence-born literature professor at St. Mary's College in Moraga, California, showed me a copy of the first adaptation of *La Divina Commedia* that she read as a girl of eight: a vintage Italian Walt Disney comic book featuring Mickey Mouse (Topolino in Italian) as Dante with Minnie Mouse as his adored Beatrice. A bicycle-riding Goofy stands in for Virgil, the great Roman poet, who guides Dante through the perils of the *Inferno*. On the final page, Mickey, Minnie, and Donald Duck (in a deus ex machina appearance) beam from a cloud in paradise.

This whimsical treatment of a stirring adventure tale made me think that I may have been wrong about Dante. I'm not the only one. Much of what the experts known as *dantisti* long assumed about the seven-hundred-something-year-old writer has proven wrong—right down to the hallmark hook in his nose. A few years ago researchers at the University of Bologna completed a meticulous reconstruction of Dante's face, based on drawings, actual historical measurements of his skull, and 3D computer technology. According to their calculations, Dante was quite ordinary-looking, with large eyes, a rounded jaw, and a pudgy nose that might have been punched and broken.

I decided to observe this noted *nasone* (big nose) firsthand by booking a table for dinner at Florence's chic Alle Murate restaurant in the Palazzo dell'Arte dei Giudici e Notai (Palace of the Guild of Judges and Notai). On the walls of this former meeting hall, restorers found large sections of frescoes, one depicting Dante as a young man in the company of other revered writers. In between courses, my daughter and I listened to an audiotaped account of the discovery of the oldest known portrait of the poet. After dinner, we climbed the stairs to stand almost nose to nose with Dante's image. Without doubt, his beak—presumably pre-punch—is long and smooth. Yet not even here does Dante smile. As photographs of his death mask attest, the grand poet died as he lived: frowning. He had good reason.

Scholars have quibbled over many facts of Dante's life—the year of his birth (the current consensus is 1265), his name (he was christened Durante—yes, as in Jimmy), and whether or not his mother's death early in his life and his father's remarriage plunged him into an unhappy childhood. Once they assumed that his muse, Beatrice (whose name can mean "blessed" or "bringer of blessings"), was a fantasy or symbol of grace on earth. But she was real, a daughter of the distinguished Portinari family. Dante first glimpsed her in La Badia, one of Florence's sweetest chapels, where lovers still leave flowers and notes at Beatrice's tomb.

Despite Dante's unrequited, undying crush, the two rarely met and barely spoke. Both entered arranged marriages. Dante's wife, Gemma, bore him at least three children, but neither she nor his offspring merit a single mention in his works. After Beatrice's death, probably in childbirth in 1290, Dante swore "to write of her what has never been written of another woman." This he certainly did, transforming the literary image of woman from evil temptress to tenderhearted, soul-saving redeemer.

But Dante could use words to wound as well. He once published sonnets claiming that a friend's wife coughed incessantly in church because of his failure to satisfy her in the bedroom. In reply, the irate husband denounced Dante as an abject coward who when confronted by a family enemy defecated in his pants an amount such that "two packhorses could not carry it." Their "low-style" dispute typifies a *tenzone*, an Italian literary contest in which two writers alternate insults, a tradition that began in the Middle Ages and continues to this day.

Drawn to Florence's raucous political life, Dante relinquished his familial claims to nobility and enrolled in the apothecaries' guild. (Writers somehow qualified, possibly by their use of ink.) The Guelfs, supporters of the papacy, had driven the pro-imperial Ghibellines from Italy, but then divided into two factions: Blacks and Whites. Dante, as a White Guelf, served as a commissioner of public works. Because he vetoed so many projects, his colleagues called him Nihil Fiat, Latin for "Do nothing," his standard recommendation.

In 1301 during Dante's term as one of the town's priors, or city councilmen, civil war ripped Florence apart. The Blacks hunted down and slaughtered the leaders of the Whites. In Rome on a papal mission, Dante escaped the bloodbath but faced trumped-up charges of misuse of public funds. The Blacks sentenced Dante and 350 other Whites—the party's intellectual elite—to lifetime exile and razed their houses, reducing central Florence to ashes. If Dante ever were to return, he would be burned to death—and, his political foes later decreed, so would his sons when they turned fifteen.

Everything Dante had worked for and earned—every shred of dignity, security, comfort, influence, and respect—disappeared overnight. At age thirty-six, he was penniless, friendless, powerless, homeless—as he put it, "a ship without sails or rudder, driven to various harbors and shores by the parching wind that blows from pinching poverty."

Wandering through the hostile countryside, Dante would hang his hat on a peg in the center of a new town and trade his services for a meal and a roof—if only in a barn or stable—for the night. For a while Dante joined with other White Guelfs in plots of vengeance, but eventually declared himself a party of one. Cursing politicians of every sort, he derided his countrymen as filthy pigs.

Around 1307 Dante began work on what he called *La Commedia* (designated a comedy because it begins in sadness and ends in happiness). No one has pulled off a comparable literary tour de force before or since. "When I taught high school students, I'd get them interested in Dante by talking about the artistic technique of rock musicians, their amazing ability to play so many notes so fast and furiously," says Giuseppe Patota, professor of the history of the Italian language at the Univesity of Siena-Arezzo. "Dante wrote poetry the way a rock star plays guitar."

The medieval virtuoso composed 14,233 eleven-syllable lines organized into one hundred cantos in three volumes: *Inferno*, *Purgatorio*, and *Paradiso*. Rejecting Latin as too elitist and regional dialects (including his native Tuscan) as inadequate, Dante fashioned a lustrous new vernacular to portray a fantastic universe that stretched from the depths of hell to the heights of heaven. A word that Dante concocted best describes how he wrote: *sovramagnificentissimamente*, in a very, very, very magnificent way.

In Dante's braided rhyme scheme, called *terza rima*, the first and third lines of every three-line *terzina* rhyme, and the second line rhymes with the first line of the next *terzina*. As a final fillip, the last line of the last canto of every volume ends with the same word: *stelle* (stars). Perhaps most remarkable of all, Dante imagined his entire glorious epic, more than 100,000 words from beginning to end, before he set quill to parchment. In this masterwork, Italian, nationless and motherless, found a father.

If I was really to understand both Italian and Italians, I realized that I had to understand Dante. Although tempted to start with contemporary cartoon adaptations, I bought an English translation of the *Divine Comedy*—several, in fact, although I'm partial to John Ciardi's. My unanticipated reaction: *Wow!* Like modern readers ensnared by the wizardly world of Harry Potter, I skidded into a fully imagined alternate world. An action-packed, high-adrenaline, breathtaking, rip-roaring yarn leapt off the pages into vivid, writhing, pulsating life.

"*Certo*," says the filmmaker Gianfranco Angelucci, who collaborated on screenplays with Fellini, the most Dantesque of modern directors, when we meet in Rome. "Dante was a born screenwriter. If he were alive today, he would be making movies far more fantastic than anything Hollywood has ever created."

Just consider the basic plot of *La Commedia* (a publisher in Venice added "*Divina*" later): Beginning on Good Friday eve in the year 1300, Dante—or "the pilgrim," as scholars refer to his first-person narrator—loses his way in a dark wood, travels deep into the earth, and enters a funnel-shaped hell with nine concentric circles spiraling down into an icy center. "Abandon hope, all you who enter here," reads its infamous welcome sign.

In this abyss of darkness and fright, the pilgrim sees and mentions by name 128 sinners and converses with 37 of them, meets thirty monsters, takes two hair-raising boat rides, faints twice, and witnesses the damned being whipped, bitten, crucified, burned, butchered, deformed by repulsive diseases, transformed into shrubs and snakes, buried alive in flaming graves, skewered into rocky ground, frozen in ice, and immersed in mud, excrement, boiling blood, or pitch.

His adventures assail every sense. Crossing steep slopes and thunderous waterfalls, the pilgrim endures terrible heat, bitter cold, and never-ceasing fiery rain. He beholds the fearsome sight of a river of blood carrying the bodies of the violent, with centaurs shooting arrows into those who dare raise their heads. He recoils from the disgusting stench of the marsh of the river Styx, where the sullen, mouths clogged with foul slime, lament endlessly.

The cast of memorable characters includes Hell's "staff" of giants, harpies, hybrids, and devils with fabulously depraved names such as Scarmiglione, Calcabrina, and Draghignazzo. Italian schoolchildren still relish the sheer naughty delight of Dante's description of Malacoda (Rotten Tail), the beastly leader of an army of devils who summons his wretched troops to battle by famously "making a trumpet of his ass" and farting. But in the *Inferno* the "beast that stinks up the world" is Fraud, who sports the face of a friendly man atop a body that is part winged hairy mammal and part reptile, with a long tail ending in a scorpion's stinger.

Not even today's cinematic wizards could top Dante's gruesome depiction of the Pisan Count Ugolino, sentenced to the ninth circle of hell for betraying his city. What you do not know, he tells Dante, who recognizes his name, "is how cruel my death was." In words that seem torn from his very soul, Ugolino describes being locked in a tower with his young sons. One morning they hear the little door through which they received food being hammered shut.

> I bit both of my hands in desperate grief,
> And they, thinking I acted out of hunger,
> All of a sudden stood straight up and wailed,
> "Father, the pain for us would be far less
> If you ate us! You put this wretched flesh
> Upon us and now you may strip it off!"

> Canto 33, lines 58–63, www.italianstudies.org/comedy/index.htm

Slowly, agonizingly, on the fourth day, the boys begin to starve to death. One collapses at Ugolino's feet, croaking, "Father, why don't you help me?" with his last breath. Weak, blind, half mad, Ugolino holds out for two days more and then crosses a point of desperation "when fasting did what grief had failed to do." Dante doesn't spell out what Ugolino does, but we find him in the depths of hell standing in a frozen lake, gnawing ferociously—his teeth as "strong on the bone as a dog's"—on the head of the archbishop of Pisa, who had ordered his cruel punishment.

The cannibal eternally cannibalizing his executioner epitomizes Dante's genius for *contrappasso*, the law of retribution in which every punishment perfectly suits the sin. Flatterers and pandering sycophants, "full of shit," so to speak, on earth, wade in their own excrement. Sorcerers and false prophets have their heads twisted around facing backward so they can only see behind, not ahead. Nimrod, the giant who defied God to build the Tower of Babel, jabbers ceaselessly in gibberish only he can understand.

Most grotesque, submerged in hell's deepest cavern, is three-headed Lucifer, the stone cold heart of darkness. Dante cannot even describe how "faint and frozen" he became at the sight of him. The flapping of Lucifer's bat wings freezes the river of tears shed as he eternally chews the three greatest sinners—Judas, Brutus, and Cassius, traitors of God and Rome—in his three rapacious mouths.

> With six eyes he wept, and from his three chins
> Dripped down the teardrops and a bloody froth.
> In each mouth he mashed up a separate sinner
> With his sharp teeth, as if they were a grinder,
> And in this way he put the three through torture.

Canto 34, lines 53–57, www.italianstudies.org/comedy/index.htm

To escape from hell, Dante and Virgil slide down Lucifer's hairy shank past "the point, at which the thigh revolves, right where the hip widens out." Following a subterranean path, they climb until through a small opening they glimpse "some of the lovely things the heavens hold. From there we came out to see once more the stars."

But the pilgrim's journey isn't over. Before him looms Mount Purgatory, an enormous island rising out of the ocean in what people of Dante's time thought was the Southern Hemisphere. In its antechambers negligent princes, excommunicants, and last-minute repenters linger before beginning the process of cleansing their unworthy souls.

In Purgatory sinners move at their own pace through seven terraces to cleanse themselves of pride, envy, wrath, sloth, avarice, gluttony, and lust (in descending order of seriousness). The proud bend low under the weight of giant stones; the envious have their eyes sewn shut; the slothful must run continually. Dante greets fellow poets, including the troubadour Arnaut Daniel (who speaks in Provençal—Dante's way of acknowledging the worthiness of another nation's dialect) and the Bolognese poet Guido Guinizelli, who initiated the "sweet new style" that Dante perfected. To reach his beloved muse Beatrice, Dante must pass through a wall of flames—the punishment for all who lust. As he finds a brief respite in the Garden of Eden, lost through the sin of Adam and Eve, the pilgrim beholds a spectacular procession representing the history of the church.

When Beatrice finally makes a triumphant entrance on a chariot, she bitterly reproves Dante for unfaithfulness to her memory after her death. Not only did he allow worldly distractions to imperil his soul, she reproaches him, but his thoughts may have strayed to another woman—something Dante conveniently forgets. Like any guy who knows he's screwed up with the woman he loves, he lets her know he's really, really sorry. And like any woman who loves an imperfect man, Beatrice forgives him. Dante leaves Purgatory "pure and prepared to leap up to the stars."

Beatrice's radiant eyes raise the pilgrim through the spheres of Paradise. Along the way he meets his crusader great-great-grandfather, Cacciaguida, a martyr for the faith who describes the miseries of exile in lines that provide our best insight into the bitterness Dante felt about his life on the lam: "You shall discover how salty is the savor of someone else's bread" (a reference to the Tuscan preference for unsalted bread) and "how hard the way to come down and climb up another's stairs."

In the last canto, Dante struggles to convey the inexpressible nature of God. He chooses the literary metaphor of a book bringing together all forms of knowledge, truth, and beauty scattered like loose pages throughout the universe. Dante's own book ends with a canto that T. S. Eliot described as "the highest point that poetry has ever reached or can ever reach." Its final line acclaims "the Love that moves the sun and the other stars."

The *Inferno* began to circulate in 1313 or 1314, at a time when books were becoming smaller and more portable. The first editions were about ten inches high, probably copied by paid-for-hire scribes on cheap paper made from old undergarments, animal parts, and hemp, boiled in a huge cauldron and then dried—a fitting medium for this earthy, often brutal masterpiece.

According to Boccaccio, his first biographer, Dante would finish six to eight cantos at a time and send them to his publisher to make copies. But at the time of his unanticipated death from malaria, he hadn't sent in all the cantos of *Paradiso*. His sons searched for them for months, then one, Jacopo, had a dream in which Dante appeared to say he was alive with a true life—not one of this world. He also gave precise directions as to where he had left the cantos: in a wall niche behind the stove in his bedroom. That's exactly where they found them.

Dante's epic was an instant sensation, with its fame spreading quickly throughout the peninsula and beyond. Its appeal was universal. Dante peopled his otherworldly realms with contemporaries (a few still living at the time), as well as classical and historical figures. Despite their atrocious suffering and barbarous nastiness, these sinners remain timelessly human—as vain, churlish, stingy, lazy, greedy, corrupt, deceitful, and immediately recognizable as the citizens of our world today. But just as compelling and vital is Dante's language.

Like a painter mixing pigments to create new colors and experimenting with different techniques, Dante, intoxicated by words, splashed his vast canvas with terms from every realm of human thought and experience. In addition to choice Tuscanisms, Dante mixes in smatterings from thirty-six (by his count) of Italy's dialects, along with Latin and a dash of Greek. Homey terms such as *mamma* and *babbo* (daddy) appear in his *Commedia*, as do words from late and medieval Latin. Classical allusions and ornate phrases rub against coarse expletives. Scientific terms clash against the sounds of street and stable. In one line Dante poetically describes people ruled by wrath on earth as "sullen in the sweet air gladdened by the sun." In another, he crudely pictures the filthy Greek prostitute Thais scratching herself "with cacky fingernails."

The richness and range of Dante's words served as testimony that the new vernacular (which he never named) could match if not outdo Latin or any other tongue as a poetic language. With *La Commedia*, the first major literary work in Italian, written barely a century after Francesco of Assisi's radiant canticle, the vernacular came of age.

More than seven centuries after his birth, Dante still rocks—literally. Bruce Springsteen, Patti Smith, and bands such as Radiohead and Nirvana cite him as an inspiration. They join an exalted chorus of famous fans, including William Shakespeare, John Milton, William Butler Yeats, James Joyce, Samuel Beckett, Ezra Pound, and Sigmund Freud. No other single piece of literature has generated more research, analysis, commentary, interpre-

tations, or adaptations—all of which keep prolifer
alarming rate," clucks the *Cambridge History of Italian Li*

It wasn't until I spent considerable time in Italy that I realized that Dante had profoundly influenced not just literature
but also Italian and Italians. Almost every day I heard echoes of
his words. A Roman described the frenetic bustle of the city at
Christmas as a *bolgia infernale*, using Dante's term for one of the
"rotten pockets" within the depths of hell, filled with rogues
such as rabble-rousers, hypocrites, and thieves. "Who are you
to look so ugly?" I heard one brother tease another at a friend's
home with a paraphrase of a line from canto 8 of the *Inferno*:
*"Ma tu chi se', che sì se' tanto brutto"*?

The better acquainted I became with Italians, the more
Dante elbowed his way into our conversations. Describing the
two passions of his life—for medicine and for his beautiful
wife—my friend Roberto quoted Dante's description of love so
strong that it permits "no loved one not to love." When I didn't
recognize the allusion, he wrote the line—*amor, che nullo amato
amar perdona*—on a card I keep on my desk. My tutor Alessandra's first suitor in Rome used the same line from canto 5 of the
*Inferno* when she was thirteen.

"What was your *Galeotto*?" our friend Mario asked my husband and me one evening at dinner. Seeing our confusion, off
he dashed to retrieve a dog-eared copy of *La Divina Commedia*
from his car and read the full story of Francesca da Rimini, a
beautiful young woman forced or tricked into marriage with
the brutish Gianciotto Malatesta. When her husband left her in
the care of his handsome brother Paolo, the two "charmed the
hours away" by reading the romantic tale of the knight Lancelot

and Queen Guinevere, wife of King Arthur. Just as Lancelot's friend Galeotto (Gallehaute in the French version) originally brought together those two ill-fated lovers, the book served as Paolo and Francesca's Galeotto. As they read of the first kiss Lancelot and Guinevere shared, Paolo breathed "the tremor of his kiss" on Francesca's welcoming lips. To this day a Galeotto signifies a pander, go-between, or seductive ploy.

In another famous canto, Dante describes Ulysses rallying his men to journey beyond what seemed the utmost limit of human voyaging by reminding them of their noble origins: "You were not formed to live like beasts." Mussolini appropriated this phrase—*fatti non foste a viver come bruti*—in his bombastic exhortations to restore the glory that was Rome. I've heard teachers use it to answer their weary students' questions of why they had to slog through yet another museum—and friends to justify an impetuous escape to Ponza or Capri to restore the soul.

The reason these words sound so natural in the mouths of Italians is that Dante meant them to be spoken. "The *Divine Comedy* was not written to be read in the sense of scanning the pages and deciphering what was written on them," says the *dantista* Steven Botterill of the University of California, Berkeley. "It was written to be read aloud for a culture in which the overwhelming majority of people were functionally illiterate." By choosing the vernacular, Dante deliberately targeted the masses—women, masons, craftsmen, farmers, bakers, millers—who didn't know Latin and might not have been able to read Italian.

Writing for the ear as well as the eye, Dante had to craft a saga so spellbinding that it would hold listeners in its thrall. And so he did. Throughout Italy's villages people gathered in the central piazza for readings of the *Divine Comedy*. Peasants memorized melodic lines and shared them as they worked the fields. In 1371, Florence, the town that had so ignominiously expelled its native son, hired Boccaccio as its first expert commentator on and reader of Dante's work.

The long tradition of listening to Dante continues to this day. As many as one in five Italians tuned in recently to hear the actor Roberto Benigni, who has performed *La Divina Commedia* for decades, read selected cantos on national television. "Can you imagine fifty or sixty million Americans glued to their TVs as Woody Allen reads Shakespeare?" asks an Italian transplanted to the United States.

Convinced that I had to hear Dante to grasp his full power, I listened to audiotapes and online translations, but these media couldn't capture the magic. And so I decided to listen to Dante as Italians do—in Italy, in the company of Italians. On a misty April evening in Rome, I managed to buy a ticket to an almost sold-out performance of Benigni's popular one-man show *TuttoDante*.

The presentation, under a gigantic navy blue tent erected in a piazza in a quiet Roman neighborhood, was a wholly Italian experience. The crowd was an eclectic mix of students, politicians, celebrities, young couples on Dante dates, and entire families—mothers, fathers, grandparents, and grade-schoolers. If nationals of other countries were in the crowd, they must have been speaking Italian. It was the only language I heard all night.

"If you don't come," the billboards advertising the show declared, "you're a *coglione*," a common vulgarity that literally translates into "testicle" but more generally means a loser or fool.

This should have prepared me for Benigni's stand-up routine, peppered with obscenities that shot over my head at bullet speed. The lines I did get—"I knew a guy who was so lazy, he married a pregnant woman"—sounded like borscht belt shtick. I cursed myself for the waste of an evening. I had expected Dante and seemed to be stuck with an Italian Jackie Mason.

Then the hyperactive Benigni settled down to deliver an uplifting language lesson, a *terzina*-by-*terzina* commentary on canto 5, the now familiar tale of Francesca da Rimini. "Listen to how Dante describes the darkness of hell," he exclaimed. "The light is mute, silent—*che bello!*" He lingered over Francesca's wistful comment that there is no greater sorrow than remembering joy in a time of wretchedness, noting how her lovely words moved Dante almost to tears. "But what am I doing?" Benigni eventually asked. "Talking about Dante in my words is like holding a flashlight to the sun."

Pausing to shift gears once more, he began a straight dramatic reading of the incandescent canto. At its end, the audience sat for a few seconds, silent except for the sound of sniffling. I looked at the teenage couple to my left. Both had tears running down their cheeks. I peeked at the family to my right. The eyes of husband and wife brimmed with tears. The grandmother was noisily blowing her nose. Every person in the theater rose to give Benigni a standing ovation.

Dante can evoke strong emotions in foreigners as well as Italians. Mary Anne Evans, better known by her pen name of George Eliot, studied Dante with her twenty-years-younger husband on their honeymoon in Venice. According to some accounts, after reading of Paolo and Francesca's passion, Evans, sixty and homely, suggested that the two take their marriage, initially a platonic arrangement, to a physical level. Her startled groom reportedly leapt from their balcony—although he and their union survived.

Percy Bysshe Shelley (1792–1822) didn't fare as well. In 1817 Dante inspired the British poet to leave London and walk in the footsteps of the exiled poet. For the sea leg to Lerici, he chartered a boat. Despite high seas and warnings from other sailors, Shelley insisted that the captain steer the boat, in full sail, into the storm. The boat sank, and Shelley's body floated to an Italian beach, where a friend cut out his heart and kept it for months in a mahogany chest in the British consul's wine cellar. (Dante, no doubt, would have appreciated this detail.)

How does Dante infiltrate his fans' very souls? "If *La Commedia* were a piece of music, Dante would have written *commosso* (movingly) instead of *maestoso* (majestically) or *animato* (spirited) across the top of each canto," says Benigni, who laughs and cries during performances along with his audiences. "Dante's genius is that he can find and create poetry in everything, even excrement. He doesn't say you should avoid evil in life—which is impossible—but you should confront it every day, because in that struggle every single human being has the potential of becoming something magnificent, a wonder of the universe."

Dante, unlike other great writers such as Shakespeare or Cervantes, is not just a literary giant but Italy's foremost national hero. No one can claim a greater hold on the Italian soul. "In countries like England and Spain, the nation came first, then the culture developed," explains Benigni, who describes *La Divina Commedia* as a great gift to Italians. Just as Americans celebrate George Washington as the father of our country, Italians cherish Dante for giving them both the foundation of their culture and the dream of a united nation.

Yet everything about Dante's ornate tomb in Florence's Santa Croce, the final resting place for Italy's *grandi*, its greatest artists and authors, strikes me as specious. First and foremost, not a speck of Dante's mortal remains lies there. Even the church's official guidebook describes the memorial as "an unpleasant work" completed in 1829 by Stefano Ricci. Dante's own words, taken from the *Divine Comedy*, serve as his eulogy: *Onorate l'altissimo poeta* (Honor the greatest poet). Atop the faux tomb sits a cenotaph, a monument erected to honor someone buried elsewhere, depicted as a brooding, bare-chested hunk. To his left, the disconsolate figure of "Poetry" mourns the loss of "the great bard," the supreme master of Italian, as the guidebook puts it.

Dante, buried in the Church of the Frati Minori in Ravenna, where he had been living, did not rest in peace. Florence, which sometimes seems to love its citizens best once they're dead, immediately asked for his corpse. Ravenna declared that by protecting and feeding the acclaimed poet in life, its citizens had earned the right to claim him in death.

A century and a half later a scion of the first family of Florence, the Medici, ascended to the papal throne as Pope Leo X and demanded that Ravenna surrender Dante's bones. "Just come get them," the city (more or less) replied. When the Florentine envoys arrived, the burial recess was empty. Ravenna's town fathers declared that either the remains had been stolen or Dante himself had reclaimed them so as to continue his roaming after death.

In 1865, in its infancy as a nation and in desperate need of heroes, Italy prepared to celebrate Dante's six hundredth birthday. A worker opening a hole between two chapels in the Ravenna church chanced upon a wooden box, half decomposed by the damp. Inside lay an almost complete skeleton, along with an official statement from a past prior of the monastery, testifying that these were Dante's bones, which he had hidden to protect them from the arrogant Florentines and the Medici pope. Dante's remains now lie in a small marble shrine, in Ravenna. Every year, on the anniversary of the poet's death, the *comune* of Firenze sends oil from the Tuscan hills to light the votive lamp that hangs above his tomb.

However, the real memorial to Italy's premier poet lies in the hearts and minds of his countrymen. In his memoir of imprisonment in the concentration camp at Auschwitz in World War II, the great Italian writer Primo Levi recalls reciting from memory a canto from *La Divina Commedia* to a young man who wanted to learn Italian. As he pronounced the poet's words, Levi felt that he too was hearing them for the first time, "like the blast of a trumpet, like the voice of God. For a moment I forgot who we were and where we were." Dante miraculously shone rays of beauty into an especially dismal ring of hell.

Just about every Italian I know can recite at least a few verses from the *Divine Comedy*. In the past, people of every station in life committed huge chunks to memory. Professor Sensi-Isolani illustrates this point with another anecdote from the Second World War: A partisan shepherd in Tuscany was ordered to shoot anyone who couldn't identify himself without doubt as an Italian. One night he stopped a professor biking outside Pisa after curfew without any identification documents. The partisan asked the scholar to prove his identity by reciting the seventeenth canto of the *Inferno*. He got to line 117 but couldn't remember the rest. The shepherd finished the canto for him.

On my last trip to Florence, I spent several hours in the Casa di Dante, a reconstructed medieval dwelling that may or may not have been the actual site of the poet's birth. The exhibits, which include a typical bedroom of the time, a plastic model of the battle against Arezzo in which Dante fought, numerous documents from his exile, and reproductions of art inspired by the *Divine Comedy*, imparts only a vague sense of the man and his life. But on the top floor, I found a continuously playing multimedia show that combines a taped reading of selected cantos with slides of Gustave Doré's fantastical nineteenth-century illustrations of the *Divine Comedy*.

Sitting alone, the sun filtering in through narrow windows, I stopped trying to translate the verses and surrendered to the tidal surge of Dante's words, the throbbing force that brings the language to life. As richly detailed images of suffering sinners and sanctified saints filled my eyes, Dante's rhythmic Italian rushed straight to my soul. I have no idea how long I sat there, but at the soaring end of the *Paradiso*, I felt that I had indeed been swept to hell and back. The only word that describes the feeling comes, of course, from Dante: *imparadisata*, or lifted into heaven.

## Italian's Literary Lions

FOR YEARS I BARELY GLANCED AT THE WHITE marble busts of Italy's *grandi* that line the shady paths of Rome's Pincio, the gardens above the Piazza del Popolo. But midway through a morning jog, I paused in front of Dante's austere visage. On nearby statues I recognized the names of other masters of Italian letters. Authors I'd known only from my readings materialized into three dimensions.

"So you really were chubby!" I thought as I beheld Boccaccio's sly grin and pudgy face. Petrarch, smug as I'd suspected, sported the poet's laurel crown he'd won mainly by dint of shameless self-promotion. With his curly hair, high cheekbones, and brawny shoulders, Leon Battista Alberti, the consummate Renaissance man, clearly qualified as the hunky centerfold of the lot, while the impressive size of Lorenzo de' Medici's nose was itself magnificent.

I've come to think of these literary lions with genuine affection as "my guys." (If a woman sits atop any of the Pincio's pedestals, I have yet to find her.) They've had a rough time of it in Rome. Vandals break off the noses of the Pincio statues so often that a local sculptor reportedly works full-time replacing them. Pollution and pigeons have stained their bases. Graffiti—silly black mustaches, horns (for Italians the mark of a cuckold), chilling swastikas—scar most of the faces. On my last trip to Rome bloodred paint coated Lorenzo's head and dripped down his neck.

My guys deserve better. These heroes of Italian's history did more than change the way their countrymen spoke and wrote. Over the course of two centuries, by bridging the gap between medieval and modern times, they changed forever the way the world thinks.

Italians refer to the trio of their most esteemed writers—the supreme genius Dante, the beguiling storyteller Giovanni Boccaccio, and the poetic purist Francesco Petrarca, whom we know as Petrarch—as *le tre corone* (the three crowns). Thanks to this trinity of talent, the fourteenth century still glows as the golden age of Italian literature. "That one city should have produced three such men, and that one half-century should have witnessed their successive triumphs, forms the great glory of Florence," the historian John Addington Symonds wrote in *Renaissance in Italy*, "and is one of the most notable facts in the history of genius."

If I had to be stranded in a snowstorm with one of these

authors, my hands-down choice would be Boccaccio. No one could spin a better yarn. Every raconteur since—from Chaucer to Shakespeare to Dickens to Twain—stands in this spell weaver's debt.

I took to easygoing Boccaccio the moment I heard his disarming nickname: Giovanni della Tranquillità. He was born in 1313—the year of the *Inferno*'s publication—and became Dante's first biographer, commentator, and public reader. Unlike Dante, who descended from an old and distinguished family, Boccaccio was the illegitimate son of a merchant, one of the newly rich Florentines. His prosperous father brought the boy into his household and arranged an apprenticeship with the Naples branch of his bank.

Boccaccio was a disaster, as completely unsuited for accounting as I would be (another reason I feel a bond with him). At his father's urging, he switched to law, which turned out to be another mismatch of temperament and talent. All Boccaccio wanted to do was write, eat (he was a lifelong *buona forchetta*, or big eater), and chase women. He fathered two illegitimate children in Naples and another in Ravenna. But the unattainable woman he pined for was "Fiammetta" (little flame), the inspiration of his early writings.

Boccaccio might have ambled good-naturedly through life, but fate blindsided him. His father's bank collapsed. Fiammetta shattered his heart. In 1348 the Great Pestilence killed a quarter of Florence's citizens, including his stepmother and numerous friends. Although he never sought the assignment, Boccaccio became the foremost chronicler of Florence's plague years.

So swiftly and fiercely did this deadly disease strike, he

recounts, that robust young men and women breakfasted with their parents at home in the morning and dined with their ancestors in the afterlife by night. Doctors and priests fell alongside those they tended. For a price men called *becchini*, for grave diggers, now the word for undertakers, carried away bodies, sometimes stacking the corpses of children atop their parents, to bury in pits without so much as a final blessing. Many believed this devastation foreshadowed the end of the world.

Boccaccio's antidote to the daily horror was the most exuberant, entertaining, death-defying work of literature the world had seen. In the *Decameron*, Italian's first great prose narrative, a group of seven young women and three young men taking refuge in a country villa swap one hundred tales—called *novelle*, for "news or novelty"—of love, lust, mischief, and treachery. As Boccaccio's "merry brigade" (*lieta brigata*, a description one of my teachers used for a particularly congenial conversation group) demonstrated, the omnipresent threat of death intensifies the love of life.

I started reading a translation of the *Decameron* during Bob's summerlong sabbatical in Italy in 2001. As we traipsed from village to village I'd look around a piazza and see characters straight from his pages: wily merchants, corrupt politicians, clever wives, henpecked husbands, and bumbling fools.

Every town, I discovered, has an unfortunate simpleton like Calandrino. In the *Decameron*, two of Boccaccio's pranksters, Bruno and Buffalmacco, convince Calandrino that he has found a magic stone, which they call a heliotrope (also the name of a plant with purplish flowers), that makes people invisible. They then casually shag pebbles at the spot where the "invisible" Calandrino is standing. In another *beffa*, or prank, they get him drunk, steal his pig, and make him pay for an elaborate lie-detecting test to prove he's the thief. When the two convince the buffoon that he is pregnant, he blames his wife, Tessa, for insisting on being on top during sex. Calandrino ends up turning over all of a recent inheritance to procure an abortion. Then the jokers get him in hot water with Tessa by arranging for her to find him in a haystack with a young girl.

While no sin goes unpunished in the *Divine Comedy*, I was glad to see that many of Boccaccio's irascible characters get off with a wink and a smile. Take Filippa, whose husband caught her with a lover in Prato, which condemned adulterers to the stake. At her trial, she asks her husband if she had ever denied him sex. No, he concedes.

"Well, then, what should I have done with the extra—thrown it to the dogs?" she demands. "Isn't it better that a noble gentleman who loves me more than himself should have it, instead of it being lost or wasted?" Roaring in laughter, the townspeople repeal their harsh statute. In another story, an abbess catches a nun in bed with a man. The young woman deftly defuses her superior's wrath by pointing out that, in her rush to get dressed, the abbess mistakenly threw the blacks pants of her lover (a priest) over her head instead of her veil.

Like most Italian men, Boccaccio had, at least in his youth, a romantic streak, which shows in his sweetest tale, that of Federigo and his falcon. This young Florentine spends his entire fortune trying to win the heart of a wealthy married woman, the virtuous Monna Giovanna. After her husband dies, the widow's young son falls grievously ill and entreats her for the one thing he thinks would make him well—Federigo's prized bird. Desperate, Monna Giovanna, planning to beg for the falcon, arrives at Federigo's house at lunchtime. In a twist that foreshadows O. Henry's touching "The Gift of the Magi," Federigo, embarrassed that he has no food to offer her, kills his prized falcon, roasts it on a spit, and serves it. Monna Giovanna's son dies, but when she learns of Federigo's selfless deed, she marries him—thereby making him rich again. "Better a man in need of riches," she decides, "than riches in need of a man."

Boccaccio's prose rivaled Dante's poetry in its range, stretching Italian from the highest to the lowest levels. His *cornici*, the luxuriously ornamented introductions that serve as the framework for the *Decameron*, are supremely elegant. Contrary to the common perception, only about a quarter of his tales have bawdy themes, but these sparkle with such earthy vitality that Italian coined the word *boccaccesco* to describe a spicy story.

I didn't fully appreciate this genre until I read my way in Italian to the tenth tale of the third day. Suddenly I thought of the U.S. Supreme Court justice Potter Stewart, who famously declared that while he might not be able to define pornography, he knew it when he saw it. I wasn't sure what *boccaccesco* was exactly, but I certainly recognized its raciness—and finally fathomed the knowing wink that accompanied Italian jokes about "putting the devil in hell." In this lighthearted tale, a young hermit, instructing a beautiful but naïve young girl, convinces her that she could best serve God by putting the devil, springing to life in his penis, into "hell," her dark and warm inferno. In a typically *boccaccesco* spin, the girl becomes so devoted to this form of worship that she wears the poor man out.

Boccaccio's zesty stories spread as swiftly as the contagion that inspired them. However, their author came to scorn them, along with the Italian vernacular, and chose instead to write turgid tomes in Latin. His girth grew, and his health deteriorated. After two marriages and countless liaisons, his love life soured to such an extent that Boccaccio derided all women in a misogynist treatise. Perhaps under the influence of religious extremists, he despaired of his literary merit and considered burning his works and his library. Petrarch stopped him.

This act is not the only reason we have for being in the poet's debt. The acclaimed thinker and writer has been described as the first humanist, father of the Renaissance, and the first modern man. His Florentine father, an ally of Dante's, was exiled in the same political purge of the White Guelfs. Born in 1304 in Arezzo, Petrarch spent many years near Avignon, home of the exiled papacy from 1309 to 1377, where both father and (eventually) son worked in various church offices.

Before being lured to Italy, Bob and I often vacationed in the countryside around Avignon, a town that always struck me as cosmopolitan and urbane. Petrarch certainly was both. Although he took clerical vows that prohibited marriage, he fathered at least two children. A man of the world, he traveled and studied throughout Europe, developing an early fascination with ancient manuscripts and cultivating friendships with anyone and everyone worth knowing—and being known by. Spinning his own life into a legend, Petrarch became Europe's first literary celebrity. Six feet tall, this towering figure felt so at home with the great men of classical times that he wrote (and published) letters to them.

When he documented his ascent of Mount Ventoux, Petrarch gained acclaim as the father of Alpine climbing. With the help of his well-placed friends, he also climbed the steps of Rome's Capitoline Hill in 1341 to accept a laurel wreath, the first bequeathed on a poet laureate since antiquity. In his acceptance speech, with characteristic immodesty, Petrarch declared that only emperors and poets were worthy of such an honor, a sentiment that seeded the apotheosis of the artist that would come in the Renaissance.

I was so put off by Petrarch's persona that I might never have read his poetry if not for Ferruccio, a mariner who captains and charters boats in Porto Ercole, a quaint port on the Tuscan peninsula called Argentario for its *argento*, or silver ore. That's what the guidebooks say, but I prefer Ferruccio's more poetic contention that the radiant sight of the full moon turning the sea to silver inspired the name.

We've been sailing the Tyrrhenian Sea off the Argentario with Ferruccio for more than a decade. From him I learned that Italian has a specific word for a ship's boy, *mozzo* (which is what Bob claims to be), and for the person who prepares food on board, *cambuso* (one of the roles of his co-captain, Erasmo). In sails to Italy's enthralling islands—Sardinia, Elba, Ponza, and Capri among them—we've passed long golden summer days and silver moonlit nights talking of anything and everything, including Ferruccio's favorite poet, Petrarch.

"No one, Diana," he insisted in his gravelly low voice, "was more romantic." Well, yes. And no. On April 6, 1327, Petrarch beheld the most beautiful woman he'd ever seen in a church in Avignon. So smitten was he with the nineteen-year-old married beauty that he began to express in writing "the boundless love for which there was no cure." His *canzoniere*, or songbook, with 366 sonnets and other verses—a leap year's worth of tributes—all dedicated to the woman he called Laura, created the model for Italian love poetry.

Yet physical love had almost nothing to do with it. "You can't imagine what Laura's leg looked like—or even her having legs," Professor Giuseppe Patota, coauthor with Professor Valeria Della Valle of *L'italiano*, a history of the language, points out. Petrarch and his long string of successors were more enamored with the language of love than love itself. He seemed rather relieved when Laura died, saying he no longer had to struggle with "an overwhelming but pure love affair." Yet Petrarch continued to polish what he dismissively called his "little songs" for her throughout his life, transforming them into literary gems.

Petrarch, a linguistic perfectionist, fashioned a new elevated language for poetry. Rather than grubby, sweat-stained syllables snatched from real life, he embroidered eloquent phrases in which water became "liquid crystal" and his beloved ("the candid rose, thorn-encompassed") an ethereal object of adoration, praised in lines such as these:

> He looks in vain for divine beauty
> who never saw of this fair one
> as she gently turns them;
> Nor does he know how Love heals and kills
> Who does not know how sweetly she sighs,
> And how sweetly talks, and sweetly laughs.

(Kay, *The Penguin Book of Italian Verse*, p. 120)

Although this may be too saccharine for modern tastes, Petrarch's verses were hailed as "pure linguistic oxygen." Migrating as quickly as quill could carry them, they made all of Europe, in a historian's phrase, "sonnet-mad." Eventually Petrarch's rarified language inspired the Renaissance poets who created another Italian literary invention, the opera libretto (see chapter entitled "On Golden Wings," page 164).

I hold Petrarch at leastly partly responsible for the disconcerting gap between Italian's written and spoken vocabularies. The popular Italian journalist and author Beppe Severgnini calls the overwrought language that Italians often write but rarely speak (except in public orations) *l'italiano parallelo.* As if hearing the voice of Petrarch in their ears, his countrymen use *autoveicolo* instead of *macchina* for "car," *precipitazione* instead of *pioggia* for "rain," and *capo* instead of *testa* for "head."

This practice mystifies foreigners like me, who must learn three different words for something as ordinary as a face: *faccia, viso,* and *volto.* It's taken me years to realize they are not interchangeable: *Faccia* is what you wash in the morning. *Viso* appears in cosmetic ads and expressions such as *far buon viso a cattiva sorte* (to smile in the face of adversity). I didn't grasp the proper use of *volto* until I saw my friend Ludovica Sebregondi's elegant art book, *Volti di Cristo* (Faces of Christ), a limited-edition, five-thousand-euro oversized volume with artistic reproductions so precious that readers are advised to wear gloves when turning the pages. No wonder Italians chuckled when I asked if I had a *sbaffo sul mio volto* (smudge on my visage).

They did the same when I used the lofty *ventre* (abdomen) rather than the everyday *pancia* (belly) when commenting about teenagers in jeans cut so low that their tummies stick out. "Don't feel bad," a friend said. "My grandmother still complains of an aching *estremità* rather than *piede*" ("extremity" rather than "foot"). She might have been a woman after Petrarch's own heart.

But even greater than his love of fancy and fanciful words was Petrarch's passion for the ancient manuscripts that were being extricated from crumbling Roman ruins and medieval monasteries. By translating and contemplating Cicero and other Latin writers, Petrarch shifted the way people thought about life itself. Rather than the medieval view of existence as a mere way station to eternity, he espoused a fuller appreciation of the dignity and potential of human life, the fundamental principle of humanism. As his reputation grew, Petrarch dedicated himself to classical studies and settled into a scholarly life. When he died working on his books, he left money for impoverished Boccaccio to buy himself a warm winter dressing gown.

Petrarch's resuscitation of classical ideals triggered an infatuation with all things ancient that had an unanticipated linguistic consequence: Latin made a surprising comeback. Once again intellectuals exalted the superiority of the classic language, and once again the vernacular fell victim to snobbish discrimination.

When I first read critical attacks on my adopted language, I took them personally. How dare the acid-tongued, sour-spirited Latinophile Lorenzo Valla, who despised almost everything and everyone, say that Italian was a purely functional instrument of communication, lacking in rules and standardization and unworthy of literary pretensions? I couldn't even comprehend the asinine assertion of one of his contemporaries that Dante was *"un ignorante,"* who used Italian—or his own version of it—because he hadn't mastered Latin.

In time, I am glad to report, the purists did themselves in. Determined to purge medieval variations from classical Latin, they concocted an even more contrived language that only the most cultivated of their effete circle could comprehend (or at least pretend to do so). Latin remained the exclusive domain of the rich and privileged, but the vernacular kept gaining ground—if only to clear up confusion. One duke mandated its use in all official correspondence after a cleric, not the falcon he'd ordered, showed up at his door in response to a request written in Latin.

Ferruccio, the Petrarch-loving sailor, also helped me understand the ancient hold of dialects. Centuries ago the Sienese claimed and colonized the craggy island of Giglio, just off the Argentario, which subsequently fell to various Italian and foreign rulers. As a boy, Ferruccio spent his summers with his grandparents, who lived on the island and spoke its dialect. When he went to university in Siena, he startled his local classmates with his intimate knowledge of what they considered their hometown tongue. In other parts of Italy, a female sibling might be a *sorella*, *suora*, *suore*, *sorore*, *serocchia*, *sirocchia*, or *sorocchia*, they thought, but only in Siena is she a *suoro*—and, it turns out, on Giglio.

The fate of the literary dialect called *italiano*, *toscano*, or *fiorentino* hinged on the fortunes of Florence, which was entering its Camelot years. As the financial capital of the world, Florence had become the richest city in Europe, with a gross national product that surpassed that of England under the great Elizabeth I. Its family-owned banks, which invented checks, letters of credit, and treasury notes, financed (at profitable interest rates) the multimillion-florin ventures of Europe's kings.

The most successful of these dynasties were the Medici. Called God's bankers because they collected money from every country in Europe on behalf of the church, they ruled fifteenth-century Florence with the power, but not the title, of princes. The Medici effect, as generous support for creative ventures has come to be known, drew the best and the brightest in every artistic and intellectual field to Florence. The humanistic ideals of their Platonic Academy sparked the great flowering of achievement known as the Renaissance. However, the language that gave it its name (*rinascita*, or "rebirth") and became its lifeblood was Italian.

The new "vernacular humanists," with melodious names such as Marsilio Ficino and Pico della Mirandola, were cultured, courtly, elegant—and so good-looking that even the driest commentators could not resist a mention of Ficino's pleasing face or Mirandola's golden hair. These glorifiers of man's every dimension were also downright sexy. After all, as J. H. Plumb comments in *The Italian Renaissance*, sex is "par excellence the expression of the individual man."

The Greeks and Romans had known this all along. Their gods were unabashedly lusty; their poetry, explicitly erotic. It was not that the vernacular humanists advocated decadence (that would come in the 1500s with Pietro Aretino and his flagrantly erotic writing), but that they recognized and embraced sexuality as central to human experience.

Too central in some cases. A portrait in the Uffizi of

Giovanni Pico della Mirandola (1463–1494) sparked my curiosity about the blond youth reputed to be the best-looking man in Renaissance Florence. This brilliant philosopher was also one of the smartest, called the phoenix of geniuses because he knew something of everything, gifted with a memory so nimble that he could recite entire books backward (and I assume forward). At age twenty-three, Pico, as he was called, developed nine hundred theses on religion, philosophy, magic, and other intellectual pursuits, which he offered to debate against all comers in Rome.

On the way to this intellectual showdown, Pico stopped in Arezzo and became embroiled in a love affair with the wife of one of Lorenzo de' Medici's cousins, which turned out badly for everyone, especially him. Attempting to run off with the woman, he was caught, wounded, and imprisoned by her husband. He was released only upon the intervention of Lorenzo himself. Pico's most famous Italian writings were his love poems, but his more esoteric Latin musings on Plato and classic philosophy brought him under suspicion of heresy, a serious crime. Fleeing to France, he was arrested and imprisoned, once again to be released into Lorenzo's custody in Florence.

Pico might have done well to follow the example of another handsome humanist, the Renaissance marvel Leon Battista Alberti, architect, mathematician, painter, poet, art critic, and writer. Alberti contributed an invaluable work to his beloved vernacular. In order to lift his language up to the stature of Latin and Greek, he spelled out rules and regulations in the first grammar for Italian—for any European language, in fact.

Convinced that Italian was capable of expressing the noblest concepts, if properly cultivated, Alberti organized a *certame coronario* (contest for the crown). On October 22, 1441, eight competitors read poems in Italian on the subject of true friendship. When the conservative, Latin-leaning judges decided that no one merited the silver laurels, Alberti protested vehemently—and proved his point by writing his most famous work, *I libri della famiglia* (translated as *The Family in Renaissance Florence*), a treatise on the fundamental Italian institution, in Italian.

In its pages, the sensible and sensitive author offers sage advice to gentlemen: "Let a man take a wife for two reasons: the first is to perpetuate himself with children, and the second is to have a steady and constant companion for his entire life. Therefore, you must look to have a woman capable of bearing children and pleasing enough to serve as your perpetual companion."

He even ventures, despite some embarrassment, to offer recommendations on the actual engendering of children. Above all, "husbands should not couple with their wives in an agitated state of mind or when they are perturbed by fears or other like preoccupations, for such emotions . . . disturb and affect those vital seeds which then must produce the human image." Another recommendation for a man: "Make yourself intensely desired by the woman."

The polymath Alberti was immediately intrigued by a newfangled German invention, the printing press, which made its way to Italy around 1460. "With these twenty-six soldiers," its inventor Johannes Gutenberg had declared, referring to the metal type of the alphabet, "I will conquer the world." His "troops" carried Italian to an ever-growing audience throughout the peninsula and the continent.

In printing centers such as Venice, a new breed of experts emerged—specialists who corrected manuscripts so they were clear, coherent, and intelligible. Under the surveillance of these editors, Italian acquired the formal characteristics of a written language, including more consistent spelling. However, punctuation remained, as the linguist Bruno Migliorini, who wrote the first history of the Italian language in 1960, put it, "scarce and oscillating," with some writers using none at all and others arbitrarily inserting a "full stop," comma, or colon wherever they chose.

Yet even as it replaced Latin in public and private documents, Italian still lacked the prestige that only the imprimatur of the highest power in the land could confer. This was the gift of Italian's glorious white knight, Lorenzo de' Medici, the most remarkable public figure of his time. I think of him as Italian's *Principe Azzuro*, or Prince Charming. A statesman and scholar, he underwrote the first printing press in Florence, contributed lavishly to the University of Florence, and purchased books and rare manuscripts for the ever-expanding Medici library.

The single word most identified with the Medici is *palle* or "balls," the family symbol, which by various accounts represent pills (the word *medici* means "doctors"), pawnbrokers' chits, or Byzantine coins, which appear on the arms of the guild of money changers to which the family belonged. In times of danger, the Medici rallied their supporters with cries of *"Palle! Palle! Palle!"*

Lorenzo, the most charismatic Medici, charmed men, women, and the masses despite his coarse features and enormous nose. At age sixteen, he fell in love with Lucrezia Donati, a girl of "rare beauty, great honesty and truly noble birth," wrote his first biographer. In her praise, Lorenzo wrote "extremely elegant verses and rhymes in the Tuscan dialect." Though he may have worshipped this fair maiden in words, he certainly didn't keep his distance from other women. Niccolò Machiavelli, the family's historian, referred to Lorenzo as "amazingly involved in sensual affairs." Another Florentine historian, Francesco Guicciardini, described him as "licentious and very amorous."

As Lorenzo pursued love and lovers, his mother, Lucrezia Tornabuoni, a minor poet herself, set about the business of finding him a wife. As the spouse of the sickly Piero the Gouty, she made good health and breeding potential the prime criteria. Clarice Orsini, a Roman princess, was not only healthy but wealthy—and noble, a nice touch for a family that lived like royalty in all but name.

To celebrate his betrothal, Lorenzo arranged a jousting tournament, the first ever in the Florentine republic. The very concept seemed so alien that Machiavelli felt it necessary to volunteer a definition: "a scuffle of men on horseback." Critics sniped that the Medici heir was not only marrying a foreign noble but taking on princely affectations.

Lorenzo, riding a white charger, appeared in a white silk mantle bordered in scarlet and a black velvet cap encrusted with rubies and a large diamond. By special privilege, he carried the French fleur-de-lis on his shield and the red Medici *palle* on his banner (along with his married mistress's scarf). The superb young athlete unhorsed every opponent. Lorenzo won not just the day but also the hearts of his countrymen, who cheered even louder at his extravagant wedding festivities, which, as Machiavelli put it, "were held with the pomp of apparel and all other manner of magnificence befitting such a man." Although *Magnifico* was a title given to every lord in those days, Lorenzo became the most *Magnifico* of all.

This magnificence rubbed off on Italian. The superbly educated Lorenzo, who succeeded his father at age twenty, could read and write the ancient languages well. However, he chose to speak only in the simple, beautiful tongue he had learned as a child, and allowed only Italian at his table, where members of his illustrious Platonic Academy, along with the young Michelangelo and other artists, joined in the conversation.

"At Lorenzo's court," note Indro Montanelli and Roberto Gervaso in *Italy in the Golden Centuries*, "the language received those finishing touches that made it the richest, most refined, and sweetest of tongues, not only in all of Italy, but—in those days—in the whole world."

Lorenzo and his humanist tutor Poliziano produced two anthologies that served as manifestos for the Tuscan vernacular. In the first, the *Raccolta aragonese* (Aragon Collection), a gift to the Aragonese royal family, Lorenzo compiled verses by Tuscan authors from Dante to himself. His dedication praised the local *volgare* as the most advanced dialect on the peninsula because of the two centuries of illustrious poets who had used it.

In the *Comento de' miei sonetti* (Comments on My Sonnets) Lorenzo contended that the vernacular is as good as Latin—if not better—for writing "high" literature. He defended this rather daring declaration (in the heydey of humanism) that an everyday language, spoken by the uneducated masses, can deal with noble subjects by citing the richness (he uses the allusive word *copia*, which translates as "abundance") that shines through in the works of *le tre corone*, as well as the earlier Tuscan *dolce stil nuovo* poets such as Guido Cavalcanti, the man Dante called his "first friend." Just as the "Florentine empire" dominated the peninsula, Lorenzo concluded, so should its language.

Florence became a literary laboratory where writers experimented with all sorts of genres. Lorenzo himself composed love poems, lusty ballads, and *canti carnascialeschi* (festive songs), some of which the censors of the Inquisition would later decry as scandalously obscene. His compositions extolled the delights of youth, women, falconry, the tranquil Tuscan countryside, and its rustic inhabitants.

"Who happy would be, let him be," Lorenzo wrote in his most famous verse. "Of tomorrow who can say?" (*"Chi vuol esser lieto sia, del doman non v'è certezza."*) In this seize-the-day spirit, the patrician poet entertained the city with masquerades, revels, pageants, and processions. Lorenzo elevated *carnascialismo*, carnival merriment, almost to the point of art. "If ever history could be happy, it was then," wrote one commentator.

History turned dark on April 26, 1478, the bleakest day of Lorenzo's rule. The Pazzi, a rival family working in collaboration with the pope, had masterminded a daring plot. At the elevation of the Communion host during Easter Mass, as the congregation in Florence's Duomo devoutly bowed their heads, the conspirators stabbed Lorenzo and his younger brother Giuliano, who died immediately. Poliziano and other friends pulled

Lorenzo, only slightly grazed, into the vestry and barred the door. The Pazzi expected the Florentines to rally to their rebellious cause. Instead the crowds shouted *"Palle! Palle!"* for the Medici.

Lorenzo's vengeance was swift and merciless. The two leaders of the coup, including an archbishop, were hanged. (The young Leonardo sketched their dangling bodies.) Dozens of conspirators were dragged naked through the streets before being executed. The head of the Pazzi family was killed, thrust into a hole, dug up again, and then dumped in the Arno.

According to the custom of time, Botticelli painted the Pazzi conspirators with ropes around their necks on the walls of the Bargello. Lorenzo, who composed rhyming epitaphs placed below each portrait, exterminated the family name, forbidding anyone even to pronounce it. The Pazzi coat of arms was erased in perpetuity, their property confiscated. In contemporary Italian, perhaps not solely by linguistic coincidence, *pazzi* refers to people who behave insanely.

The attempted coup and its many ramifications challenged Lorenzo's leadership. The Medici's vast financial enterprises foundered as a result of mismanagement and bad loans. In his early forties, Lorenzo began to suffer complications of gout, the disease that had killed his father. A slow fever, probably caused by spreading infection, attacked, as Poliziano recorded, "not only the arteries and veins, but the limbs, intestines, nerves, bone, and marrow." Doctors brewed what they hoped would be a cure: a concoction of pulverized pearls and other precious stones that may well have hastened his death in 1492 at age forty-three.

Two years later, Lorenzo's son Piero, lacking his father's

charisma and political acumen, fled the city. That year, at the urging of the conniving lord of Milan, the French invaded the peninsula and marched into Florence. But when the French king Charles VIII demanded an extortionary sum, the Florentines refused to pay the full amount. When he threatened to sound his trumpets to call his troops to arms, a magistrate shouted the phrase that became a local proverb: *"Se suonerete le vostre trombe, noi suoneremo le nostre campane!"* ("If you sound your trumpets, we will ring our bells!")

Soon hatred for the occupying foreigners brought together an unprecedented coalition of city-states, duchies, and papal forces in the peninsula. Troops speaking a dozen dialects rallied for "the liberty of Italy"—as if "Italy" really existed. The Military and Sovereign Order of the Knights of Saint John more precisely declared that they were fighting for "the Italian language." The decisive battle, at Fornovo on July 6, 1495, marked a catastrophic turning point for Italy. Two-thirds of the soldiers who died that bloody day were Italian; the French escaped. This rout set the stage for nearly four hundred yeas of foreign occupation.

In the dark days that followed, Florence fell under the sway of the fanatic friar Girolamo Savonarola (1452–1498), who wielded words like a whip. Claiming that he personally conversed with God, Savonarola stirred his followers (derided as *piagnoni*, or snivelers and whiners, by his critics) into a frenzy with his fiery sermons. They would stream into the streets singing songs with lyrics such as "crazy, crazy for Jesus." In the infamous Bonfire of the Vanities, the snivelers rounded up and burned books, sumptuous clothing, fine furniture, jewelry, gaming tables, musical instruments, poetry, mirrors, makeup, and works of art (including paintings by Botticelli, thrown on the pyre by his own hand).

In 1498 Savonarola's opponents, known as the Arrabbiati (the Angry Ones), dragged the mad-eyed monk, charged with heresy, from his cloister. As if a single death were not enough, the Florentines tortured him on the rack for three days (breaking almost every bone in his body, except the hand he needed to sign a confession), hanged him, and then cremated his body in a giant bonfire that burned for hours in the Piazza della Signoria—the same site where he had incinerated the works of others.

Several years ago, during my Italian history studies in Florence, I walked past the plaque commemorating the last of Savonarola's blazes on my way back from dinner at the Caffè Concerto Paszkowski, my favorite of the famed writers' hangouts in the Piazza della Repubblica. On the chill, foggy evening, a young man standing nearby was playing a spirited violin concerto. The music echoed through the Piazzale degli Uffizi as I passed among Florence's statuary tributes to Dante, Boccaccio, Petrarch, and the other masters of Italian art and literature.

All Italian cities have ghosts, but Florence's seem to me to be always speaking. As I mulled over the words of its giants, I realized that I was unconsciously moving my hands beneath my cape in the very same ways that I do when I speak Italian. And I *was* speaking Italian—to myself! My teachers had predicted that someday this milestone of a moment would come, that I would start thinking, reacting, even dreaming in Italian. I didn't believe them. Yet here, in the cradle of the language, in the shadow of Italy's *tre corone*, I crossed some invisible membrane into a world that at once was entirely familiar yet completely new. Springing to life in my brain, Italian had traveled to my fingertips and set them aflight.

# The Baking of a Masterpiece

HE'D LOST HIS NOSE. HIS EYES WERE MERE holes; his mouth, a rough slit. When workers paving a neighborhood in Rome around the turn of the sixteenth century dug up the battered ancient statue, they heaved him upright on a busy street corner near Piazza Navona. In celebration of the feast of San Marco on April 25, 1501, a cardinal draped a toga around the armless torso and attached Latin epigrams to its base. Jocular Romans followed suit, covering this unofficial community bulletin board with anonymous satiric jibes that lampooned church and state.

The "talking statue" called Pasquino, Rome's oldest social and political commentator, hasn't been quiet since. *Meno male* (thank goodness)—for Italian's sake. Clever *pasquinades*, copied on sheets of paper called *cartelli* and widely circulated, managed to keep all the world talking about Italians—and Italian—throughout the ill-fated *Cinquecento*. During the years we call the 1500s, warring princes, foreign invaders, and outbreaks of the plague all but destroyed the peninsula, its people, and their language. The ultimate horror came in 1527: the sack of Rome, an unparalleled orgy of lust, wanton destruction, and unspeakable cruelty by Spanish troops and German mercenaries. "In truth," the Dutch humanist Erasmus wrote, "this was rather the fall of a world than of a city."

My friends Carla and Roberto Serafini introduced me to Pasquino, the stone survivor of the best and worst of Roman times, one night en route to their favorite pizzeria. But when Roberto commented that he was curious about what *"il grillo parlante"* was saying these days, I was confused.

"The talking cricket?" I asked.

Many Romans posting *pasquinades*, often in Romanesco dialect verse, assume this pen name, Roberto explained, describing it as a metaphor for someone *piccolo ma spiritoso* (small but witty). *"Come te"* ("Like you"), he teased. That night the musings attached to Pasquino's statue dealt mainly with a proposal to extend equal political and legal rights to unmarried couples, including gays. The topic inspired all manner of puns and parodies, many so outrageously obscene that Roberto, ever the gentleman, refused to translate them.

"They're for Aretini," he said, referring to the followers of the most famous and flamboyant of *pasquinade* authors, Pietro

Aretino (1492–1556), whose name translates into Peter, citizen of Arezzo. This self-confessed scoundrel created the prototypes of today's gossip columns and celebrity magazines.

The illegitimate son of a cobbler liked to say he was born "with the spirit of a king." Without family, fortune, or formal education, Aretino pioneered the use of language to garner attention, acclaim, and riches. After wandering through Tuscany and Umbria, he settled in Rome in 1517 and recruited the faceless Pasquino as the perfect foil for his talents. His acid pen, for hire by bankers, cardinals, aristocrats, and popes, honed the coarse *pasquinade* into a rapier-sharp weapon. When Hanno the elephant, pet of Pope Leo X, died in 1514, Aretino composed "The Last Will and Testament of the Elephant Hanno." The fictitious document, which cleverly mocked Rome's leading political and religious figures, kick-started his scandalous literary career.

In another broadside, Aretino expressed no surprise that it was taking so long for the papal conclave of 1521–22 to choose a new pontiff. After all, he sniffed, one cardinal had a wife, another couldn't keep his hands off boys, and the rest were heretics, thieves, traitors, counterfeiters, or spies. And, yes, Aretino named names—unless he was paid not to. He blatantly accused Cardinal Alessandro Farnese of having prostituted his sister to the Borgia Pope Alexander VI in order to obtain the regal crimson hat and robes of a "prince" of the church.

At times Aretino pushed the limits too far. In the libidinous *Sonetti lussuriosi* (Lewd Sonnets), he wrote bawdy dialogue for an artist's explicitly erotic engravings of copulating couples. The manuscript caused a sensation across Europe and provoked ecclesiastical ire. The church threw the artist in jail, and Aretino lost his papal patronage and protection. A would-be assassin, hired by a victim of his trenchant wit (or his cuckolding ways), knifed the pioneer pornographer and left him for dead on the banks of the Tiber.

Aretino, who survived but lost two fingers in the attack, relocated to a more hospitable venue: Venice, which he fondly described as the "seat of all vices." For almost thirty years, amid its labyrinthine streets and murky waters, Aretino indulged in every variety of lascivious activity, with a menagerie of mistresses, secretaries, boys, parasites, servants, and groupies. Despite—or perhaps because of—his outrageousness, he achieved an extraordinary position of international power and political influence. Emperor Charles V knighted him, and the pope bestowed ecclesiastical honors (although not the cardinal's noble rank that he had dared hope for). Aretino became a brand name for everything from pieces of Murano glass to horses.

"I live by the sweat of my ink pot," the freewheeling freelancer declared, churning out verses, essays, and epic poems commissioned by vain nobles hungry for flattery and fame. The Duke of Gonzaga underwrote Aretino's lavish lifestyle for years as he toiled away on a biographic ode. The leaders of France and Spain each hired him to spread scurrilous gossip about the other.

Proclaiming himself "the secretary of the world," Aretino possessed the raw talent to become one of the leading writers of his time, but lacked the discipline—and the desire. "I am a free man," he wrote. "I do not need to copy Petrarch or Boccaccio. My own genius is enough. Let others worry themselves about style and so cease to be themselves. Without a master, without a model, without a guide, without artifice, I go to work and earn my living, my well-being, and my fame. What do I need most? With a good quill and a few sheets of paper, I mock the universe."

Aretino couldn't resist mocking the Platonic humanists and their discourses on love and language. He set one of his parodies in a brothel, where an old prostitute expounds on the obscene activities of women in the three roles available to them in the Renaissance—wives, nuns, and whores. This unabashedly bawdy work, which would have made Boccaccio blush, became wildly popular throughout Europe and inspired an entire genre of ribald writing.

Born centuries too soon to blog, the "scourge of princes," as the Renaissance poet Ludovico Ariosto described him, produced a steady stream of letters oozing extravagant compliments and thinly disguised demands for hush money. He "kept all that was famous in Italy in a kind of state of siege," wrote the nineteenth-century historian Jacob Burckhardt, who condemned Aretino's work as "beggary and vulgar extortion." But even the celebrities he bedeviled couldn't resist reading him. Aretino was the first European author to publish letters in a vernacular tongue—some three thousand of them, collected into six volumes, each an immediate success.

The celebrated artists of the day were natural targets for Aretino's attention. He spread malicious insinuations about why it took Leonardo several years to finish his signature portrait of the winsome La Gioconda, third wife of a much older and very rich husband, and slavishly begged Michelangelo for drawings since, as he wrote, "there are many kings but only one Michelangelo." The artist declined Aretino's unsolicited suggestions for his *Last Judgment* in the Sistine Chapel, but noted that the gossipmonger described doomsday as if he had already witnessed it. Some see Aretino's features in Michelangelo's apocalyptic painting on the face of St. Bartholomew, while the artist himself appears on the martyr's flayed skin.

The artist Titian painted Aretino three times. The most famous of these portraits hangs in Florence's Pitti Palace. Everything about the huge figure is excessive: the massive belly, the shaggy long beard, the sumptuous velvet robes that envelop him. The French king gave Aretino the thick gold chain he wears, bearing a Latin motto that may be translated "His tongue will always speak falsehood."

Aretino died of a stroke at age sixty-four, but a widespread rumor claimed that the aging libertine's last laugh killed him. Roaring over a juicy tale, he supposedly threw back his head and fatally knocked himself out. His exit was well timed. Three years later the Inquisition placed his complete works on its Index of Prohibited Books. His secretary Niccolò Franco, whose writings were even more defiant and decadent, suffered a crueler fate: the Inquisition sentenced him to death by hanging.

Aretino represented a new literary and social phenomenon. With publishing flourishing, particularly in Venice, members of the "meritocracy"—called *poligrafi* for their multiple talents—could earn a living as writers, editors, translators, and anthologizers. Thanks to their efforts at standardizing the vernacular, by the end of the sixteenth century readers could no longer identify an Italian author's home region by his language, and punctuation assumed a more or less modern form. The *Cinquecento* also saw the invention of the enthusiastic exclamation point, dubbed *un punto affettuoso*, an affectionate period, by an editor of the time.

Throughout the peninsula, Latin and Italian remained uneasy bedfellows. Correspondents wrote letters in Italian but used Latin for headings, addresses, and dates. Lawyers questioned witnesses in Italian, but court records mixed Latin with the verbatim vernacular. Elementary and technical schools used Italian manuals, but universities remained fortresses of Latin, with no instruction in Italian. A new comic style called "macaronic" language, named for the rustic pasta, lampooned the "barbarous Latinity" of pompous pedants by presenting verses that looked like proper Latin but were chock-full of coarse expressions and vulgarities in Italian or dialect.

As the *Cinquecento* unfolded, language became a much more serious matter. Lacking their own king, court, or constitution, Italian speakers placed supreme value on their imperiled tongue. "Living with the Spanish, turning in time with the Spanish [dancing to their tune, that is]," one writer wistfully observed, "have almost taken away my language." Other Italians feigned indifference to their foreign rulers. As a dismissive saying in dialect put it, "France or Spain, as long as you eat." But a consciousness of belonging to a common civilization began to bubble up like yeast, and with it a new awareness of Italian as the vehicle for a single national culture.

Although Italian was clearly established as a literary language, Renaissance writers faced a dilemma as to which language to use on a daily basis. If they were Florentines, they could use the lively vernacular they spoke on the street. Or they could employ the more contrived and formal language of the aristocracy and courts. Or they could resurrect the classic *fiorentino* created by Dante, Petrarch, and Boccaccio in the fourteenth century.

A less practical option for non-Florentines was to write in their own dialect. The poet Ludovico Ariosto (1474–1533) of Ferrara did so in creating the greatest chivalric epic of the Italian Renaissance, *Orlando Furioso* (*Orlando Enraged*). In this sprawling saga, set against the background of war between Charlemagne and invading Saracens, the hero goes mad with unrequited love for a pagan princess. Because so few people could read his own regional dialect, Ariosto decided to rewrite the entire saga in a more Tuscan Italian—a decision that turned his life into a love-mad drama.

In Florence, Ariosto caught sight of a woman named Alessandra di Francesco Bettucci. So dazzled was he by her appearance that he noticed nothing else in the city. "I remembered little and little do I care," he wrote in an impassioned letter. "I was left with just the immortal memory that in all that fair city I saw no fairer thing than you . . . [not] anyone who could equal you in beauty, in modesty, courtesy and noble semblance, much less surpass you."

Inconveniently, Alessandra was married at the time to the nobleman Tito di Leonardo Strozzi, a member of the court of Ferrara. Eventually Ariosto achieved a happy ending. His rewritten romance finally found widespread acclaim, and after her husband's death, he married Alessandra in 1528.

A more important but lesser known *sostenitore* (supporter) of Italian was an odd fellow named Pietro Bembo (1470–1547)—

known today mainly for the typeface named for him—the well-educated son of a Venetian nobleman. This humanist scholar was utterly smitten by Petrarch and his elevated way of writing. At the turn of the sixteenth century Bembo created a *petrarchino*, the first of the little books clutched by so many lords and ladies in Renaissance portraits. (One writer described them as "the prayer books of a lay culture.") Bembo's original pocket book reproduced in type Petrarch's final handwritten copy of his Italian works, a priceless manuscript, now in the Vatican Library, that was Bembo's most cherished possession.

I began to understand Bembo, who loved falling helplessly, hopelessly, deliriously in love, after Bob and I visited the charming town of Asolo, in the Veneto, where Bembo spent part of his career. On our first visit, when Bob disappeared in search of parking, I informed the concierge at the Hotel Villa Cipriano that I had lost my husband. "Don't worry, *signora*," he beamed. "We will find you another."

Bembo was an early master of such swift substitutions. Enamored of a Venetian girl, Bembo tenderly recounted every *spasimo* of longing and frustration in letters to his admiring friends. In time he became attracted to Lucrezia Borgia, the pampered daughter of the decadent Borgia pope Alexander VI and wife of the Duke of Ferrara, Alfonso d'Este. A visit from her when he was sick with fever inspired Bembo to write steamy verses crammed with literary allusions to every pair of lovers who ever lived in print—Aeneas and Dido, Tristan and Isolde, Lancelot and Guinevere. Yet Bembo, wary of the watchful and jealous men in Lucrezia's life, restricted his passion to pen and paper.

Bembo's letters, which one critic describes as "informed, mannered, obscure, and so loaded with spiritual effusions on love, beauty, God and women that they are almost unreadable," brought him to the attention of the widow of the king of Cyprus, who presided over a "musical comedy court," as it is often described, both charming and zany, in Asolo. He became a long-term fixture and glorified the townspeople in his best-known work *Gli Asolani*, which earned him a critic's coronation as "the archpriest of love."

Bembo had a real knack for getting himself into—and out of—delicate situations. At the court of the bookish Elisabetta Gonzaga in Urbino, he enjoyed declaiming on love costumed as an ambassador of Venus, the love goddess. When he won a legitimate diplomatic post as ambassador of Venice to Florence, he became a *cavaliere servente* (a kind of Renaissance "walker," a man who escorts married ladies) and flagrantly courted the alabaster-skinned Ginevra de' Benci, the subject of a famous portrait by Leonardo now in the National Gallery in Washington, D.C. Eventually securing a post as papal secretary, Bembo settled in Rome, found a new illicit love, and fathered three children. Despite his illegitimate brood, Bembo earned a cardinal's princely robes.

The real love of Bembo's life, however, was the Italian language. On a boyhood trip to Florence, he became infatuated with the Tuscan way of talking, which he affected as an adult. To preserve and exalt his adopted vernacular—although some say it was mainly to impress a mistress—Bembo created the first rules of grammar for writing in Italian. Linguists consider his *Prose della volgar lingua* (Writings of the Vulgar Tongue), published in 1525, a watershed in the history of the Italian language.

Every literary author, Bembo argued, should write for posterity and should therefore choose the best available language. Just as Petrarch had used Latin and Greek classics as his models, Bembo sought to "purify the language of the tribe" by using Italian's most edifying models—Boccaccio for prose and Petrarch for poetry—without any contamination from Latin or dialect. Disdainful of Dante's "rough and dishonoured words," Bembo endorsed the use of only the more refined terms in the *Paradiso*.

Bembo influenced several women Renaissance poets, including Vittoria Colonna (1490–1547), whose *Rime della Divina Vittoria Colonna* was the first published book of Italian poetry by a woman. Virtually unknown outside of Italy today, Vittoria Colonna was as great a celebrity as Michelangelo (her devoted admirer) in their day—recognized, gossiped about, petitioned, pandered to, plotted against. Born into one of Rome's oldest and most powerful noble clans, the *marchesa* lived at the political, intellectual, and artistic epicenter of the times. Aretino, of course, bombarded her with sycophantic missives.

Another *Cinquecento* woman also exerted influence on book production and design. Isabella d'Este (1474–1539), "the first lady of the Renaissance," attracted the greatest talents of a golden age to her court at Mantua. Besotted by books, she collected first editions and luxurious hand-illustrated books and commissioned the first print runs of Petrarch and other poets. At her insistence, the printer added something new—page numbers—to these volumes.

Isabella's "insistence" was famously formidable. When her husband, Francesco—described by contemporaries as "short, pop-eyed, snub-nosed, and exceptionally brave"—was imprisoned in Venice, Isabella's grit, particularly in dealing with the ruthless Cesare Borgia, kept Mantua from being invaded. Upon his release, her less-than-grateful spouse declared himself "ashamed that it is our fate to have as wife a woman who is always ruled by her head." Isabella stalked out but returned to rule Mantua for twenty years after Francesco died of syphilis, contracted from prostitutes, in 1519.

Yet despite the obvious talents of Renaissance women, literary life remained very much an old boys' club—nowhere more so than in Florence. In 1541 Duke Cosimo I, a distant cousin and successor of Lorenzo il Magnifico, conferred on the Florentine Academy "the authority, honor, and privilege for an official compilation of the rules of the Tuscan language." Its distinguished but stodgy members pontificated about their vernacular in ever-more-abstruse talks and treatises. Two quintessentially Italian passions saved the language from their deadly deliberations: language and food.

I've spent enough time observing rowdy groups of bantering young men in Florence's cafés, restaurants, and piazzas to imagine how their late-Renaissance counterparts came up with a tongue-in-cheek approach to the language question. At the time an unheralded but invaluable invention was transforming Italian agriculture: *il frullone*, a sievelike device that separated wheat from chaff to produce flour. In a land where pasta and *pane* (bread) had long sustained its people, the *frullone* was as important a breakthrough in its own way as the printing press.

"Only pigs eat everything," Florence's intellectual young turks declared. Why not become human *frulloni* and separate the literary *fior di farina*—the flower (a pun in English, but not

Italian, on "flour") of the wheat—from the *crusca* (chaff or bran)? Meeting in a building that now houses an Irish pub, they proclaimed themselves the Brigata dei Crusconi (Brigade of Crusty Ones). The members playfully gave themselves names related to farming, cooking, baking, and bread, such as Lievito (yeast or leaven), Macinato (milled into flour), Sollo (soft or spongy), and Grattugiato (grated).

Each Cruscone also selected a related symbol, such as a sieve or sheaf of wheat, which was embossed in vibrant colors upon a wooden *pala*, a shovel-like paddle bakers used to slide loaves of bread from an oven. Seated on ceremonial chairs constructed from wooden flour storage barrels, the crusty ones referred to their lighthearted meetings as *cruscate*, playful conversations of little import, like bread crusts.

The Crusconi might have done nothing of substance if not for the arrival of an ambitious *cervellone*, or "big brain" (as the Italian linguistics professor Giuseppe Patota describes him to me) named Leonardo Salviati. L'Infarinato (covered in flour), his "Cruscan" name, had gained dubious repute for his work on the *"rassettatura"* or "reordering" of the *Decameron*—the literary equivalent of painting loincloths on Michelangelo's nudes. Church censors had first taken a crack at expurgating Boccaccio in 1571, with disastrous results. Duke Cosimo I, with papal backing, brought in Salviati to reduce the damage. The new, less mutilated edition came out in 1582.

A year later Salviati joined the Crusconi and reorganized them into L'Accademia della Crusca, today the oldest scholarly academy in Europe. His mission was to create something no one had ever before produced, the first great dictionary of officially recognized words in any European tongue. Some charged that Salviati sought mainly to curry favor with the pope, but his fellow word lovers took up the gauntlet and continued the project after his death in 1589.

Theirs was no dry academic venture. French may have its "immortals" of the Académie Française, the superior souls who protect their proud linguistic heritage, but the Italian language police have always had much more fun. La Crusca's voluminous archives teem with menus, skits, plays, puns, jokes, and rhapsodic odes to the academy and its members.

Among La Crusca's traditions was an annual *stravizzo*, a term members defined with understatement as "eating that happens together with pleasant conversation." A modern dictionary may be more accurate when it defines the verb *straviziare*, derived from the word for "vice" (*vizio*), as "to indulge or be intemperate." The menu from one *stravizzo* presents five staggering courses that included veal, tongue, prosciutto, pigeon, chicken, capon, lamb, meat rolls, soup, several varieties of pasta, artichokes, Parmigiano, strawberries, pears, peaches, biscotti—and *stuzzicadenti* (toothpicks). The goal the Crusconi gluttonously pursued was *abbofarsi*, or stuffing oneself to the bursting point.

Despite their jocular tone and boisterous banquets, La Crusca's founding brothers took their mission seriously. Over decades of research, discussion, and debate, they created the *Vocabolario degli Accademici della Crusca*, published by a Venetian printer on January 20, 1612. The 960 oversize pages of the first such compendium in any language contained only words that qualified as "*belle, significanti e dell'uso nostro*" ("beautiful, noteworthy, and of our use," that is, from Italian authors, mainly the three crowns—Dante, Petrarch, and Boccaccio—and other Florentines).

Unlike previous dictionaries, the *Vocabolario* defined words rather than listing synonyms and traced their origins and history through prose and poetic citations, largely from the fourteenth-century masters of the language. Although critics sniped that the choices were too Tuscan and dated, the *Vocabolario* so impressed international scholars that France, England, and Germany set to work on similar compendiums. For Italians, La Crusca's *Vocabolario*, like Dante's *Divina Commedia*, became a *gran libro della nazione*, another literary substitute for a unified political state.

La Crusca's ongoing work to expand and embellish the language attracted the great thinkers of the times, including Galileo Galilei (1564–1642). Best known as the founder of modern science, this remarkably talented man of letters also wrote poetry and learned commentaries on Dante and Petrach. Although scholars of his day continued to write in Latin, Galileo deliberately chose the vivid, lucid Tuscan vernacular because of his commitment to spreading knowledge to all people.

In one of his works, Galileo compares the universe to *"un grandissimo libro"* ("an enormous book") that one can read and understand only if you know the language in which it was written: mathematics. "Even after four centuries," the linguists Valeria della Valle and Giuseppe Patota note in *L'italiano*, their biography of the language, "neither his concepts nor his Tuscan way of writing seem distant from us." Galileo muttered his most famous statement in Italian—*"Eppur si muove"* ("And yet it moves")—under his breath when he was forced to refute his heretical assertion that the earth circled the sun.

A lesser known but no less lively scientist, Francesco Redi (1626–1698), physician to the Medici grand dukes, brought a touch of scandal to the increasingly distinguished L'Accademia della Crusca. His most famous scientific contribution was his research disproving the theory of the spontaneous generation of maggots from rotting meat. In his experiments—among the first with modern scientific controls—Redi put a substance, such as chunks of dead fish or raw veal, into pairs of jars. He covered the tops of one group with fine gauze so only air could get in but left the other jars open. After several days, maggots appeared on the material in the open containers, but not on the gauze-covered ones, indicating that the vermin had developed from tiny eggs deposited by flies when they flew into the jars.

Redi was less conscientious in his designated task of adding scientific terms to La Crusca's *Vocabolario.* Many of the examples and citations he submitted for new words, researchers discovered centuries after the fact, had come from his own work, not from the authors whose manuscripts he had claimed to possess. Perhaps his research in another area affected his thinking. Redi is best known for *"Il Bacco in Toscana"* ("Bacchus in Tuscany," a poetic ode of praise for Tuscan wines and a diatribe against water:

He who drinks water,
I wish to observe,
Gets nothing from me;
He may eat it and starve.
Whether it's well, or whether it's fountain,
Or whether it comes foaming white from the mountain,

I cannot admire it,
Nor ever desire it . . .
Wine, wine is your only drink!

(www.elfinspell.com)

As foreign powers seized control of Italy, La Crusca, dedicated to a language without a political state, closed down. An Italian most people think of as French eventually came to its rescue: Napoleon Bonaparte (1769–1821), born of Italian parents in Corsica the year after France annexed it. The great military and political leader spoke French with an Italian accent throughout his life and never mastered its spelling. After defeating the Austrians at the Battle of Marengo in 1800, Napoleon appointed himself king of his linguistic homeland.

In 1809, recognizing what the citizens of Florence would hold most dear, Napoleon conceded to them the right to use their language as well as French. He also established an annual prize for authors "whose works contribute with the greatest effect to the maintenance of the Italian language in all its purity." In 1811 Napoleon reopened L'Accademia della Crusca and paid the salaries of its scholars. La Crusca flourished once more—until Mussolini's propaganda machine took over the policing of the language. The scholars who had been working for decades on the fifth edition of the *Vocabolario* got only as far as "o." The last word of this unfinished volume is *ozono*.

La Crusca, which reopened in 1955, now maintains its *sede*, or central seat, in the austerely elegant Villa Medicea di Castello, a favorite residence of Lorenzo il Magnifico. Botticelli's *Primavera* and *Birth of Venus* hung there in the sixteenth century. The surrounding gardens, planted in 1540, remain among the most re-nowned in Italy.

In my pilgrimage through the Italian language, La Crusca was my mecca. I planned my first visit in 2005 months in ad-vance. With my friend Stefania Scotti's help, I composed an ex-tremely courteous request for an interview with its president. "Chiarissimo Professor Sabatini," she instructed me to write, using an honorific that literally means "most clear" but trans-lates as "illustrious." La Crusca's press officer replied promptly to set a date and time.

"La Crusca?" my Italian friends asked, stunned by my au-dacity at daring to enter the fortress of their language, a place in which most Italians would fear to open their mouths. I began to think they were right. I nervously prepared a list of questions in English (for my sake) and Italian (for the interview). I dressed in business black, wrapping myself in my magic shawl. My hands trembled as I reviewed my notes a final time. At the historic villa, I slipped on a small staircase, spiraling one of my high heels into the air. The shy young press officer gallantly re-placed it on my foot.

"I feel like Cinderella," I said in English before remember-ing that I was standing (well, sitting at the moment) on Italian's most hallowed ground. *"La Cenerentola,"* I translated, and he smiled.

Stepping into the grand Sala delle Pale (the room of the baking shovels), I sensed the spirit of the boisterous founders of the crusty club. Like shields emblazoned with coats of arms their brightly painted *pale* gleamed from the walls. I
their ceremonial chairs and the cabinets, called *sacch*

tained official documents. A large oil painting immortalized Salviati, who inspired the literary irregulars, seated between two fetching beauties, one representing La Crusca and the other, the Florentine Academy of Art and Design.

Even more impressive was the vaulted, hushed library, a veritable cathedral of books with more than 138,000 Italian volumes dating back to the 1500s. Here lies Italian's genome, constructed of words chosen specifically and deliberately to please the ear, the eye, and the soul. They are, as La Crusca's motto states, the language's "loveliest blooms."

When I finally touched a first edition of the *Vocabolario*, I turned its stiff, dry pages with gentle reverence. No less than the artists laboring in a Renaissance *bottega* to fashion works of astounding beauty, I realized, the language "bakers" of La Crusca had painstakingly created a living masterpiece. And I finally grasped why their language has such special significance for Italians.

Down through the centuries conquerors stole much of what Italians created. Emperors and kings routinely packed up paintings, sculptures, and jewels—a practice that continued into the twentieth century, when the Nazis filled railroad cars with pieces of Italian art. The one treasure no one could loot from Italians was their language, which La Crusca had elevated to a living art. Because of its efforts, the fourteenth-century dialect of Florence, with inevitable modifications in grammar and additions to the lexicon, lives in Italy's classrooms, offices, shops, and restaurants.

"If Dante appeared in this room today, you could talk

with him," La Crusca's then-president, Francesco Sabatini, a tweedy, silver-haired scholar with an aquiline nose, assured me.

"I can't imagine what I would say," I replied, intimidated just to be speaking to him.

"But I can guess what he would say to you!" Professor Sabatini said in his deep God-the-Father voice. "Just imagine. More than seven hundred years after he lived, a woman comes from a continent he never knew existed, a woman with a nation and a language of her own who wants to learn about the language he spoke and wrote . . ."

He paused to contemplate the significance of my odyssey and then leaned forward with an enormous smile and a twinkle in his dark eyes.

"*È un miracolo!*"

My love of Italian, a miracle? Could Dante himself have put it more poetically?

# How Italian Civilized the West

"RUGGERO IS THE CONSUMMATE ITALIAN GENTLE-man," said the former professor's colleagues in the Department of Italian Studies at the University of California, Berkeley, who urged me to visit the charming, sophisticated *dantista* (and ladies' man). After retiring from the faculty, Ruggero Stefanini had returned to his hometown north of Florence to write poetry. Then he was diagnosed with advanced stomach cancer. "I get sometimes just a little weak," he advised me by e-mail. "Come early."

When I arrived on a wintry March morning, Ruggero, pale and gaunt, was far frailer than his friends in America had suspected. He grimaced in pain as he shifted in his chair and rested one hand on the other to stop its trembling. I tried to cut the interview short, but he insisted on taking me to his favorite *trattoria* and ordering the local specialties for my lunch.

Afterward we walked through the damp streets as he talked of "the language that was [his] life." Of Dante: "As a writer I admire everything about him; as a man, almost nothing." Of why he chose English for one of his poems: "I was very much in love with an American woman and Italian does not have a word for what I wanted to express: 'togetherness.' " Of what Italian, more than any other language or literature, can teach: "how to live."

When we said goodbye, he gave me a book of his poetry inscribed with a phrase I couldn't immediately decipher. On the bus ride back to Florence, I worked out the translation: "You are a breath of the spring I will not live to see." Within a few weeks I learned of his death, and I realized that he had given me a lesson in how to die.

Ruggero's gallantry embodies a concept that defines the Italian character: *fare bella figura.* Foreigners mistakenly think they can translate this term into pat phrases such as "making a good impression" or "keeping up appearances." *Fare bella figura* goes far beyond these superficialities to describe a refined code of behavior that Italians taught the world.

Humanism, the intellectual movement that glorified man's potential, arose in Italy, which became "the richest, most dazzling, cultured, irreverent, and intelligent nation of Christendom," Luigi Barzini wrote in *The Italians.* "Italians had transformed the universe, or, at least, man's ideas about the universe and his place in it." People no longer looked to the saints as role models. Instead they turned to the heirs of classical Rome and the inventors of the

Renaissance to show them how to live in the manner to which they aspired.

Then as now, the essence of *italianità* was language. "In our present times," observed the Florentine playwright Giovan Battista Gelli in 1551, "many diverse people of intelligence and refinement, outside Italy no less than within Italy, devote much effort and study to learning and speaking our language for no reason but love." These acolytes included Elizabeth I of England, Francis I of France, and Emperor Charles V, who once declared, "I speak Spanish to God, Italian to women, French to men, and German to my horse."

John Milton and other British poets wrote sonnets in Italian. William Shakespeare based many of his plots on Italian *novelle* and set twelve of his forty plays in Italy. Italian artisans and artists, traveling to other countries, left behind words and phrases of their lyrical language along with the paintings, buildings, and sculptures that Mary McCarthy likened to "dropped handkerchiefs of marvelous workmanship." Italian became the hallmark of a person of education, refinement, and sophistication—and a prerequisite for anyone aspiring to such status. "The Italians had all Europe for their pupils, both theoretically and practically in every noble bodily exercise and in the habits and manners of good society," the nineteenth-century historian Jacob Burckhardt observed.

Social graces remain woven into the fabric of Italian. Even the chipper Italian *ciao*, which does double duty as "hi" and "bye," reflects centuries of *bella figura*, as I discovered on my first trip to the most serene city of Venice. A waiter at the café where I came every day to sip espresso and watch the pigeons swoop across the Piazza San Marco joked that my *ciao* sounded too Tuscan.

Coaching me in the Venetian pronunciation, he explained that the word itself was a local invention. In La Serenissima's glittering heyday, correspondents signed letters, "*Il Suo schiavo*" ("your slave"). Meeting on the street, acquaintances would bow and repeat the same ingratiating words. However, in the Venetian dialect, which softens the hard sound of *sch* (pronounced *sk* in other regions) to a chewy *sh* (as in "show"), *Suo schiavo* came out *sciao*, which melted into *ciao* as it migrated to other parts of Italy.

When I traveled to the south, I discovered that the mellifluous Neapolitans, who can make a menu sound like music, were even more effusive. "I am the last button on the livery of your least lackey," an unctuous marchese would intone when he took his leave. The proper response: "The last button on the livery of my least lackey is a diamond."

Italian Renaissance authors taught the world how to act with the same flourishes of grace and style—and, when need be, cunning. The most widely read books in sixteenth-century Europe were what we would call self-help manuals. Niccolò Machiavelli's *Il Principe* (*The Prince*) served as a primer for those hungry for power and a survival manual for those trying to hold on to it. Baldassare Castiglione's *Il libro del cortegiano* (*The Book of the Courtier*) instructed gentlemen and their ladies in the ways of talking, acting, and interacting that would enhance their social status. Giovanni della Casa's *Il Galateo*, the f book for the masses, taught the burgeoning midd chant classes that good manners could serve them not better than—mere money. So influential did these three works become that Emperor Charles V of Spain kept Machiavelli's *Prince* and Castiglione's *Courtier* next to the Bible at his bedside, and the word *galateo*, with a small *g*, remains synonymous in Italy with etiquette.

I wish that all three were required reading today. "Do you realize that we would never have ended up in Iraq if George Bush had read Machiavelli?" I said to my somewhat startled husband a few years ago. In *The Prince*, Machiavelli (1469–1527) clearly spells out that if a ruler is thinking of invading a foreign state, he had better be prepared to send in an ample army, take up residence there himself, or set up a well-armed permanent colony to keep the natives in check.

The names of few authors have penetrated the global vocabulary as profoundly as Machiavelli, an international byword for political cunning and pragmatism; yet no one, as T. S. Eliot observed, "was ever less Machiavellian than Machiavelli." As a civil servant in the Florentine republic, which held power for fourteen years after Savonarola's overthrow in 1498, Machiavelli served in various diplomatic and administrative roles, including minister of defense, which gave him firsthand experience with power. When the Medici returned in 1512, their supporters accused Machiavelli of conspiracy and tried, tortured, and exiled the republican patriot.

Frustrated in his forced retirement to his modest country home, Machiavelli began work on *Il Principe*. At the time the Medici pope Leo X, son of Lorenzo il Magnifico, and his brother Giuliano seemed likely to form an Italian alliance, perhaps even a nation-state. As Machiavelli saw it, a Medici pope (or prince) who heeded his advice could bring a better future to Italy and perhaps even take up arms to liberate the peninsula from its "barbarian" invaders—a vision of unification almost 350 years before the fact. More pragmatically, Machiavelli hoped that a clear-eyed, no-nonsense tactical handbook would serve as a job application, a display of his political acumen that could gain him a position in the Medici government.

Machiavelli's dreams, personal and political, never materialized. He died—"of a surfeit of failure," one historian stated—before the printing of his masterwork. But by analyzing affairs of state dispassionately, with logic and objectivity, Machiavelli did more than create a classic. As professors like to quip, he put the science into political science. He thought that it should be possible to devise general rules about politics because the same desires and fears motivate all people in all places. Machiavelli, as Francis Bacon observed, teaches "what men do, not what they ought to do."

Five centuries after Machiavelli's time, *The Prince* still compels and shocks readers for two reasons: what its author said and how he said it. "A prince must, if he wants to keep power, learn to be able not to be good and use or not use this ability according to need," Machiavelli argued. Conventional virtues, such as generosity, kindness, and keeping one's word, might undermine his power, whereas qualities that appear to be vices could be essential to his survival.

What if a ruthless prince lost the adulation of his people? Better to be feared than loved, shrugged Machiavelli, who observed that since men are generally ungrateful, vacillating, cowardly, and greedy, they might promise their souls to a prince yet desert or betray him because love is fickle, whereas fear is not. Machiavelli never agonized over whether the ultimate end might justify any means. He was sure it would.

As a case in point Machiavelli cited the ruthless Cesare Borgia, called Il Valentino from his title as Duke of Valentinois. When his father, decadent and opportunistic, assumed the papacy as Alexander VI, the two conspired to take over much of central Italy. Machiavelli coolly describes how Borgia, to subdue unruly Romagna, "full of thefts, fights, and of every other kind of insolence," hired a "cruel and able" henchman and gave him full authority to do whatever was necessary to impose order.

Once the province was pacified, Borgia wanted to show the resentful populace that "if any form of cruelty had arisen, it did not originate from him but from the harsh nature of his minister." So one morning the local citizens awoke to discover their hated overlord "placed on the piazza in two pieces with a block of wood and a bloody sword beside him." Borgia had deftly accomplished his objective. "The ferocity of such a spectacle," Machiavelli wrote, "left these people satisfied and amazed at the same time." The Borgias' ambitious scheme unraveled when Alexander VI suddenly sickened—perhaps the result of poison—and died. Cesare, having lost everything and everyone, ended up a babbling madman and died in his early thirties.

Just as remarkable as *The Prince*'s unflinching pragmatism is its language. Considered by some the finest Italian stylist of the *Cinquecento*, Machiavelli wrote in a clean, stiletto-sharp vernacular that echoed the everyday speech of his fellow Florentines (including, in some of his more ribald works, their earthiness).

So proud was he of his local tongue that, in one of his lesser-known essays, Machiavelli resurrected Dante. In a richly imagined debate, the poet conceded that the language of *La Divina Commedia* is actually Florentine. Why call it anything else, Machiavelli asked, if it has simply absorbed a few non-Florentine words from other sources?

In his finest Florentine, Machiavelli, who, as one biographer put it, "felt the shame of Italy like a wound," mourned most eloquently for his fatherland—"leaderless, lawless, beaten, despoiled, torn apart, overrun, and subjected to every manner of desolation"—and yearned for a chance to make and not just write its history. When the Florentine republic returned to power in 1527, Machiavelli applied for his old post but was rejected.

Shortly before his death that same year, the heartbroken political strategist wrote to a friend, "I love my country better than my very soul." His country, which ignored him in life, didn't know quite what to say of him in death. His appropriately monumental tomb in Santa Croce, the burial site for Italy's titans of history, reads simply, "To so great a name, no epitaph can do justice."

Machiavelli, whose satiric play *The Mandrake* is still revived and performed around the world, couldn't resist mocking the pretensions of some of his newly prosperous countrymen. In his own twist on *bella* and *brutta figura*, he r
of a character named Castruccio. A man from
to dinner at his house, which—thanks to a
he has just remodeled in the most ostentatiou

During the meal Castruccio suddenly spits in his host's face. Rather than apologize, he explains that he did not know where else to spit without damaging something valuable.

I can picture Machiavelli's smirking expression as he told this tale. In his portraits, you can spot tiny cynical creases hovering at the edge of his mouth, a counterpoint to the crafty gleam in his eyes. My hunch is that his sardonic demeanor played some role in his undoing. Surely the impeccable Castiglione, every inch the perfect courtier he portrayed in *Il libro del cortigiano*, would never have indulged in such dangerous self-revelation.

If princes lived by the sword, courtiers survived by the word. Unlike medieval knights who proved themselves on battlefields, the men and women of Renaissance courts had to maneuver through the more treacherous turf of palace intrigues and power plays. Count Baldassarre Castiglione (1478–1529), named for one of the magi, or wise men, never lost his footing.

Castiglione lived the way Petrarch and his admirer Bembo wrote: on a loftier plane, above the messy banalities of ordinary life. In 1504, after serving the Duke of Mantua, Castiglione moved to the place he called "the very abode of joyfulness," the court of Urbino, home of the artists Raphael and Bramante and one of the most civilized places in the Renaissance world.

Its Duke Federigo da Montefeltro, most famous for the portrait in the Uffizi of his hatchet-nosed profile, epitomized an ideal Renaissance ruler—scholar, warrior, and patron of the arts. Duchess Elisabetta Gonzaga became Castiglione's idolized, ideal-
platonic inspiration. He hid her portrait and the verses she
behind a mirror in his room. "Never be it spoken with-

out tears," he wrote years later, finally exp
ments, "the Duchess, too, is dead!" (Williar
romantic, claimed, "[This phrase] often m
dimmed.")

Castiglione won me over with a single word he created to
describe the essence of courtly behavior: *sprezzatura*, the studied
carelessness that "conceals art and presents everything said and
done as something brought about without laboriousness and almost without giving it any thought." The closest English comes
is "nonchalance," which fails to capture the behind-the-scenes
preparation and hard work that underlies the ability to carry off
"things that are exquisite and well done"—be it a duel, debate,
or dance, executed with such ease that it inspires "the greatest
wonder." This is the essence of *bella figura*: "acting" the gentleman, playing a role in the world's eyes, prizing appearance over
reality.

In a series of dialogues and discussions, based on his own
experiences and observations, Castiglione fleshes out his ideal
gentleman as if he were painting a portrait. He must be a manly
man, physically accomplished, proficient in arms and horse-
manship, courageous in battle, but above all a man with *grazia*,
or gracefulness, in all he does. Yet Castiglione doesn't advise
courtiers to be insincere or opportunistic solely out of self-
interest. By making the best possible impression, he emphasizes,
they are more likely to succeed and become effective advisors to
their princes.

Although a courtier requires a superb education in letters,
music, and the fine arts, Castiglione cautions against an excess
of excellence so as not to provoke jealousy. With Machiavellian

rewdness, he advises a courtier to be bold in battle—but only under his lord's eyes, so he gets proper recognition for his bravery. Above all, he exhorts gentlemen to speak well, avoiding any affectation in language, and to entertain others with witty remarks, urbane stories, and clever jests.

A lady of the court, Castiglione notes, must guard her virtue and reputation, avoid unsuitable activities (such as sports), and cultivate a sweetness and gentleness that "shall always make her appear the woman without any resemblance to a man." Castiglione didn't mince words: looks matter. "That woman lacks much who lacks beauty," he comments. But any woman could learn to be charming and delightful in conversation, vivacious, warm, affable, "far from prudish but never bawdy nor lascivious."

At age thirty-eight Castiglione found all these comely qualities in Ippolita Torelli, a pretty fifteen-year-old noblewoman, whom he married. His adored wife bore him three children before dying four years later. Overwhelmed by grief, Castiglione renounced courtly life and entered the priesthood. Pope Clement VII sent the silver-tongued sophisticate as his ambassador to the Spanish court of Emperor Charles V in 1524.

Three years later the emperor's mercenaries invaded and pillaged Rome. Cornered in the Castel Sant' Angelo, the pope raged against Castiglione, accused him of a "special friendship" with the emperor, and blamed him for not averting the catastrophe. Charles V's court rationalized Rome's misfortunes as divine retribution for the many sins of its clerics. Caught in the middle, Castiglione fell into a debilitating depression. Through

eloquent letters, he eventually regained the favor
and emperor, but his spirit was broken.

Although he shared his manuscript with respected friends,
Castiglione might never have allowed publication of *The Book of
the Courtier* in 1528 if the poet Vittoria Colonna hadn't circulated
it widely, despite his request that she not. The *marchesa* brushed
off his protests with coy compliments. "I do not wonder that
you have formed a perfect courtier," she cooed, "since you had
only to hold a mirror to yourself and reflect what you saw
there."

In 1529, exhausted and demoralized, the "ornament of
every court" died in the Spanish city of Toledo, where he was
buried in its opulent cathedral, then the most sumptuous
church in Christendom, with utmost pomp. "One of the best
gentlemen in the world is dead," Charles V remarked to his
courtiers. Eventually Castiglione's family brought his remains
back to Italy to lie next to his wife's in the family chapel in
Mantua.

Castiglione's bible of refined behavior took on a life of its
own. The book was soon translated into Spanish, German,
French, and English, and 108 editions were published between
1528 and 1616. (Of course, Pietro Aretino created a smutty parody, *La cortigiana*.) Castiglione's readers devoured his book so
compulsively that, to the pope's alarm, a gentlewoman in Urbino
reportedly became so rapt in reading and rereading *The Book of
the Courtier* that she died without receiving the last rites. Yeats
poetically praised the idealized court as "that grammar school of
courtesies / where wit and beauty learned their name." Samuel

Johnson told Boswell that *Courtier* was "the best book that ever was written about good breeding."

*Etichetta* remains so vital to social survival in Italy that the same word translates into both "etiquette" and "label." To this day the way you present yourself in Italy marks you even before you open your mouth (another reason not to tromp through its cities in T-shirt and shorts).

However, nothing constitutes a greater act of *brutta figura* than sounding or acting *maleducato*, a word that foreigners often mistake for "badly educated" but that translates as "ill bred" or "rude." This word served me well when I was bumped off an overbooked flight from Rome several years ago. The ticket agent showed not a shred of sympathy until I added that the clerk had been quite rude. *"Maleducato!"* he repeated in horror. The next thing I knew, I had a hotel reservation for the night and an upgraded seat on the next morning's flight.

An Italian observing a display of graceless behavior is more likely to say that the offender "doesn't know his *galateo*," a reference to the first etiquette guide, written by Giovanni della Casa (1503–1556). This Florentine patrician, who admired Petrarch and befriended Bembo, moved to Rome in 1528 to pursue the genially decadent life of a gentleman poet.

In the same spirit as Florence's Crusconi, Della Casa and his witty friends established the Accademia de' Vignaiuoli, the Academy of Vineyard Workers. In addition to stylish sonnets, he published clever, sophisticated, and (much to his subsequent regret) fashionably obscene verses, along with a treatise on whether a gentleman should take a wife. His answer, in this humorously misogynist rant, was a resounding no, especially if the man had scholarly or political ambitions.

Della Casa had both. Like many talented men of his times, he entered the priesthood solely for its professional opportunities. Well spoken and well connected, he rose rapidly up the clerical ranks, eagerly accepting assignments less ambitious prelates might have dodged. As a papal taxman, Della Casa zealously collected tithes from all the Florentine territories. In his next posting, he established the Venice branch of the Inquisition and vigorously prosecuted heretics, including a bishop who taunted him with his unsavory early writings. Back in Rome, he drew up the city's first Index of Prohibited Books, which included Machiavelli's *The Prince*.

The ambitious prelate seemed so clearly destined for glory that his friend, the poet Pietro Bembo, at the height of his fame, dedicated what proved to be his final sonnet—"a masterly farewell to poetry and to life," his editor declared—to the man he crowned as his literary successor. It begins with a play on Della Casa's name: "*Casa* [house], in which the virtues have their illustrious dwelling." In an inflated style meant to convey his moral earnestness, Bembo praises their past achievements and links what he predicts will be their illustrious futures. "What worthier destiny can a couple hope for?" he asks.

Della Casa was hoping someday to wear a cardinal's crimson, which he yearned for so fiercely that he wrote verses about the nobility of the color. But the risqué poems of his youth, along with an illegitimate son (less of a problem), blocked his ascension. With the election of a new pope, Della Casa lost his patronage and retired to a country abbey in 1552. Only after his death, with the publication of his poetry, did he gain the acclaim he so craved. Some consider him the century's best poetic stylist.

Della Casa's most famous and influential work, with a title immortalized in the Italian language, was *Il Galateo, Ovvero de' Costumi* (*The Galateo, or On Manners*), derived from the name of his friend Bishop Galeazzo Florimonte, who urged him to write a manual of proper behavior, based on consideration, politeness, and pleasantness. Its first word—*conciossiacosachè*, a pretentious literary term for "since"—became one of the most infamous in Italian literature. This tongue twister so irritated a famous Italian dramatist that he hurled the slim volume out his window. It also convinced many people that this entertaining treatise is pedantic and boring.

*Il Galateo* is anything but. Assuming the persona of an *idiota*, an ignorant old man, instructing a youngster, Della Casa doles out wise, witty, and timeless recommendations in folksy colloquialisms: Don't bray like an ass when you yawn. Don't shamble, stomp, or shake your bottom like a peacock wiggling its tail. Don't drone on about your senseless dreams or adorable children. Don't interrupt, lie, bad-mouth, flatter, brag, pick your teeth, scratch yourself in public, or make fun of the deformed.

Emily Post herself could not offer a more sensible observation than this: "When you have blown your nose, you should not open your handkerchief and look inside, as if pearls or rubies might have cascaded from your brain. This is a disgusting habit which is not apt to make anyone love you, but rather if someone loved you already, he is likely to stop there and then."

Surely anyone who's ever dined at a rib joint on dollar night would recognize the voracious eaters Della Casa describes as "totally oblivious, like pigs with their snouts in the swill, never raising their faces nor their eyes, let alone their hands, from the food in front of them."

After *Il Galateo*'s publication in 1558, Della Casa's little book of graces became must-reading for all aspiring to hoist themselves a rung higher up the social ladder. Its regularly updated versions remain essential self-help guides to modern-day dilemmas. The most recent edition exhorts both sexes not to engage in online bickering (the onomatopeic *battibecco*), reminds women who dye their hair to touch up their roots, and directs men to remove black socks when otherwise nude and not to put their feet on a table as if they were a Texas oilman (*petroliere texano*). I've taken to heart its thoughtful suggestion of never closing the front door after guests leave but waiting, as well-bred Italians do, until they walk or drive away.

Della Casa, I discovered by chance, is buried in Sant' Andrea delle Fratte, which stands across the street from my apartment in Rome. I think of him whenever I hang my lingerie out to dry on the balcony overlooking the church and worry, Would he take offense at this somewhat immodest display?

Yet for all the advice the Italian equivalents of Miss Manners dispense on the subject of *le buone maniere* (good manners), none has helped me with what I consider one of the most confounding aspects of Italian: how to address another person. While you are always "you" in English, regardless of age, gender, rank, or number, in Italian you might be *tu*, *Lei*, *voi*, or (if you happen to be royalty or a pontiff) *Ella*. As a direct or indirect object, "you" becomes *te*, *ti*, *La*, *Le*, or *vi*. Other languages that distinguish between formal and informal terms of address also pose a problem for English speakers, but only in Italian can the choice of a second-person designation spell the difference between *bella* or *brutta figura*.

In the living room of her gracious apartment, with a view across the Tiber toward the Piazza del Popolo, I ask the linguist Valeria della Valle why Italian has made the straightforward task of starting a dialogue so damnably difficult. Don't blame the Romans, she tells me. They used *tu a tutti*, the casual "you," to everyone, from slave to emperor. In the Middle Ages, their Italian descendants, wanting to accord special respect to worthier persons, began using the plural *voi* for someone as valuable as two lesser *tu*'s.

Dante provides some excellent examples. In the *Divine Comedy*, his pilgrim *"dà del tu"* (gives the informal "you") to almost everyone. The exceptions are characters of great importance, such as the father of his poet friend Cavalcante Cavalcanti and the intellectual Brunetto Latini, whom Dante considered his *maestro*—although he damns him nonetheless. When he comes upon Latini with the sodomites in hell, he displays great surprise and asks, using the plural "you" form, *"Siete voi qui, ser Brunetto?"* ("Are you here, Sir Brunetto?"). Until the twentieth century children and grandchildren said *voi* out of respect when talking to their parents and grandparents. Many southern Italian dialects that date back to medieval times still use *voi* as a polite form of address.

Sometime in the 1500s, probably in the resplendent courts of the day, *voi* gave way to *Lei*, the word for "she." Contrary to a common assumption among Italians, *Lei* did not derive from the Spanish (who used *usted* for their formal "you"), but is *"una forma italianissima,"* says Professoressa della Valle, that stands for *la Sua eccellenza* (Your Excellency), a feminine noun. And so when you are talking to someone with whom you are not, as she puts it, *"in confidenza,"* or familiar with, you address him or her as a woman and use the third-person rather than the second-person verb forms.

If this explanation seems complicated, imagine figuring out these social and grammatical niceties dozens of times a day with every person you meet. And heaven forbid you should get thirsty in Italy! One of my grammar books provides a list of sixteen ways to ask for a glass of water (*bicchiere d'acqua*)!*

All convey the desire for a drink, but their use depends on where you are and whom you're asking. *"Le sarei grato se avesse la cortesia di darmi un bicchiere d'acqua,"* which translates as, "I would be grateful if you would have the courtesy of giving me a glass of water," might win you an invitation to dine with a duke. *"Ohè, questo bicchiere d'acqua, me lo porti!"*—"Hey, that glass of water, bring it to me!"—might get you tossed out the door.

When I first started studying Italian many years ago, I de-

---

*Le sarei grato se avesse la cortesia di darmi un bicchiere d'acqua.
Abbia la cortesia di darmi un bicchiere d'acqua.
Vorrei un bicchiere d'acqua.
Mi dia un bicchiere d'acqua.
Le dispiacerebbe darmi un bicchiere di acqua?
Avrei bisogno di un bicchiere d'acqua.
Dammi un bicchiere d'acqua.
Portami un bicchiere d'acqua.
Da'qua questo bicchiere d'acqua.
Chi mi dà un bicchiere d'acqua?
Un bicchiere d'acqua, per favore.
Che ne diresti di un bicchiere d'acqua?
Vorrei un bicchiere d'acqua.
Che voglia di un bicchiere d'acqua!
La disturbo se le chiedo un bicchiere d'acqua?
Ohè, questo bicchiere d'acqua, me lo porti?

cided to dodge the formal-familiar dilemma entirely by learning only the polite *Lei* form of address. I honestly figured I wouldn't get to know anyone well enough to need *il tu*. (This happily turned out not to be the case.)

One day when I was jogging on a country road in Tuscany, an agitated man ran up to me and explained that his dog was trapped in a steep ravine. He could push him from behind, but would I call the dog to come to me? He, of course, addressed me in the respectful *Lei* form. And I, knowing no other, did the same with the dog. The man nearly fell over laughing at the sound of my oh-so-polite imprecations, which translated as, "Mister Dog, would you please be so kind as to come to me?"

Mussolini, seeking a more virile language for his megalomaniacal vision of the Italian nation, substituted the comradely *voi*, the plural "you all," for *Lei*. Throughout the Fascist era, *voi* was obligatory in schools, public offices, movies, radio, and public ceremonies. Failure to use *voi* constituted an unpatriotic act and could result in the favored form of intimidation: huge doses of castor oil, which ignominiously destroyed any trace of *bella figura*. (The reputed originator of this demoralizing practice was the poet, novelist, and self-declared "superman," Gabriele D'Annunzio.) After the war, *il voi* as a form of address for just one person survived only in the mouths of American movie stars. Thanks to Italian dubbers, Cary Grant, Audrey Hepburn, Jimmy Stewart, and Grace Kelly always addressed their costars as if they were Fascist loyalists.

As a woman, I've learned that when talking to a man I must be the one to suggest that we *darci del tu* (give each other the informal "you")—unless, like most of my sources, he is more important than I or he's Roberto Benigni, who used *il tu* in our first conversation. Professoressa della Valle, now my friend Valeria, was the first distinguished scholar whom I tentatively asked about "*tu*-ing each other." "But Diana," she said sweetly, "I have been using *il tu*." I'd been so busy concentrating on the gist of the interview that I hadn't noticed.

Perhaps Italians are innately more fluent in the language of courtesy. I have never entered an Italian's home, however humble, without being offered something to eat or drink. An Italian guest has never arrived at my doorstep empty-handed. At the beginning of an interview, many Italian men take a dramatic moment to reach inside their coat jackets, retrieve their cell phones, and switch them off with a courtly flourish.

*Troppo bello, meno buono.* Too much of the beautiful and less of the good, some of my Italian friends say cynically. But I relish the flourishes of *bella figura*, each an opportunity to transform minor interactions into memorable interludes. When I confide my perspective to Enrico Paoletti, president of the Società Dante Alighieri in Florence, his elfin face lights up.

"Ah, *signora*, you are learning the Italian secret!" he exclaims.

"And what is that?"

"Our greatest art: the art of living."

# La Storia dell'Arte

FOR CENTURIES "ITALY" HAS BEEN SYNONYMOUS with art. An estimated 60 percent of the world's designated art treasures resides within its borders, and Italian paintings and sculptures grace museums and collections around the globe. But Italy did more than inspire masterpieces: it developed the visual language of Western culture and changed forever our concepts of beauty and its creators.

A thousand years ago Italian—or, more precisely, the Florentine dialect of the time—had no words for "art" or "artist." *Arte* meant "guild," a collective of specialists in a certain field. (The greater "arts" were judges and notaries, cloth weaving, exchange, wool, silk, physicians and apothecaries, and furriers. The lesser "arts" included butchers, shoemakers, carpenters, innkeepers, bakers, and so on.) Painters, who belonged to the same guild as doctors and apothecaries, and sculptors, members of the guild of stone masons and woodworkers, were *artigiani*, or artisans, anonymous craftsmen who worked with their hands, usually for low pay and little, if any, recognition.

This began to change in the late-thirteenth century with the emergence of a painter unlike any who had come before. We know him as Cimabue (Ox-head), a nickname his stubbornness may have earned. In Florence in 1286 Cimabue completed a panel of the Madonna surrounded by angels for the Church of Santa Maria Novella. The large figures, more lifelike than any previous works, so stunned the townspeople that they carried the painting with great rejoicing and the sounding of trumpets in a triumphant procession through the city streets to the church.

Cimabue (c. 1240–c. 1302) may have been the first celebrity artist, but an even greater talent, his apprentice Giotto di Bondone (1277–1337), soon eclipsed him. "In painting Cimabue thought he held the field," Dante Alighieri wrote in the *Divine Comedy*, "and now it's Giotto they acclaim." Cimabue himself, observing his pupil's remarkable progress, commented, in a phrase still used in Italy, *"L'allievo ha superato il maestro"* ("The pupil has surpassed the teacher"). Within a few years, painters throughout Italy were trying to emulate Giotto's ability to make paintings breathe.

As Giotto's fame grew, the pope sent a representative to Tuscany to learn more about the artist and his work. When asked for a sample to take to the pontiff, Giotto dipped a brush in red, pressed his arm to his side to make a compass of it, and with a turn of his hand made an impeccable circle on a piece of paper.

"Am I to have no other drawing than this one?" the flummoxed courtier asked.

"It's more than sufficient," answered Giotto.

As soon as the pope learned how Giotto had created the sample, he immediately realized that the artist did indeed surpass all other painters of his time. As this tale spread, it gave rise to the expression *"più tondo dell'O di Giotto"* ("rounder than Giotto's O"), for someone slow or dense.

Two centuries after Giotto, the greatest artistic flowering the world has ever seen took place in Italy. The man who gave *la rinascita* (for rebirth), or the Renaissance, its name was a prolific (if prosaic) painter and respected architect, Giorgio Vasari (1511–1574), who wrote the first book of art history. He called artists *artefici*, creators of beauty like God himself, touched with the same genius that lifted poets above less noble souls.

As a young apprentice, Vasari saved one of the Renaissance's artistic icons. In 1527, in a pitched battle in the heart of Florence, the republican forces in power at the time threw a bench from a window of the Palazzo Vecchio, the city hall, onto Medici loyalists attacking the building. It struck the town's prized symbol of freedom, *Il Gigante*, Michelangelo's colossal David, and broke its arm.

When the fighting subsided, Vasari darted out of the besieged *palazzo* to retrieve the pieces. After keeping them safe for years, he finally repaired the mutilated sculpture in 1543, after Duke Cosimo I de' Medici, a distant cousin of Lorenzo il Magnifico, came to power. Vasari became Cosimo's cultural impresario and oversaw massive construction projects, including the Uffizi (offices), home of many Renaissance treasures, and painted dozens of often monumental works.

Yet Vasari would surely have been overshadowed by his more dazzling contemporaries if not for a dinner conversation at Rome's Palazzo Farnese around 1543. The A-list dinner guests, swapping reminiscences of the artistic giants who had beautified Italy, worried that their stories might soon be forgotten and lost forever. A scholarly bishop agreed to compile a learned treatise about them in Latin, but he soon turned the project over to the boundlessly energetic Vasari. After traveling widely to contemplate works of art and to interview people who had known artists of earlier times, he told their stories in an engaging, reportorial Italian that illuminated both the masterpieces and the masters behind them.

The first edition, entitled *The Lives of the Most Excellent Italian Architects, Painters, and Sculptors, from Cimabue up to Our Own Times: Described in the Tuscan Language* but referred to simply as *Le vite* (*The Lives*) in Italian, came out in 1550; a second, more inclusive version, in 1568. Although dates and details have proven unreliable, Vasari did something no one else had: he made artists as immortal as their works. As the aging Michelangelo wrote in a laudatory sonnet, Vasari had brought the dead back to life and prolonged the life of the living—or the half-living, like himself, he added.

Vasari's language captured the vision of Michelangelo and his contemporaries, who prized *la difficultà* (*difficoltà* in contemporary Italian), the technical and aesthetic challenges of creating works of beauty. (Lorenzo il Magnifico argued that *la difficultà* was also what imbued the Italian vernacular with dignity.) Michelangelo considered sculpture superior to painting because of both its *difficultà* and the need for greater *giudizio dell'occhio* (judgment of the eye).

Both painters and sculptors strove not just to overcome *la difficultà* but to do so with *la facilità*, the artistic equivalent of Castiglione's *sprezzatura*, or seemingly effortless ease. When they succeeded, their works inspired reactions such as *meraviglia*, a sense of marvel or extraordinary delight, and *stupore*, which David Summers defines in *Michelangelo and the Language of Art* as "the state resulting from the perception of a thing that exceeded the limits of the senses."

I experienced both these sensations in the Brancacci Chapel in Florence's Santa Maria del Carmine Church. Like generations of artists, I sat before the murals painted by Tommaso Guido (1401–1428), mesmerized by their raw emotional power. However, only in reading Vasari did I discover that their creator was so on fire with *"le cose dell'arte"* (literally "the things of art" or artistic matters) that he paid no attention to the clothes he wore, the food he ate, the money he received or owed—and went down in history as Masaccio, or Messy Tom.

The painter known as Sandro Botticelli (1445–1510), nicknamed for his brother's trade as a barrel maker, emerges in Vasari's pages as a clever practical joker. In one elaborate prank, he arranged to sell a *tondo* (a circular painting) of the Virgin Mary surrounded by angels by his apprentice Biagio for six gold florins. He instructed Biagio to hang it high in good light so they could display it to the potential buyer in the morning.

That evening Botticelli and one of his pupils made eight red paper hoods, similar to those worn by the *Signoria* (governing body) of Florence, and attached them with wax to the heads of the angels. When Biagio arrived along with the potential buyer (who was in on the joke), he was horrified. But the buyer praised the work, and Biagio followed him home to get his payment. Meanwhile Botticelli removed the hoods so that "his angels had become angels again and were no longer citizens in hoods."

"Master, I don't know if I'm dreaming or if this is real," Biagio said when he returned. "When I came here those angels had red hoods on their heads and now they don't—what does this mean?" Botticelli convinced him that the money must have gone to his head.

"If what you say were true, do you think the man would have bought the painting?" he asked.

The sensual stylist who conjured Venus from the sea and scattered hundreds of Tuscan wildflowers through *Primavera*, his exaltation of spring, was also a serious literary scholar. In Vasari's opinion, Botticelli "wasted a great deal of time" illustrating and writing a commentary on Dante's *Divine Comedy* and squandered whatever money he did earn. Swayed by Savonarola's fiery rhetoric, he reportedly threw some of his own works on the infamous Bonfires of the Vanities in the late-fifteenth century. If not for the financial support of Lorenzo il Magnifico and his friends, the impoverished artist—who became so infirm that he hobbled about on two canes—might have starved.

The words of other artists, as Vasari recorded them, provide insight into their characters. When Donatello (1386–1466), christened Donato di Niccolò di Betto Bardi but so lovable that his family's fond diminutive nickname stuck, showed Filippo Brunelleschi a crucifix he had painstakingly carved in wood, he expected a compliment. Instead the blunt Brunelleschi (1377–1446) asked him why he had put the body of a peasant rather than that of the divine son of God on the cross.

"If it were as simple to create something as to criticize, my Christ would look like Christ to you and not a peasant," Donatello snapped. "Take some wood and try to make one yourself." Brunelleschi, trained as a goldsmith and clock maker, did exactly that, bringing his crucifix to "the highest degree of perfection," according to Vasari. When it was done, he positioned it carefully in optimal light on a wall in his home and instructed Donatello to take the fixings of a simple lunch there. The moment Donatello caught sight of the superbly crafted carving, he dropped his apron, filled with eggs, cheese, and bread, and stood before it in awe.

"How can we have lunch if you have spilled everything?" Brunelleschi demanded when he arrived. Donatello begged off, saying, "I've had enough for this morning. It's for you to make Christs and for me to make peasants."

Donatello, who later claimed that the constant carping of Florentines spurred him to greater accomplishments, traveled to Rome with Brunelleschi. The pair—often mistaken as grave robbers—spent years poking about the ruins to study the techniques of ancient artists. In the Pantheon, the architectural wonder of imperial Rome, Brunelleschi found the secrets to a puzzle that had baffled Florence's finest minds for half a century: how to complete the mammoth dome for the city's Basilica of Santa Maria del Fiore.

Winning the commission for this task proved almost as challenging as the work itself. Brunelleschi argued so fervently and relentlessly for the job that at one point the "Great Council," which consisted of guild leaders, appointed trustees, and consultants, had the volatile "ass and babbler," as one called him, forcibly thrown into the street as if he were a lunatic. He complained that he was afraid to walk through Florence for fear of hearing people say, "Look! There goes the madman."

When the project trustees demanded that Brunelleschi reveal the technical details of his plans, he responded with an egg. Whoever could make it stand on end, he contended, should win the contract to build the dome. When all his rivals failed, Brunelleschi took the egg, cracked its bottom on a table, and made it stand upright. His competitors argued that they could have done the same thing because it was so obvious. That, Brunelleschi countered, was why he refused to show them his blueprints before the assignment was his. "By a vote taken with beans," as Vasari describes it, the trustees named Brunelleschi the Duomo's *capomastro*, or principal master builder.

Time and again, faced with a seemingly insurmountable challenge, the most extreme *difficultà*, Brunelleschi invented something entirely new: a hoist, a crane, even a way of installing stoves on the dome so his workers could eat well without wasting valuable time descending to the street. (He reportedly watered their wine to keep them sober.) The townspeople quoted a phrase from Dante's *Paradiso—de giro in giro*, circle by circle—as they beheld the dome's soul-stirring ascent into the Tuscan sky.

After its completion in 1436, they began introducing themselves with the proud words *"Io son fiorentino del Cupolone"* ("I am a 'Florentine of the Big Dome"). To appreciate just how big Brunelleschi's dome is—142 feet in diameter, 300 feet high—climb the 463 steep steps between its two vaults to the narrow gallery above the cathedral. But avoid the dizzying mistake I made: Don't look down.

The last creature I expected to come upon in Vasari's tales was a Barbary ape, the cherished pet of the painter Fiorentino Rosso (1494–1540), nicknamed *"Il Rosso"* for his fiery complexion. The highly intelligent beast, who "possessed a spirit more human than animal," became enamored with Batistino, Rosso's handsome young apprentice, who communicated with the ape through gestures. He taught the ape to scramble down a trellis to pluck the plump San Colombano grapes growing in the adjacent garden of the friars of Santa Croce. When the ape's paws were full, Batistino pulled him up with a rope sling.

The prior, incensed by the theft, lay in wait and seized a rod to beat the robber. The terrified ape grabbed on to the trellis and shook it so mightily that the entire structure landed on the cleric. The irate prior, "muttering things that are not in the Mass and full of rage and animosity," complained to the feared Office of the Eight. These Florentine judges ordered Rosso to attach a weight to his pet to restrict its movements.

Rosso devised a roller that turned on a chain so the ape could lumber about the house but not climb into the garden. The clever animal, as if he had figured out the culprit behind this punishment, every day practiced jumping down the steps while holding the weight in his hands. One day when he was alone in the house and the prior was singing vespers, the ape leapt onto the friars' cloister and made his way to the roof above the prior's room. There he dropped the weight and romped about for half an hour, "leaving not a single tile or gutter unbroken." Three days later it rained, and the prior's outraged screams echoed through the neighborhood. Rosso and his ape retreated to Rome.

In Florence, innovations such as *prospettiva* (perspective) and *proporzione* (proportion) changed the way artists thought, worked, talked—and sometimes lived. The painter Paolo Uccello (1397–1475), for example, became so engrossed by studies of perspective that he often would refuse his wife's requests to join her in their bedchamber so he could linger with what he called his "odd mistress." By the late fifteenth century, the period called the High Renaissance, artists were pursuing beauty like a drug, and their talents, combined with technical advances, lifted art to unparalleled levels of *dolcezza* (sweetness), *leggiadria* (gracefulness), and *grazia* (grace).

The painter who achieved *graziosissima grazia*, the most graceful grace, was Raphael of Urbino (1483–1520), the epitome of the ideal gentleman his friend Baldassare Castiglione described in *The Book of the Courtier.* The doe-eyed painter was talented, affable, kind, and drop-dead gorgeous.

Raphael's artistic genius sprang from his uncanny ability to reproduce a master's style so adroitly that he first equaled, then surpassed him. Criticized for a lack of majesty and grandeur in his pretty paintings, he knew the perfect tutor: the ferociously solitary Michelangelo, who had locked himself in the Sistine Chapel to paint scenes from the creation on its ceiling. When Michelangelo, squabbling with the pope, stalked off to Florence in 1511, the sculptor Bramante, who had the keys to the chapel, smuggled his friend Raphael in for a clandestine visit. After viewing the work in progress, Raphael immediately added a Michelangelesque figure (believed to be the master himself) to his current painting, *The School of Athens.* "All that Raphael knows of art, he got from me," Michelangelo later thundered. (Raphael, for his part, described his tempermental critic as "lonely as a hangman.")

In Raphael's defense, he did seek out his own inspiration—and in the process added new words to both Italian and English. While he was working in Rome, archaeologists were excavating the Domus Aurea, Nero's golden house, near the Colosseum. In order to study firsthand the vividly colored decorations painted on its walls, Raphael had himself lowered into the cave, or *grotta.* The designs that he reproduced in his works came to be known in Italian as *grottesca*; their ornate, stylized forms gave rise to the English "grotesque."

As the toast of Rome, Raphael lived like a prince, showered with lucrative commissions, sought after by the rich and powerful, even offered a cardinal's niece in marriage. This "very amorous man," as Vasari delicately puts it, "was fond of women . . . and always quick to serve them." When an infatuation distracted Raphael from a deadline, his patron moved his mistress into the palazzo where he was working. His pursuit of *amore* proved Raphael's undoing. After a night of even more "immoderate" indulgence than usual, Vasari reports, he returned home with a very high fever. Because he didn't tell his doctors of "the excesses he had committed," they bled him in such a way that he grew progressively weaker and died. He was thirty-seven. All of Rome wept, except for Michelangelo, whose only comment was "My thief is dead."

Standing before a captivating Raphael in Florence's Pitti Palace, I overhear an Italian guide speculate that a sexual infection killed the painter. "Did he die of AIDS?" a precocious young boy asks. The docent locks eyes with the lad's flustered mother. "You can blame his death," he says diplomatically, "on the orgy that was Rome."

Just as he had done with Michelangelo, Raphael devoted himself to appropriating some of Leonardo's hallmarks, such as expressive faces, graceful figures, and delicate shading. He "came nearer to Leonardo than any other painter," Vasari tells us, but he never equaled or surpassed him. Then again, no one did.

Unlike artists who let their works speak for them, Leonardo da Vinci (1452–1519) left a rich legacy of words—an on-going conversation with himself that covered more than five thousand surviving manuscript pages gathered into *libricini*, combination sketch and notebooks, written in his idiosyncratic right-to-left "mirror script." True to his mantra of *saper vedere*, to know how to see, Leonardo's incomparable volumes crackle with a lifetime of astute observations, set down without punctuation or accents, often with several short words run together into a long one or a long word divided in half. *"Dimmi"* ("tell me"), Leonardo would doodle when breaking in a new pen nib. In the margins of his notebook, another phrase appears, "Tell me if anything was ever done," scribbled time and again by an artist who left a legacy of largely unfinished projects.

An illegitimate son of a Florence *notaio* and a countrywoman, Leonardo bounced back and forth between his father's city home and his mother's farmhouse. Largely self-taught, he described himself as an *"omo senza lettere,"* a "man without letters," but he took pride in his independent thinking and nimble mind. "Why are we supposed to worship the Son," he once asked caustically, "when all the churches are dedicated to the mother?" Although he admired the human body as a marvel of nature, he disdained its owners as "sacks for food" and "fillers-up of privies."

In Florence in the 1470s Leonardo hung out with a group of vernacular writers known as poets *alla burchia* (which translates as "in a hurry," "piled up at random," or "higgledy-piggledy"). These rap artists of their day improvised verses in a slangy, ribald, satirical style called *burchiellesco* (from *burchia*), the antithesis of Petrarch's labored sonnets. His eclectic treatises include the memorably titled "Why Dogs Gladly Sniff One Another's Bottom" (*"Perché li cani odoran volentieri il culo l'uno all'altro"*). The reason: the smell lets them know how well fed a dog is. A whiff of meat indicates a powerful and rich owner—and a need for deference.

Leonardo delighted in puns, wordplay, complex codes, spoofs, and pictograms (sketches, for instance, of the letter *o* and the drawing of a pear—*pera* in Italian—to represent the word *opera*). He also jotted jokes in his notebooks. In one, a painter is asked how he depicted such beautiful images of dead things and yet produced such ugly children. The punch line: He made his paintings by day and his children by night. In a riddle, Leonardo asked which men walk on treetops and which on the backs of great beasts. The answer: It depends on whether they are wearing wooden clogs or ox-leather shoes.

Perhaps Leonardo's jokes were the secret behind his signature creation: Mona Lisa's smile. To entertain this fetching young model, Vasari records, Leonardo brought in musicians who played or sang and clowns to make her merry. Italians refer to this most recognizable of portraits as *"La Gioconda,"* with its double meaning of "Signor Giocondo's wife" and "a merry or joking girl." The artist spent so much time in her company that gossips, such as Aretino, speculated about the reasons why. But the time and effort paid off. "The portrait was painted in a way that would cause every brave artist to tremble and fear," wrote Vasari.

Except one—Michelangelo Buonarroti. In a telling incident in Florence's Piazza Santa Trinita in 1504, a group arguing over a passage in Dante asked the opinion of Leonardo, who was walking by. Spying Michelangelo, who had entered the piazza, Leonardo replied by calling out that the sculptor could advise them. Taking this as an insult, Michelangelo, in a scathing reference to Leonardo's aborted project for the Milanesi (whom he refered to as *caponi,* big heads, insinuating stupidity or obstinacy), retorted, "Explain it yourself—you who designed a horse to cast in bronze, and couldn't cast it, and abandoned it out of shame." He then abruptly spun around—"turned his kidneys," as an observer put it—and stomped off, while Leonardo's face reddened.

After stints in Milan and Rome, Leonardo moved to France and spent the last three years of his long life in the comfort of a Loire château. His patron, King Francis I, delighted in conversations with this extravagantly gifted thinker and talker. (Despite his fondness for the artist, the king did not—as Vasari reported—cradle his head as he died.) When Napoleon invaded Italy, he claimed Leonardo's notebooks as the spoils of war and transferred them to the Bibliothèque Nationale. They've since scattered to libraries throughout Europe.

Leonardo's fellow genius and archrival, Michelangelo (1475–1564), who wrote his name as Michelagnolo, an old Tuscan spelling, in a defiantly bold script, left an indelible artistic and architectural signature on Florence and Rome. Born into a poor Florentine family, he told Vasari that he had imbibed an affinity for stone in the breast milk of his wet nurse, a mason's wife. His father tried to beat artistic inclinations out of the boy, but his obvious talent won him an invitation to live and study in the home of Lorenzo il Magnifico, his first and most beloved patron.

Michelangelo's genius exploded in youth and blazed into robust old age. Through almost a century of tumults—uprisings, assassinations, civil wars, sieges, conspiracies, and invasions— he battled with popes, broke with the Medici, and after the fall of the Florentine republic (for which he oversaw fortifications) railed against his fellow citizens. Yet he worked ceaselessly, producing unequaled masterpieces in painting, sculpture, and architecture and earning the accolade of *Il Divino*, the divine one.

The word most associated with the brusque artist is *terribilità*. Michelangelo's temper was indeed so fierce that the Medici pope Leo X, who had known the artist since boyhood, called him *"troppo terribile,"* "too terrible to deal with." But in the artistic language of the Renaissance, *terribilità* conveyed awesomeness, virtuosity, force, vehemence. The *terribilità* of Michelangelo's *figura serpentinata*, such as the anguished, writhing, tormented souls in his *Last Judgment* over the altar of the Sistine Chapel, represented art at its most sublime. (Italians derided the artists who later added "corrections" to clothe these naked figures with the mocking word *braghettoni*, or "big underpants makers.")

The historian and poet Benedetto Varchi described Michelangelo's works as "so new, so unusual, so unheard of [*inudita*] in all cultures in all countries . . . that I for myself . . . not just admire, not just am stupified [*stupisco*], not just am astonished and amazed, and almost reborn; but my pulse trembles, all my blood turns to ice; all my spirits are shocked, my scalp tingles with a most sacred and never before felt horror to think of him."

Thousands of books, treatises, poems, dissertations, plays, and novels have dissected every dimension of Michelangelo and his art. Yet what intrigued me most was the sole regret this titan of titans expressed: that he had kissed only the hand and not the face or lips of the poet and noblewoman Vittoria Colonna as she lay dying.

When I first read this anecdote, I did a mental double take, stunned that a woman had evoked such a tender sentiment from a man whom I had assumed was homosexual. Scholars still debate the unanswerable question of whether the artist's well-documented infatuations with young men were platonic or physical. A contemporary, viewing his sensuous Bacchus, commented, "Buonarroti could not have sinned more with a chisel."

According to his pupil and biographer Ascanio Condivi, beauty in either sex of any age shot straight to Michelangelo's heart. He himself wrote that Vittoria's *bel volto*, or beautiful countenance, spurred him to rise "beyond all vain desire" so that he saw "death in every other beauty."

At age sixty-three, the most venerated artist of the day met the most acclaimed female poet of the Renaissance, then forty-eight, in Rome, after admiring her Petrarchian verses for years. A widow esteemed for her intelligence and saintly virtue, Vittoria attracted the liveliest intellectual and religious leaders to her circle. To Michelangelo, she became, as Michael Besdine writes in *The Unknown Michelangelo*, "the most important woman in his adult life, the dominant influence of his later years, the good mother, and intellectual companion for whom he had longed."

Francisco de Hollanda, a visiting Portuguese painter who spent several Sundays with Michelangelo and Vittoria in a church garden overlooking Rome, recorded almost verbatim transcripts of conversations between the two intellectual soul mates. During these spirited discussions, Vittoria, always affectionate but alternately provoking and cajoling, drew out the reticent genius on a variety of subjects. Words, I realized as I read these dialogues, were the gift she gave to, and inspired in, Michelangelo. Although he had written all his life, Michelangelo composed most of his muscularly energetic sonnets and madrigals between the ages of sixty and eighty and dedicated many to Vittoria. Historians rank him as one of the finest, if not the finest, of Italian Renaissance poets.

"Those who do not know you," Vittoria once wrote to him, "esteem only the least of you, which are the works of your hands." To her he revealed something even more precious—a glimpse of his very soul. "Save me," Michelangelo entreated Vittoria, "from that old me, self's black abyss."

This is exactly what she did, in a relationship so intriguing that I considered writing a book about the aging artist and his middle-aged muse. As I accumulated research, Michelangelo and Vittoria became so real to me—and so realistic in my conversations about them—that my husband began irreverently referring to them as "Mickey B." and "Vicky C." I dropped the book idea once I realized that their involvement was nothing but reverent.

In one of his poems Michelangelo says about listening to Vittoria, "I am at last made such that I can never be my own again." He compares her spiritual influence over him to the power of an artist over his material. Just as he reworked a clay model or rough sketch until it finally resembled the original idea, Vittoria shaped to her idea of virtue the "unprized" form of Michelangelo, carving away excess just as he did with a sculpture to reveal the innate form within.

In a tender letter to Vittoria, Michelangelo writes, "[I] wanted to do more for you than for anyone I have ever known on earth. But the great task [painting *The Last Judgment*] that I had and still have on hand prevented me from letting your Ladyship know this." Vittoria's death in 1547 shattered Michelangelo, who wrote a sonnet comparing her to a fire that had scorched him and left only embers.

Yet Michelangelo never stopped working—or writing. "You will surely say that I must be old and mad for wanting to write sonnets, but since so many people say I'm in my second childhood, I wanted to act the part," he wrote to his "dear friend"

Giorgio Vasari in 1554. In the twilight of his life, Michelangelo produced some of his most haunting sculptures and ambitious architectural designs, including the dome of St. Peter's.

For a recent birthday, my daughter gave me a book of Michelangelo's letters that reveals another side of him. A shrewd businessman, he bought up real estate for his brothers and nephews and, as an act of personal charity, provided dowries for poor Florentine girls so they could marry or buy their way into convents. But when angered, Michelangelo lashed out, warning his nephew Lionardo about "certain envious, scandal-mongering, low-lived scoundrels who write you a heap of lies because they can't cheat or rob me. They are a bunch of vultures. . . . Don't bother about my affairs, because I know how to look out for myself, and I'm not a child."

Michelangelo never flinched from what he was. "I am ill in body with all the ills that usually plague old men—the stone so that I can't urinate, pains in my side, pains in my back, so that often I can't climb the stairs," he wrote. "Writing is very hard on my hand, my eyesight, and my memory. That's what old age does!" The elderly artist became increasingly preoccupied with death. In a poignant verse, he wrote of being "betrayed by these fleeting days of mine, and by the mirror, which tells the truth to all who gaze in it." He died a few weeks shy of his eighty-ninth birthday in 1564.

Immersed in papal and civic projects in Rome, Michelangelo hadn't set foot in Florence in two decades. Vasari claimed the "bad air" kept him away. However, the city fathers had no intention of allowing another celebrated son to spend eternity beyond its walls (as Dante does, in Ravenna). The pope had pledged to honor Michelangelo with a grand memorial in St. Peter's, but the artist's nephew spirited the corpse out of town.

The great Florentine returned home twenty-five days after his death. Crowds surged into the basilica of Santa Croce for a glimpse of history's most famous artist. A lieutenant overseeing the transport of the casket to the sacristy, unable to resist his curiosity, ordered that it be opened. According to Vasari's eyewitness account, Michelangelo's body showed no signs of decomposition, but looked as if he were "only resting in a sweet and most tranquil sleep."

Almost immediately tributes in Latin and Italian— epitaphs, sonnets, verses, letters, odes—flooded the church. Michelangelo's adoring fans couldn't say enough about him. On Duke Cosimo's orders, this display was left standing for many weeks as a tribute to the beloved artist. Michelangelo's funeral, as majestic as a monarch's, and his grandiose tomb in Santa Croce testified to the lofty status that Italian artists had attained since Cimabue's day.

No Italian artist has ever equaled this level of achievement or acclaim. "So does the story of the golden age of Italian art end with Michelangelo?" I ask my friend Ludovica Sebregondi, a professor of art history at the University of Florence. She hesitates a minute before mentioning another worthy name: Michelangelo Merisi da Caravaggio (1571–1610). Through her, I found myself swept into a four-hundred-year-old mystery surrounding his death.

Caravaggio, a baroque painter famed for his dramatic compositions and bold use of chiaroscuro, the contrast of darkness and light, dazzled Rome with his brilliance. His personal life oscillated between light and dark. Forever arguing and brawling, he killed a young man in a fight and had to flee Rome with a price on his head. For years he careened around southern Italy until he ended up in a prison in Malta. Caravaggio escaped, and the fugitive, wearying of life on the run, eventually won a papal pardon. However, his plans to return to Rome with paintings for his powerful patrons went terribly wrong.

Thrown into jail in a small coastal town, Caravaggio bought his freedom with a large bribe, only to discover that the boat with his paintings and possessions had sailed north. He set out in pursuit, traveling by whatever means he could find, including by foot, in the midsummer heat. According to folklore, the desperate artist collapsed on the beach and died in the fishing village of Porto Ercole on the Tuscan coast. The paintings disappeared.

Caravaggio's death is the town's sole claim to historic fame. I know. Every summer since 1990 Bob and I have come to this picturesque port, named for the mighty Hercules but lacking any distinguished museum, church, or work of art. However, its humble church may add more clues to the lingering mystery about the painter's final days.

As a special privilege, its pastor—who set the village buzzing when he honored us, mere itinerant Americans, by coming to dinner at our rented villa—allowed Ludovica to examine the official parish record book. We gathered around her as she opened the stained cover of the oversize ledger, which dates back to 1590.

Ludovica turned the tattered pages slowly until she came to an envelope containing a torn piece of paper. As she read the bold black script out loud in Italian, I translated the words into English: "Here in Porto Ercole, 18 July 1609, died Michelangelo Merisi da Caravaggio, painter, in the hospital, of an illness."

Was this the definitive answer to Caravaggio's demise? Not at all. Historians were still haggling over the details of his death, Ludovica informed us. If this notice is genuine, the accepted historic date of the celebrated artist's death—July 18, 1610—might be wrong. If it's a fake, who inserted the bogus notice into the record book? When? And, most perplexingly, why?

"*Molto emozionante!*" ("Very exciting!"), Ludovica exclaimed after hours of scrutinizing the yellowed document. The gleam in her dark eyes reminded me that art in Italy doesn't just hang on walls or pose on pedestals but speaks across time and space. On that serene summer day, I too felt the thrill of entering— however distantly and indirectly—the *storia* of an artist, a creator of the beauty that never dies.

# On Golden Wings

"ARE YOU A MIMI OR A MUSETTA?" ASKS MAE-
stro Mario Ruffini, a musicologist and composer in Florence, referring to the leading
ladies—sweet-souled Mimi and coquettish
Musetta—of Giacomo Puccini's La bohème. An
American might have tested my temperament
(more Musetta than Mimi) with a choice between fiery Scarlett or placid Melanie from
Gone with the Wind. But of course an Italian, especially one who spent years as an opera conductor, would think in terms of this wholly
Italian invention.

Opera, a splendid confection of music,
words, drama, costumes, sets, special effects,
and complete suspension of disbelief, could
not have emerged in any other country. "Italian opera is the ultimate expression of the col-

lective Italian genius—the Italian sun captured in sound," says Maestro Ruffini. "It stems from the Italian nature, the Italian voice, the Italian soul."

Nothing looks like Italian opera. Nothing sounds like Italian opera. And no one (not even Petrarch, who inspired its language) speaks or has ever spoken the elevated idiom found in the libretto (little book) of virtually every classic Italian opera. As soon as she steps on stage, a *donna* (woman) becomes a *beltà* (beauty)—no matter how plain the singer—with *lumi* (lighted candles) for eyes. Rather than a *chiesa* (church), she goes to a *tempio* (temple), where *sacri bronzi* (sacred bronzes) ring instead of *campane* (bells). Stage directions for battle scenes invariably call for the firing not of a *cannone* but of a *bronzo ignivomo* (fire-vomiting bronze). An impassioned suitor entreats his beloved, "*Stringimi al seno*," usually translated as, "Draw me to your bosom." But *seno*, a Roman physician informs me, refers more precisely to the delicate spot between a woman's breasts.

Absurd though it may be, opera's *stile gonfiato*, or inflated style, can enchant—no less than the golden wings of music that carry the poetic words aloft. I fell under its spell long before I knew a single sentence in Italian. As a graduate student at Columbia, I would buy standing-room tickets to the Metropolitan or the New York City Opera and sidle into empty seats, working my way ever closer to the stage. At certain magical performances, the melding of words and music bypassed my ears and shot straight to my heart. I could actually feel it fluttering in my chest, directly beneath my *seno*.

When I moved to San Francisco to marry a man who had never even been to an opera, I won him over slowly. On

Saturday evenings we would anchor our little sailboat off Belvedere Island in the San Francisco Bay, watch the stars, and listen to broadcasts from the Metropolitan Opera on a portable radio. Without the benefit of supertitles or a libretto, we had to listen with our hearts, intuiting what the singers were saying. Within a year, Bob was hooked, and we had student tickets (he was a psychiatry resident at the time) to the Friday-evening series at the San Francisco Opera.

Back then I thought that learning Italian would help me understand opera better. Instead, the more I learned about *la lirica*, as Italians refer to opera, the better I understood Italian—and Italians. Phrases from its overwrought libretti percolate through the language. Every Alfredo sooner or later is implored, *"Amami* [Love me!], *Alfredo!"* from *La traviata,* and every Aida becomes *"celeste Aida,"* for Verdi's celestial heroine. Men who shake my hand on a chilly day break into *"Che gelida manina!"* ("What a cold little hand!") from *La bohème.* Thanks to *la lirica, vendetta* (vengeance) is always *tremenda* (terrible) as in *Rigoletto,* while *lacrime* (tears) are *furtive* (hidden) as in *L' elisir d'amore,* and *spiriti* (spirits) *bollenti* (boiling hot), as in *La traviata.*

Yet the source of these phrases, the opera libretto, remains the neglected stepchild of this most extravagant of arts, and librettists—who often lived as outrageously as their larger-than-life characters—have been eclipsed by composers, conductors, and, most of all, superstar singers. This was not the way things were some four hundred years ago when opera was born. The word—and its writers—came first.

In the twilight of the Renaissance, a group of Florentine

poets, philosophers, and professional musicians, who called themselves *La Camerata* (the salon), devoted themselves to recreating something that hadn't been heard since ancient Greece— stage drama set to music. One evening in the late 1590s they presented *Dafne*, the story of an innocent maiden turned into a laurel tree to escape Apollo's lustful pursuit, with a libretto by the poet Ottavio Rinuccini. The composers may have included Vincenzo Galileo, father of the illustrious astronomer, as well as Jacopo Peri, a young tenor nicknamed Zazzerino (long hair) for his mane of red-blond hair, who moved listeners to tears with his voice. The aristocratic audience had no idea they were listening to the first *opera in musica*, or work in music.

In 1600 this new art form took another major step with the performance of the Greek myth *Eurydice*, with a libretto by Rinuccini and music by Peri, at the monthlong festivities for the wedding of Grand Duke Ferdinando de' Medici to Christine de Lorraine. But opera's true father was Claudio Monteverdi (1567– 1643) of Cremona, Europe's foremost composer of madrigals, love songs for several voices. The premiere of his *Orfeo: favola in musica* (*Orpheus: A Fable in Music*) on February 24, 1607, at the Gonzaga Palace in Mantua marked the debut of both the first modern opera and the first modern orchestra.

Collaborating closely with Rinuccini, Monteverdi presented solos, duets, trios, and declamatory passages sung by small choruses. Italian gave names to these operatic inventions, such as *aria* (air), for a song sung by one singer; *recitativo* (recitative), for a semi-sung passage between set pieces of music; and *arioso*, for a cross between an aria and recitative that was very popular in early opera. Accompanying them was what seemed an outlandish assemblage of three dozen instruments, which became the model for all orchestras that followed.

The new musical sensation spread throughout the peninsula as quickly as motion pictures would in the twentieth century. In Rome, the infatuated Barberini family built a three-thousand-seat theater to share opera's pleasures with their friends. Clerics, including popes, cardinals, and their retinues, became devoted fans. Music-loving Naples enthusiastically welcomed the new diversion, which soon traveled throughout Europe.

However, no city embraced opera with greater fervor than cosmopolitan Venice, which built the first public opera theaters and attracted a new, more egalitarian audience. "Monteverdi's Venetian successors went on to create more operas with real people as subjects, further secularizing the art form and making it open to new themes and styles, including comedy," writes Fred Plotkin in *Opera 101*. Thanks to them, Venice, "the New York City of its day," became the first great city of opera.

By the end of the 1600s, Venetians were thronging to some sixteen opera houses, each located in a different parish of the city. Their appetite for new works—often different compositions based on the same libretto with new scenic effects—was insatiable. "It didn't take long for the middle class to hijack what had been an aristocratic entertainment," says Kip Cranna, musical director of my favorite company, the San Francisco Opera. Operagoers, who often came to the theater every night, ate dinner in their boxes or the less pricey *parterre* (the open area in front of the stage). During the performances, they gossiped, flirted, or played cards, pausing to marvel at an especially eye-popping special effect or intoxicating aria.

To capture their distracted audience's attention, librettists exaggerated everything. Huge casts tramped across the stage. Tortured plots usually showcased a knightly hero enduring arduous tribulations. Trapdoors opened with a hellish red glare to release or swallow demonic spirits. But everything always turned out for the best. For the requisite *lieto fine* (happy ending), a deus ex machina ("god from a machine" in Latin), such as the allegorical figure of glory, would descend from the rafters to save the day.

By 1700 nearly four hundred different operatic works had been produced in Venice, but even its staunchest admirers agreed that ever-more-outlandish stunts were turning opera into a parody of itself. The librettist who came to its rescue once sang and recited verses for strangers on the streets of Rome—or so goes the most operatic version of the childhood of Pietro Trapassi. A wealthy intellectual adopted the boy and changed his name to Metastasio (from a Greek word meaning "change"). When his benefactor died, the twenty-year-old singer and poet inherited a fortune—which he quickly dissipated.

The penniless Metastasio (1698–1782), renouncing feckless pursuits, went to work for a lawyer in Naples. After a few years he began writing anonymously for the Neapolitan theater. His alleged mistress, a famous soprano known as La Romanina, encouraged him to write his first libretto, *Didone abbandonata* (The Great Dido Abandoned). Its engaging verses hushed the noisiest opera house in Europe. Returning to Rome, Metastasio produced so many triumphant librettos that his name—often stamped on every page—became synonymous with *opera seria* (serious opera). In 1729 the Austrian emperor named him to the most prestigious musical post in Europe, that of Caesarean Poet in Vienna.

As the cultural impresario of a powerful monarch, Metastasio wielded more influence than any librettist before or since. This purist, upholding the traditions of Greek tragedies, stripped opera of "vulgar" comic scenes, thundering choruses, and almost all movement. Metastasio's verses, which he often read to admirers before they were set to music, practically swooned with Petrarchian imagery. "The waves that murmur between the shores," a typical lyric read, "the air that trembles between the bows, is less fickle than your heart." Almost every scene in his operas ended in an exit aria. The flamboyant *castrati* or *voci bianche* (white voices)—talented young boys castrated at puberty to preserve their remarkable singing range—exploited these to showcase their vocal pyrotechnics.

Audiences looking for lighter fare turned to *opera buffa*, or comic opera, which first flourished in Naples. There local theaters presented comic operas, both in Italian and in dialect, on their own or as *intermezzi* between the acts of a serious opera. The cast, made up of actors who could sing rather than trained professional singers, portrayed stock characters from the traditional *Commedia dell'Arte*: stingy merchants, crafty servants, star-crossed lovers, lecherous old fools, pompous doctors, and flirtatious maids. The librettists, who mainly cobbled together classic comic situations, remained anonymous.

The one exception was Carlo Goldoni (1707–1793), a Venetian playwright who adapted his works and others' into comic operas. Although less influential than Metastasio, he revolutionized *opera buffa* by insisting on less improvisation and greater adherence to the written libretto. Goldoni's spirited characters were as recognizable as next-door neighbors—toothpaste sellers, custodians of public baths, café owners, hunters, peasants. Rather than musing chastely about love, they engaged in lively give and take, punctuated with folksy epithets such as *"Birboncello!"* ("Rogue!"), *"Bricconaccia!"* ("Rascal!"), and *"Furbacchiotto!"* ("Trickster!").

Milan staked its claim as music capital of Italy on August 3, 1778, with the opening of Il Teatro alla Scala on *"una serata afosa"* (a hot muggy night). Newspaper reports described the theater as *"magnifico, innovativo,"* with tier upon tier of ornate boxes (*palchi*) and a compressed gallery of cheaper seats called *loggione.* People gambled in the foyer, exchanged visits from box to box, and ate dinner at a restaurant on the mezzanine or an *osteria* near the *loggione.* The servants of patrician families toted dinner from their houses.

"For many years," a journalist of the time wrote, "it was an adventure to walk under the windows of La Scala because from above rained down everything—leftover food and other things, too." Performers were also in firing range. The opera-mad *loggionisti* not only voiced their dissatisfaction with catcalls and boos but hurled tomatoes and other alimentary missiles at the stage—a tangible expression of their *"passione musical-teatrale."* (The food flinging has stopped, but the vociferous booing has not.)

By the end of the eighteenth century, the names of librettists began to disappear from printed librettos. Writing fast and furiously, they may not have had time or energy to worry about recognition. In addition to impresarios' deadlines, composers' dictates, and divas' demands, librettists had to contend with church and state censors. Some banned the name Maria because it suggested the Madonna; others required such picky substitutions as *nubi* (clouds) for *cielo* (heaven).

Censors were the least of the threats that menaced Lorenzo Da Ponte (1749–1838) in his breakneck romp of a life. Born Emanuele Conegliano to a Jewish family north of Venice, the *spiritoso ignorante* (clever ignoramus) essentially educated himself by reading old books stored in the family attic, including Metastasio's verses. When he was eleven, his widower father, hoping to better the family's position, converted to Catholicism. As was the custom, Emanuele, the eldest son, took the full name of Bishop Lorenzo Da Ponte, who had received them into the church.

The new Da Ponte, sent to the local seminary, quickly acquired Latin, Hebrew, and Greek, but his greatest passion was for Italian literature. Memorizing much of Dante and Petrarch, he wrote poems by the thousands. But when his sponsor died, Da Ponte's only hope of continuing his education was to train for the priesthood, a calling he described as "wholly contrary to [his] temperament, [his] character, [his] principles." Six months after his ordination in 1773 at age twenty-four, the handsome prelate bolted to Venice.

To support himself, Da Ponte became an *improvvisatore*, a sort of street poet who spontaneously declaimed hundreds of lines of verse to musical accompaniment. Like Casanova, the philanderer whom he later befriended, Da Ponte feverishly pursued women, wine, cards, and trouble. In 1779 his debauchery reached such extremes that the unrepentant rake was convicted of *mala vita*, or bad living, and exiled from the Venetian republic for fifteen years.

Two years later Da Ponte showed up in Vienna, where Emperor Joseph II's Italian opera company was in need of a "poet," or house librettist. During his job interview, Da Ponte confessed that he had never written a full opera libretto. "Good, good," Emperor Joseph said. "We shall have a virgin muse." In this post, the anything-but-virginal Da Ponte, who reportedly read twenty opera texts to prepare for his new trade, met the most famous composer in Europe, Wolfgang Amadeus Mozart (1756–1791). The two collaborated on three of opera's crowning glories: *Le nozze di Figaro, Don Giovanni,* and *Così fan tutte.*

When I ask Maestro Ruffini about this unlikely creative pairing, he describes it as a partnership made in operatic heaven: "Who but someone brazen, malicious, peevish, lying, vulgar, vain, servile, and hypersexual could write librettos like the ones that Da Ponte provided to Mozart?" he replies, noting that Mozart prized Da Ponte's firsthand knowledge of *loscaggine*— a suggestive word that roughly translates as "the slimy underbelly of society." The libertine librettist also brought to the collaboration a strong sense of plot, intriguing characters, and immensely singable, witty, economical verse.

"And what did Mozart bring?" I venture.

Mozart, says Ruffini, brought Mozart: "If it is true that the libretto is finished when the music is finished, Da Ponte's Italian librettos are drenched in the genius of Mozart."

After Emperor Joseph's death, the arrogant, argumentative Da Ponte was hounded out of Vienna—or as he saw it, "sacrificed to hatred, envy, the profit of scoundrels." He lost more than his sinecure. When he developed abscesses in his mouth, he treated them with a potion containing nitric acid. The abscesses disappeared, along with all his teeth. But in Trieste the serial seducer fell in love for the last time.

"At the age of forty-three, penniless, toothless, and with no prospects," Rodney Bolt writes in *The Librettist of Venice*, Da Ponte won the heart of sweet, beautiful, British-born Ann Celestine Grahl, known as Nancy, twenty years his junior. The couple, whose marriage would endure for forty years, settled in London and had five children. Da Ponte hopscotched from one doomed entrepreneurial venture to another. In 1805, tipped off that creditors were pressing for his arrest, Da Ponte boarded a ship to America.

In New York City, Da Ponte launched a string of enterprises, including a grocery, pharmacy, and dry goods store. In a casual conversation with a customer, he delivered such an erudite oration on Italian literature that the stranger—Clement Clarke Moore, who later wrote *'Twas the Night Before Christmas*—offered him a job teaching Italian literature at the house of his father, the president of Columbia College. In time Da Ponte became the college's first professor of Italian—the first, in fact, in the United States. But Italian wasn't an academic requirement or much of a draw, and few students showed up. Undeterred, Da Ponte lobbied intensely for an Italian opera house in Manhattan. It opened its doors in 1833 and closed them in 1836.

The would-be impresario took American indifference to Italian and to opera personally. "I, the creator of the Italian language in America," he wrote to a friend in Italy, "I, the poet of Joseph II, the author of thirty-six dramas, the inspiration of . . .

Mozart! After twenty-seven years of hard labor, I no longer have a pupil." Yet Da Ponte, who died at age eighty-nine in 1838, felt that importing Italian culture to America was an even greater contribution than the operas he wrote for Mozart.

Da Ponte may have been ahead of his time. With nineteenth-century romanticism, opera, always extravagant, reached new heights—and depths. Ever more intense, Italian opera became known as *melodramma*, a generic term for any story set to music that took on new meaning as the scope of the plots considered *operabile* (suitable for opera) expanded. Death, once banished from the stage, moved front and center. Corrosive hatred, which engenders a greater range of scabrous emotions, trumped plaintive love. Opera halls echoed with burning cries such as *"Vendetta!"* ("Vengeance!"), *"Io tremo!"* ("I tremble!"), and *"O rabbia!"* ("Oh, rage!").

New operas were written and performed at an astonishing rate—five hundred, according to one count, in a single decade of the early nineteenth century. All of Italy seemed seized by *melomania*, a mania for music. Every city boasted at least one opera house; traveling companies brought operas to towns and villages. No other form of entertainment could compete with opera's wild popularity.

The quality of the libretto didn't always justify such enthusiasm. "If you want to write a smash-hit opera," Carlo Pepoli, a composer of the time, counseled with caustic irony, "write an outlandish libretto in seven parts, which has a weird and terror-filled subject. Give it the most horrible title. Don't bother about the epoch or the whys and wherefores: only muddle up everything without any continuity, neither verse nor prose, and it will be like a steamship, which gives off spume, spray, smoke, and noise."

But one popular form of romantic opera—*bel canto* (beautiful singing)—was anything but noise. Its premier composer, Gioacchino Rossini (1792–1868), son of a musician and singer, began his musical training early and produced the first of his thirty-nine operas, *La cambiale di matrimonio*, at age eighteen. For an opera he called *Almaviva*, Rossini turned to the same libretto that another composer of the day, Giovanni Paisiello, had used for his popular *Il barbiere di Siviglia (The Barber of Seville)* more than twenty years previously. Rossini composed the music at lightning speed in twelve days, by his account. Paisiello's fans were so irate that they sabotaged the premiere in Rome in 1816 by whistling and shouting during the entire first act. But not long after the second performance, the opera scored such great success that the title *Il barbiere di Siviglia* permanently attached itself to Rossini's score.

Rossini, whose more serious operas include *Otello* and *William Tell* (with its rousing overture), had other priorities. After *Il barbiere*'s tumultuous opening night, Rossini wrote to its soprano (who would later become his wife), "What interests me more than music is the discovery that I have made of a new salad, which I hasten to send to you."

A reference to pasta actually made its way into the libretto of *Il barbiere*.

"*Siete ben fortunato*," Figaro tells the Count. "*Sui macheroni il cacio v'è cascato.*" ("You are very lucky; the cheese has landed on the macaroni.") This phrase, instantly understood by any Italian, is the English equivalent of "landing butter-side up."

Although he lived the last thirty-nine years of his life as a revered cultural icon in Paris, Rossini would eat only pasta from Italy—and, according to an oft-repeated tale, rebuked a Parisian shopkeeper who tried to sell him pasta from Genoa when he had asked for Neapolitan pasta. "If he knows his music as well as he knows his macaroni, he must write some beautiful stuff," the merchant commented. Rossini considered this one of the greatest compliments he ever received.

The sophisticated gourmand inspired a host of recipes *alla Rossini*, including tournedos, cannelloni, filet of sole, and pheasant supreme—all, as one chef put it, "worthy of the great gourmet-musician."

No dish, however sublime, might seem worthy of Giuseppe Verdi (1813–1901), the Michelangelo of Italian opera. In more than thirty operas this maestro of maestri (nicknamed Peppino by generations of fans) gave "Italians" a unifying language and helped meld the patchwork of independent states and occupied territories into a unified nation.

The son of a poor tavern owner in a bleak village near Busseto in Emilia-Romagna, Verdi described himself as "the least educated" of composers. Yet he read voraciously and memorized large chunks of the Bible. At age twelve the musical prodigy became the village organist and wrote hundreds of pieces for the local band and church choir. Milan's prestigious music conservatory rejected his application, but after private training, Verdi qualified to become Busseto's music director. He fell in love with the daughter of his first patron, married, had two children, and wrote two operas—one a moderate success and the other hissed off the stage at the Teatro alla Scala.

Then, in the span of three tragic years, Verdi's young children and cherished wife died, probably of infectious diseases. On "the threshold of nothingness," as one biographer put it, words pulled Verdi back into the world of music—and back to life. One night an impresario in Milan shoved a rejected libretto into his hands. Alone in his room, Verdi threw the manuscript onto a table.

"Without my knowing why," he later recalled, "I found myself staring at the paper in front of me and saw these verses: 'Va, pensiero, sull'ali dorate.' 'Go, thought, on golden wings.'" Although intrigued by the phrase from the biblical story of Egypt's Hebrew slaves yearning for their home, Verdi forced himself to go to bed. "I couldn't sleep. I got up and read the libretto not once but two or three times, so that by morning I knew all of it by heart."

The libretto became *Nabucco*, which premiered in 1842. The chorus *"Va, pensiero,"* the poignant lament of the enslaved captives longing for their homeland, became an unofficial anthem for Il Risorgimento (the resurgence), a nationalistic movement that was sweeping the fragmented peninsula.

"The tune made him, then and for all time, the singer of his people's liberty," wrote an early biographer. Verdi gave voice to his countrymen's longing for freedom and unity. The day after *Nabucco* opened, people were singing the song in the streets. Another nationalistic opera, *La battaglia di Legnano (The Battle of Legnano)*, began with the cry of *"Viva Italia!"*—enthusiastically echoed by audiences. At the end of the third act, the hero Arrigo, locked in a tower, decides to risk death rather than the dishonor of missing the fateful battle. Donning his sash, he

cries, *"Viva Italia!"* and jumps from the window. At one performance, a young man carried away with patriotic fervor leapt
from a fourth-tier box into the orchestra pit. (Or so the story
goes.)

As nationalism grew, its advocates shouted, *"Viva V.E.R.D.I.!"*
and scrawled the letters on walls across Italy—not only in homage to the composer, but as an abbreviation for *"Vittorio Emanuele
Re D'Italia,"* the Piedmont king who had promised to liberate Italy
from its foreign occupiers. *Attila*, one of Verdi's lesser works, included a line that stirred millions of patriotic souls: "You may
have the universe if I may have Italy." I personally concur, but
Alessandra, the opera diction coach who knows every nuance of
Italian librettos, puts her own spin on this phrase: "You may have
the universe if I may have Verdi." She convinced me to use his
music as the soundtrack of my life as I worked on this book.

With his greatest hits (and there are many) downloaded
onto my iPod, for many months I worked out, ran errands,
drove the California coast, hiked the Marin headlands, folded
laundry, and flew back and forth to Italy with Verdi in my
head—and eventually in my heart. Not a day goes by without
*"Va, pensiero"* wafting into my brain. The thumping anvil chorus
from *Il trovatore* has kept me from screaming during many a traffic jam. In moments of pure bliss, *"Io son, io son felice"* ("I am, I am
happy") from *La traviata* floats through my mind.

When my daughter and I saw an unforgettable production
of *Rigoletto* in Florence's Boboli Gardens on a summer night, we
couldn't stop humming the duke's infectious *"La donna è mobile"*
("Woman is flighty"), nor could others in the audience. We kept
hearing snatches of the refrain as we walked back to our apart-

ment on the Arno, as if the great maestro had come back to life for an encore (a *bis*, from a Latin term for "two times," in Italian).

Verdi brought a new quality to opera: *ruvidezza*, a roughness, a pounding, a grinding, an underground rumbling that produced a visceral effect aptly called *furore*. I think of it as the musical equivalent of Michelangelo's *terribilità*. As his often scathing letters to his beleaguered librettists reveal, Verdi intervened in every stage of preparing a libretto, from the content and structure of individual scenes to the vocabulary of the lyrics. Once the libretto was finished, he would recite it over and over as he stomped around his farm in the Po Valley until music finally flowed from the words.

Verdi haggled over every syllable of *La traviata* (which translates as "she who strayed") with the librettist Francesco Maria Piave. Then he had to take on the censors. *"Una puttana deve essere puttana"* ("A whore must be a whore"), he wrote, complaining that they wanted to make the courtesan Violetta *"pura e innocente."* "If the night shone like the sun," he argued, "it would no longer be night." After the opening-night audience in Venice laughed pitilessly at the final curtain, the maestro wrote, "Was it my fault, or the singers'? Time will tell." Time has spoken: I doubt if a week passes without a performance of this masterpiece somewhere in the world.

Verdi insisted on strong situations, strong emotions, strong contrasts, and the strong language he called *parole sceniche*, dramatic words "that carve out a situation or a character." In *La traviata* (the opera I would want with me if I were stranded on a desert island), *croce e delizia* (torment and delight) sear themselves on our hearts as Violetta *(sempre libera,* always free) yields to *quell'amor,* the love that pulses through the universe.

What were the theatrical words, *le parole sceniche,* of Verdi's life? *Croce,* for sure, caused by crushing losses. *Delizia,* also, with his companion Giuseppina Strepponi, the soprano who first sang his *Nabucco,* in a half-century-long relationship that scandalized his hometown. *Vendetta?* Verdi's operas vibrate with hate, and he held fierce grudges for decades. *L'Italia,* without a doubt. *"Siamo Italiani, per Dio! In tutto! Anche nella musica!"* ("We are Italian, for God's sake—in everything, including our music!"), this proud Italian thundered as Wagner's influence seeped into Italy.

Verdi's genius glowed long and bright. Working with the librettist Arrigo Boito, a poetic virtuoso, he composed *Otello* at seventy-four and *Falstaff* at eighty. On January 21, 1901, at age eighty-eight, Verdi, whose music seemed as vital as air to generations of Italians, died. According to the maestro's precise instructions, his funeral was simple and silent, "without singing or music."

The transfer of the maestro's body to its final resting place at the Casa di Riposo, the rest home he had built for retired opera singers, provided an opportunity for a more fitting *addio.* Hundreds of thousands, including the royal family and government officials, joined the cortege. At the cemetery, Toscanini led a chorus of more than nine hundred singers in *"Va, pensiero."* Without prompting, the entire crowd joined in the chorus that had helped forge a nation.

A new generation of composers, including the Milan iconoclasts called *scapigliati* (the messy-haired or disheveled ones), demanded *verismo*, which translates as both "truth" and "realism." Rather than creating grand epics, they strove to express the real passions of real people. *Verismo*'s voice "does not speak or sing— it yells! yells! yells!" said Pietro Mascagni, an impoverished music teacher in Apulia who became an overnight sensation with the landmark *verismo* opera, *Cavalleria rusticana*. When I watched a DVD of this opera at a seminar on Italian opera at ItaLingua, my language school in San Francisco, I could barely keep track of who betrayed whom, but the "yelling" was divine.

The first Italian composer to sweep me off my feet in my grad-school days was the last of Italy's operatic princes, Gia-como Puccini (1858–1924). "Almighty God touched me with his little finger and said, 'Write for the theatre—mind you, only for the theatre,'" Puccini said. "And I have obeyed his supreme command." This incorrigible bon vivant was, as one biographer commented, perfectly equipped—mentally, emotionally, and musically—to make his spiritual home "in that place where erotic passion, sensuality, tenderness, pathos, and despair meet and fuse."

Describing himself as an instinctive composer with "more heart than mind," Puccini wanted to express *"grandi dolori in pic-cole anime"* ("great sorrows in little souls"), as he put it. He was forever searching for a libretto "that will move the world"—all the while pursuing lovely ladies, fast cars, and the wild geese he hunted at his beloved Torre del Lago near the Tuscan coast. Local farmers and fishermen jokingly referred to him in dialect as *"il maestro cuccumeggiante,"* the composer of harlot music.

On three of his most cherished operas—*La bohème* (1896), *Tosca* (1900), and *Madama Butterfly* (1904)—Puccini (who had

worn out previous librettists) collaborated with Giuseppe Giacosa, an intellectual and poet, and Luigi Illica, a temperamental
young playwright who considered a libretto nothing more than
a sketch produced, as he put it, for the convenience of the deaf.

Puccini tortured this writing team during the composition
of *La bohème*, which he insisted on being word-perfect. Sometimes he would write doggerel verse or sing nonsense words to
give his librettists a sense of the meters and rhythms he was
seeking. When they did as asked—or so they complained—he
would change his mind. Puccini liked to compose late at night,
often in the company of friends, playing a hand at cards and
then going to the next room to bang out a few bars on the
piano and jot some notes before returning to the game. He converted a ramshackle hut next to the local tavern into *"Club La bohème"* for the convenience of his drinking buddies.

In *La bohème*, written in a lively idiom that sounds colloquial compared to conventional libretti, Puccini created poetry
of ordinary things. A worn overcoat becomes a treasure; a
dropped key, a ruse for romance; a simple seamstress and starv-
ing writer, the spinners of soulful dreams. Although it sounds
effortless, none of it was. Giacosa complained of "messing up
more paper" and "racking his brain more" on the exuberant Café
Momus scene for *La bohème* than on anything else he wrote.

Although I was fascinated to find Puccini's notes, letters,
and libretti (as well as his hat collection) on display at his un-
pretentious home at Torre del Lago, now a public museum, I
was even more intrigued by his operatic love life. After a scandalous affair, he ran off with the pregnant Elvira Gemignani,
his piano student, the wife of a friend, and the mother of

two young children. They married in 1904 (after her husband's death), but Puccini's eye never stopped roving. On a visit to America, he wrote his sister that New York women "could make the Tower of Pisa stand erect." Even though Elvira spied on him, he added, he "got away with everything."

Elvira's suspicions intensified over the years. In an incident that became an international scandal, she hounded and publicly harangued their young maid Doria, whom she accused of sleeping with her husband. Doria, protesting her innocence, swallowed a toxic disinfectant and writhed in agony for five days before dying. In her suicide note, she proclaimed her innocence and begged her family to take revenge (*vendetta!*) on Elvira but not Puccini. The town gossiped that Doria had died of an abortion, but an autopsy revealed that she was a virgin. With such drama in his personal life, is it any wonder that Puccini so masterfully told tales of "tenderness mixed with pain"?

Puccini wanted his audience to experience his music as if they were living it and not watching it onstage. He achieved this sublime feat in part because of his meticulous attention to detail. For the prelude to the third act of *Tosca*, set on the ramparts of Rome's Castel Sant'Angelo at dawn, Puccini went to the historic fortress on the Tiber in the early hours of the morning so he could replicate the multitude of matin bells ringing over the hushed city.

Puccini's pursuit of the ultimate libretto led him to London and a play by David Belasco, an American playwright, theatrical director, and producer, about a geisha of the time abandoned by a cavalier naval officer. After the performance, Puccini rushed backstage, kissed Belasco, and declared on the spot, in a flood of tears, that he would write an opera about little Butterfly.

Puccini, who never came close to mastering English, made this commitment with little or no regard to Belasco's words. But as always, he did his research, studying books on Japanese customs, religion, and architecture and consulting collections of Japanese music. Puccini persuaded the wife of Japan's ambassador to Italy to sing for him and Japan's leading actress to recite lines in order to capture the "peculiar high twitter" of the Japanese female voice.

On February 17, 1904, *Madama Butterfly* opened at La Scala. The applause for the lilting love duet at the end of act 1 was subdued, and the rambunctious *loggionisti* in the cheap seats booed at the curtain. In act 2 all hell broke loose. When Butterfly's kimono billowed, people in the audience shouted that she was pregnant (by the opera's conductor, Toscanini, the in-the-know *loggionisti* yelled). In the almost mystical vigil scene when Butterfly waits for her "husband" until sunrise, Puccini had arranged for actual birdsong. The audience answered with its own birdcalls, rooster crows, and mooing. At the final curtain they hissed and shouted at what critics called "a diabetic opera."

Puccini, who felt that *Madama Butterfly* was his best work, the only opera he could bear to hear over and over, was stunned. His publisher and producer had La Scala cancel all performances, refunded a sack of money, and sent agents to music stores to buy up all copies of the libretto. The creators

got to work snipping and tucking. A more streamlined, less saccharine *Butterfly* reopened in Brescia and moved on to triumph
in Paris and around the world.

At my first production of *Madama Butterfly* in San Francisco, I remained dry-eyed until the very end, when Butterfly
blindfolds her little boy before taking her own life. As I came to
understand the words—and anticipate the plot—my heart
started to break ever earlier in the opera: at Pinkerton's *"Addio,
fiorito asil,"* his farewell to their flowered asylum of love, then
even sooner when Butterfly, brimming with love and hope,
sings of the "one fine day" (*un bel dì*) when her beloved husband
will return to her. Last season, in a particularly captivating production, I got as far as the couple's love duet at the end of act 1,
when Pinkerton concedes, *"Un po' di vero c'è,"* that there's some
truth in Butterfly's fear that an American who catches a butterfly pierces its heart with a pin. I wanted to cry out to the naïve
*farfalla* to fly away while she could.

The word that Americans most associate with Puccini,
thanks to Luciano Pavarotti and the Three Tenors' concerts, is
*"Vincerò!"* ("I will win!") from the aria *"Nessun dorma"* in *Turandot.*
Everything about this tale of a venomous, man-hating princess
whose suitors lose their heads as well as their hearts is over the
top—the score, the singing, the sets, the even-less-logical-than-
usual libretto. Yet I have loved every one of the half-dozen pro-
ductions of *Turandot* I've seen, even—as often happens—when
the supposedly ravishing empress looked like John Belushi as
the samurai warrior. (I have never found a definitive answer on
how to pronounce the name Turandot. Some opera purists in-
sist on articulating the final *t*, as Italian usually does with a con-

sonant ending, but according to the first soprano to sing Turandot, Rosa Raisa, neither Puccini nor his conductor Arturo Toscanini ever did.)

Puccini died of complications of throat cancer treatment before completing *Turandot*, although he left dozens of pages of notes for its end. At its premiere at La Scala on April 25, 1926, a year and five months after Puccini's death, Toscanini put down his baton in the middle of act 3 and said to the audience, *"Qui finisce l'opera, perchè a questo punto il maestro è morto"* ("Here the opera ends because at this point the maestro died").

Subsequent performances have used a pleasant, if uninspiring ending fashioned by the composer Franco Alfano, with considerable input from Toscanini. Almost everyone agrees that Puccini would have come up with something grander—but who knows? "What a sad irony," comments William Berger, author of *Puccini Without Excuses*, "that the whole magnificent tradition of Italian opera should end not with a bang or a whimper but a big, fat question mark."

For years I dreamed of celebrating Italian opera's long tradition by attending an opera at La Scala. My chance came when I scheduled a research trip to Milan. *Adriana Lecouvreur*, a tragic love story about a French actress by the Italian *verismo* composer Francesco Cilea, was scheduled for performance on my only free night. The very minute that online tickets went on sale (at nine a.m. in Milan, midnight in San Francisco), I snagged the best available seat.

I booked a room at the Grand Hotel et de Milan, where Verdi lived off and on throughout his life. After the triumphant premiere of his *Otello*, fans unhooked the horses from his carriage and pulled *il maestro* back to the hotel themselves. The crowd shouted Verdi's name until he appeared at his balony with the opera's tenor, who sang a few arias. When Verdi suffered a stroke in his rooms at "The Milan" in 1901, updates about his health were posted in the lobby, and the streets outside were covered with straw to deaden the clatter of carriages and horses so as not to disturb his final days. Verdi's apartment remains unchanged, and his music plays continously, even on the hotel's stylish Web site.

The afternoon before the performance, I toured the La Scala museum, where I was most fascinated by death casts of Verdi's and Puccini's graceful hands, and portraits of the women in their lives. At lunch at the adjacent La Scala café, I couldn't resist a *panino* called *La traviata*, a disappointingly prosaic ham-and-cheese sandwich.

When I arrived at the gleaming, recently restored theater, I discovered that my "box" was exactly that—a dark cube with floor-to-ceiling walls that blocked a clear view of the stage except for the two seats in the front row (one of them mine). After I took my chair, a young Asian couple—she in a floor-length silk gown, he in a leather bomber jacket with several cameras slung over his shoulder—entered the box. We all bowed to each other. The husband ungallantly took the good seat next to me; his wife, the inferior one behind. Minutes before the performance two German-speaking women—one so stunning that I assumed she was one of Milan's many runway models, and her mother—burst into the box.

The older *frau*—upset that she couldn't see the stage from her second-row seat (probably a third the cost of mine)—

rammed her chair into the minuscule space between the Asian man and me. Thrusting her shoulders between us, she craned forward, so close that if I turned my head we would have touched. After about ten minutes, her neck muscles gave out and she retreated.

Half an hour into the opera I heard a sound not in the score—loud snoring from the Asian man, who had sagged in his seat in a deep sleep, his head cushioned on the balustrade. Then I glimpsed an amazing sight: the German woman, kneeling sideways on her chair, had splayed herself, Spider-Man fashion, against the side of the box. With both arms outstretched, she had inched her torso along the wall so she could just manage to peek out toward the stage. The jet-lagged gentleman sputtered in his sleep. Spidey clung for dear life to the wall. And, of course, the band played on.

This was not the glamorous night at La Scala that I'd expected, but it was likely to be the only one of my lifetime, so I resolutely focused on the stage and the singing. And then it happened. The ineffable melting of words into music, the timeless thrill of spectacle and song, worked their magic. Italian opera once again carried my heart aloft on golden wings.

# Eating Italian

In 1860, THE CHARISMATIC GENERAL GIUSEPPE Garibaldi led a band of one thousand red-shirted irregulars (half under age twenty-five) into the region he called *Mezzogiorno*, the hot land of the midday sun. As they marched in triumph across Sicily, Garibaldi, wearing the trademark poncho and sombrero of his campaigns against Latin American dictators, spotted a robust youth dozing on a little stone wall in the shadow of a carob tree.

Reining in his horse, he asked, "Young man, will you not join us in our fight to free our brothers in southern Italy from the bloody tyranny of the Bourbon kings? How can you sleep when your country needs you? Awake and to arms!"

The young man opened his eyes and

silently flicked the fingers of one hand under his raised chin. The timeless gesture (which can still be observed in any Italian piazza) translates into "I don't give a ****" (insert the expletive of your choice). Garibaldi accepted his wordless dismissal and rode on.

"We have created Italy," one of its founding fathers sighed after the unification of the nation in 1861. "Now we must create Italians." It seemed an impossible challenge. The liberating troops often couldn't understand each other's dialects. Crowds cheering "*La Talia*," as they pronounced the unfamiliar word *l'Italia*, thought it was the name of their new queen. No one could imagine how Italy's people could ever unite to salute the same flag in a national language all could understand. "It will be spaghetti, I swear to you," Garibaldi predicted, "that will unite Italy."

He was right. Pasta, in its seemingly infinite varieties, did indeed bring Italians together—and then proceeded to conquer more people in more countries than any dish from any cuisine. "What is the glory of Dante compared with spaghetti?" the twentieth-century journalist Giuseppe Prezzolini dared to ask. Yet one of the glories of Italy's food is that when we eat pasta, we ingest a bit of its culture too.

Italy's food and language meld together as smoothly as *cacio sui maccheroni* (cheese on macaroni). Both boast a rich and rollicking history dating back to ancient times. Both vary greatly from region to region, even from village to village. Both reflect centuries of invasion, assimilation, and conquest. And both can transform daily necessities into vibrant celebrations.

Italians have long realized that we are, quite literally,

what we eat. *Sapia*, Latin for "taste," gave rise to Italian's *sapienza* (wisdom). In pursuit of divine wisdom and saintly virtues, as Carol Field recounts in *Celebrating Italy*, Italians developed the tradition of "eating the gods." Through the yearly cycle of church holidays, they devour *dita degli apostoli* ("fingers of the apostles," crêpes filled with sweetened ricotta), *minni di Sant' Agata* ("breasts of Saint Agatha," stuffed with marzipan), *occhi di Santa Lucia* ("eyes of Santa Lucia," circles of durum bread), and at Christmas *cartellate* (the cloths that cradled the baby Jesus, made of flour, oil, and dry white wine).

I have adopted a similar strategy of "eating Italian" to make the language part of me. I read aloud the lilting words for simple culinary techniques, such as *rosolare* for make golden, *sbriciolare* for crumble, and *sciacquare* for rinse. I revel in the linguistic pantry of pasta shapes: little ears, half sleeves, stars, thimbles—and the tartly named *lingue di suocera* ("mother-in-law tongues"), and *strozzapreti* ("priest stranglers," rich enough to sate ravenous clerics before the expensive meat course). Desserts such as *zuccotto* (sponge bombe filled with ice cream), *ciambellone* (ring cake), *sospiro di Monaca* (a nun's sigh), and tiramisu (pick-me-up) glide so deliciously over my tongue that I agree with cooks who claim they can *fare respirare i morti* (make the dead breathe). Only Italians would christen candy sugar pearls filled with the same sweet syrup parents serve children for a toast on special occasions *lacrime d'amore* (tears of love).

Italian's gastronomic words—like the dishes they describe—do more than tease or appease the appetite. They spice up daily conversations. Italians deftly describe a busybody who noses into everything as *prezzemolo* (parsley), someone uptight as a *bac-*

*calà* (dried cod), a silly fool as a *salame* (salami), and a bore as a pizza or a mozzarella. Gotten yourself into a mess? You've made an omelet (*fatto una frittata*). Fed up and can't take any more? You're at the fruit (*alla frutta*). Have a crush on someone? You're cooked (*cotto*). Italians dismiss a story told time and again as *fritta e rifritta* (fried and refried), a worthless or banal movie as a *polpettone* (large meatball), and something that's all sizzle and no steak as *tutto fumo e niente arrosto* (all smoke and no roast).

Italian cuisine, like Italian itself, has many tongues. Rather than *una cucina italiana*, every region developed a *gusto della geografia*, a geographic taste based on climate, topography, local products, and distinctive ways of baking bread, growing olives, aging cheese, and shaping pasta. The wives of Ligurian fishermen, for example, created *la cucina del ritorno* ("homecoming cooking") that includes a marvelous *torta marinara*, which is not a fish pie but a savory flan served to welcome their men back from the sea. Sardinian bakers rolled flat breads so thin that shepherds could fold the almost transparent *carte da musica* (sheets of music) and carry them in their pockets for a snack. Different regions use slightly different recipes and names for the fried pastries served at Carnevale: *cenci* (rags), *chiacchiere* (gossips), *lattughe* (lettuce leaves), *nastrini* (ribbons), and *nodi degli innamorati* (lovers' knots).

When I asked a waiter about the golden hue of *risotto alla milanese*, he claimed its origins dated back to the construction of Milan's multispired Duomo, which began in the fourteenth century. A young apprentice glassmaker working on windows for the cathedral created such radiant colors that his colleagues relentlessly teased him about adding saffron to the pigments to make them so brilliant. To retaliate, he mixed saffron with the rice for his master's wedding. The appetizing result proves the wisdom of one of my favorite Italian proverbs: *Anche l'occhio vuole la sua parte* (the eye too wants its part). In Italy food must be *bello* as well as *buono*.

Although I enjoy cooking, in Italy I prefer the company of wonderful women such as Maria-Augusta Zagaglia, who transforms the matchbook-size kitchen at L'Ercolana, the villa we rent each summer, into a culinary Merlin's cave. Bob and I gobble up her featherweight *fiori di zucca* (fried zucchini flowers) before they have a chance to cool. Our guests tell us—and I certainly believe them—that she makes the best *pappardelle al cinghiale* (pasta in a sauce of wild boar), a local specialty, in the west Tuscan region called the Maremma.

I have never asked Maria-Augusta for a recipe because such a request might seem *brutta figura*. After all, could any ordinary cook replicate her delicious dishes just by following standardized directions? Not I—especially since she, like many Italian cooks, measures out oil by the *dito* (finger) and flour by the *pugno* (fist). But as we mixed a salad together one day, Maria-Augusta did share an old Italian axiom for flavoring a salad perfectly: find *un prodigo* (a spendthrift) to pour the oil, *un avaro* (miser) to add the vinegar, *un saggio* (a wise man) to add the salt, and *un pazzo* (a crazy man) to mix them all together. But she has kept her secrets for handmade pasta to herself.

This "paste" of flour and water (with an egg thrown in to make a "Sunday pasta") remains the common denominator at Italian tables. At the Pasta Museum in Rome, tucked into a tiny piazza on the Quirinale Hill, I learned of pasta's legendary origins: Once upon a time the muse Talia inspired a man named Macareo to construct a metal container with many tiny holes from which long strings of dough emerged as if by magic. He immediately cooked these *maccheroni* and served them to some hungry poets. Talia entrusted the secret of this wondrous device to the siren Partenope, who founded the city of Naples in the sixth or seventh century B.C.

Based on more scientific archaeological research, we know that the early Romans subsisted on a diet of barley porridge and a pastalike dough mixture called *langanum* or *lagana*, which may have been the earliest form of a lasagna noodle (a word derived from the Latin *nodellus*, or "little knot"). As the city's population grew, the government banned cooking fires in its crowded tenement apartments to prevent catastrophic blazes. Their occupants often brought home dishes from hot food stalls—the original takeout.

When in Rome, I do as the ancient Romans did and buy fresh, piping hot pasta from Tony, an Egyptian cook who immigrated to Italy thirty years ago and sells delicious dishes *da asporto* (to carry away) to my apartment around the corner. Yet even when I ask for a single serving, Tony always packs up enough food for two (or more). I know why: eating alone is almost too sad to contemplate in Italy.

Italian proverbs testify to the national antipathy to a table for one: *"Chi mangia solo crepa solo"* ("Who eats alone dies alone"). *"Chi non mangia in compagnia è un ladro o una spia"* ("Who doesn't eat with a companion is a thief or a spy"). *"Chi mangia solo si strozza a ogni mollica"* ("Who eats alone chokes on every bite"). Sometimes these jests are playful ways of inviting a solitary diner to join a group. Often when I eat alone in Italy, entire families in a restaurant cordially lift their glasses to wish me a *"buon appetito!"* *"È tradizionale,"* a waiter once explained, as if he feared I'd take offense.

The Italian tradition of writing about food dates back to the publication of the first known cookbook in the Western world in the fourth or fifth century: *On Culinary Things*, referred to as *Apicius*, for the Roman *buon gustaio* (food lover) Marcus Gabius Apicius. He probably wasn't the author, says Gabriella Ganugi, who named her prestigious Apicius Culinary Academy in Florence in his honor, but he embodied the thoroughly Italian passion for eating well. When I find out that Ganugi, smart in every sense of the word, had studied law before pursuing a career as a chef, I ask about the origins of her passion for food. "Ah, *signora*," she says, flicking back her long black hair, "surely you know: We do not so much pick our passions as they pick us."

The ancient Romans' passion for unusual dishes inspired the first truly international cuisine. In an empire that stretched to the corners of the known world, all culinary roads led to Rome. Foods from conquered territories (and cooks to prepare them) made their way into the kitchens of the privileged and powerful—artichokes from Africa, cherries from Asia, pistachio nuts from Syria, ham from Gaul, dates from Egypt.

*Apicius* conjures up scenes of lavish banquets where guests, reclining on couches around low tables, dined on exotic entrees such as camel, flamingo tongues, and roasted swan or parrot, all washed down with wine scented with rose leaves. Some Italian desserts date back to ancient times. According to culinary lore,

Nero and other ancient Romans enjoyed flavored snow from nearby mountains—the original gelato.

In the brutal Dark Ages after Rome's fall, the staple that kept the population alive was *minestra*—soup brewed of roots, weeds, plants, and bits of meat (if any), stretched into an entire meal or a day or week of meals. The word *minestra* became synonymous with survival and a metaphor for what one does to get by in life. If you have the means to act as you wish, you can have any *minestra* you want, including a minestrone, or big hearty soup. If not, you have to settle for *minestra riscaldata*, the same old reheated fare. When you have used all your options, *mangia la minestra o salta dalla finestra*—eat the soup or jump out the window.

Pasta reemerged in the Middle Ages. In an early travelogue written around 1154, an Arabian geographer described the production and drying of thin noodles he called *itriyya* (an Arabic word that Italians translated into *vermicelli*, or "little worms") in a village in Sicily. Sailors probably transported this durable food to Genoa and Pisa, where *maccheroni* and *vermicelli* appear in personal wills and inventories—some on display at the Pasta Museum. These documents, its curators emphasize, clearly refute what they consider a preposterous claim—that pasta didn't arrive in Italy until 1295, when Marco Polo introduced noodles from China.

I can offer further (albeit unscientific) evidence in the form of a twelfth-century folktale a teacher gave me when I was struggling (as I still do) with the *passato remoto*. Written entirely in this arcane tense, it tells the story of a beautiful princess

who lived in a castle with many cooks to prepare her meals—
but none who could make a marinara sauce to her liking. One
day a handsome young peasant offered her his recipe in return
for her throne. After a taste of his sauce, she agreed. He grew
old and tired governing the kingdom, while she enjoyed herself
and lived to the age of one hundred. *La morale della favola* (the
moral of the story): Sometimes it's better to eat like a king than
to be one.

Medieval *cucina principesca* (princely cooking) tipped toward
ostentation more than taste. Banquets featured exotic foods and
expensive spices (so valuable they often served as currency) that
testified to a host's wealth and prestige. Veritable food orgies featured leather-tough eagles or peacocks, boiled and then roasted
and smothered under pungent sauces. Royal cooks, who com-
manded astronomic salaries, handed recipes down orally like
family secrets from one generation to the next. Among the few
written in vernacular Italian was one that belonged to a dis-
solute young nobleman in thirteenth-century Siena.

Renouncing his licentious life, this youth turned over to a
nun his last prized possessions: a bag of precious spices and a
recipe for a sumptuous sweetmeat that made generous use of
them. The extravagant delicacy struck the good sister as unfit
for a convent, so she gave the recipe to a bishop, who shared it
with other food-loving clerics. Eventually it made its way to a
cardinal's brother named Ubaldino, a cook so renowned that
Dante immortalized him as one of the insatiably hungry glut-
tons in his *Purgatorio*. Ubaldino's downfall may have been the
dish he created by adding almonds, hazelnuts, and candied

fruits to the original recipe—the famed Sienese *panforte* (strong bread).

About the same time, food made a spectacular literary debut in Giovanni Boccaccio's *Decameron*. This lifelong *buongustaio* conjured up *il Paese di Bengodi* (the land of good and plenty), where "there was a mountain made entirely of grated Parmesan cheese, on whose slopes were people who spent their time making macaroni and ravioli, which they cooked in chicken broth and then cast to the four winds. The faster one could pick it up, the more one got of it. And not far away, there was a stream of Vernaccia wine, the finest that was ever drunk, without a single drop of water in it."

With the dawn of the Renaissance, kitchens became the workshops of culinary artisans. The cooks of Duke Ercole d'Este invented the golden eggy noodles called fettuccine as a culinary tribute to his son's blond-tressed bride, the notorious Lucrezia Borgia. The navel of Venus inspired the cardinal of Bologna's cook to fashion tortellini, although local gossip claimed the beguiling belly button actually belonged to an innkeeper's daughter.

The Renaissance increasingly emphasized simple, fresh, locally grown ingredients prepared in ways that brought out their true flavors—the essence of modern Italian cooking. The man behind this culinary revolution was Maestro Martino da Como, a combination of Mario Batali and Alice Waters, who cooked for a *reverendissimo* monsignor in Rome. Many details about this fifteenth-century master chef, including the years of his birth and death, remain unknown. However, his groundbreaking *Art of Cooking* took much of the mystery out of food preparation by disclosing tricks of the trade that chefs had long kept hidden.

Unlike previous manuals, which merely listed recipes and ingredients, Martino's specified amounts, utensils, times, and techniques and spelled out every step of the cooking process. Dessert lovers should thank him for pioneering the use of large quantities of sugar (previously treated as a condiment like salt) to make sweet dishes.

If Martino were alive, I have no doubt the Food Network would base a series on his culinary special effects. In a presentation of his "flying pie," live birds, placed into a baked crust containing a smaller "real" pie, flitted into the air on serving—echoing the nursery rhyme about "four and twenty blackbirds baked in a pie." To create a fire-spewing peacock, Martino roasted the animal whole, replaced its feathers, and stuffed its beak with alcohol-soaked cotton, which he then set ablaze.

Who wouldn't tune in to watch a celebrity chef tackle Martino's directions for "How to Make a Cow or Suckling Calf or Deer Appear to Be Alive?" After butchering and skinning the animal, he instructs, "make sure the hooves remain attached to the skin and flesh." Use irons large enough to hold the beast standing up, then roast it slowly in an oven or over an open flame. When the meat is cooked, nail the irons to a large table and dress the animal with its skin to hide the irons. "Note," he adds, "that in order to prepare animals with such ingenuity, the cook must be neither a madman nor a simpleton, but he must have a great brain."

Bartolomeo Sacchi, better known as Platina, certainly had one. A humanist scholar, Vatican librarian, and contemporary of

Martino, Platina obtained one of the few manuscripts of Martino's book, written in vernacular Italian. Translating Martino's recipes into Latin, he added ten of his own, along with a treatise on his humanist, life-savoring beliefs. His combination cookbook and philosophical treatise, *De honesta voluptate et valetudine* (*On Right Pleasure and Good Health*), published in 1494 in the universal language of Latin, became the first international culinary best seller.

No one might have known of Martino's contribution if not for an American chef and hotelier named Joseph Dommers Vehling. In 1927 this bibliophile purchased a copy of Martino's original manuscript (one of five known to exist) from an Italian antiquarian and recognized the recipes. His scholarly work, *Platina and the Rebirth of Man*, published in 1941, finally rescued Maestro Martino from anonymity. Stefania Barzini, a Roman chef and food historian, updated Martino's recipes for a recent English edition of *The Art of Cooking* published by the University of California Press. She includes instructions for "how to dress a suckling pig," but none for a flame-breathing peacock or standing calf.

In the Renaissance the men who butchered and carved meat became as celebrated as chefs. At courtly banquets—occasions for theater as much as taste—the *scalco* (carver) played an all-important role: he sliced each guest's serving on the basis of his or her social rank, an exacting assignment that inspired Italian's elaborate vocabulary for cuts of meat. A duke might rate a *fesa* (a tender cut from the top side of the hindquarters); a lesser dignitary, a *scamone* (top rump).

In honor of our all-American holiday, the Fourth of July, Lina, the cook at the *castello* of Monte Vibiano Vecchio, prepared *tacchino* (turkey)—not a Thanksgiving-style whole stuffed roasted bird, but a massive turkey leg, which she grilled in the enormous fireplace. After carrying out the huge *brontosauro*, as she called it, she immediately turned to Bob and handed him the carving knives.

"*Allo scalco!*" the Italians at the table cried out. "To the carver!"

The first person to export the Italian way of cooking, eating, and entertaining was Catherine de' Medici (1519–1589). Already a *buona forchetta* (hearty eater) at age fourteen, when she married the future French king Henry II, she took along chefs, bakers, confectioners, and cupbearers as well as recipes. As the wife of one king and the mother of three others, Catherine changed what the French ate (introducing foods such as artichokes and spinach Florentine style) and the way they ate it, although her husband never got the hang of the newfangled forks she brought to the table. Parisians quickly strove to dine *à la mode de la Reine*, and French cooking soon became the dominant international cuisine.

The English didn't take as readily to Italian culinary innovations. A British tourist, noting that "all men's fingers are not alike clean," praised the Italian *forchetta*. However, many of his countrymen mocked the pronged food piercer as pretentious and lampooned its users as "forkifers."

A British ex-pat in Florence once tried to convince me that English roast beef had inspired the city's sizzling specialty, *bistecca alla fiorentina*. "*Non è vero*" ("It's not true"), said the waiter who served my daughter and me a sensational slab of Tuscany's fine *Chianina* beef at a restaurant right on the Arno called

Golden View (local friends had recommended it despite its cheesy English name). The Medici, he explained, would cook and serve these tender steaks to the people of Florence on the feast of Saint Lorenzo, the family's patron. Some English travelers in the throng once eagerly cried out for servings of what they called "beef steak." Italians took up the chant of *"bistecca,"* and the English derivative stuck to *"la fiorentina."*

When pasta officially reached England after "the peace of 1763," as one historian recorded, it quickly earned a place in London's new restaurants. However, their bewigged, foppish clients—along with dandified British tourists besotted with all things Italian—were mocked as "macaroni," a taunt that made its way into the verses of "Yankee Doodle Dandy."

Neapolitans, once called *mangiafoglie* (leaf eaters) for the green vegetables in their diet, gained the nickname of *mangiamaccheroni* (macaroni eaters) in the eighteenth century. Street vendors called *maccaronari* cooked spaghetti on rustic stoves and sold them, seasoned only with grated cheese, by the handful. Prints from the time, hung in the Pasta Museum, show ragged urchins dangling the long strands high above their heads and dropping *il ghiotto cibo*—which translates as both the "appetizing" and the "greedy" food—into their open mouths. "The difference between the king and me is that the king eats as much spaghetti as he likes," an old Neapolitan saying goes, "while I eat as much as I've got."

Neapolitan cooks were the first to pair pasta with its perfect mate, the tomato, an import from South America. The *pomodoro*, or golden apple, moved north with Garibaldi's troops, who first sampled pasta with tomato sauce in their march up the peninsula. Naples's other specialty—pizza—also merits a mention in Italian's history.

The Bourbon king Ferdinand I, ruler of Naples in the nineteenth century, became so addicted to the creations of a certain Antonio Testa that he would dress up in shabby clothes to sneak into his pizzeria. His successor Ferdinand II invited another *pizzaiolo*, Don Domenico Testa, to come to his palace and bake pizzas for the ladies of the court. As a tribute he bequeathed to Testa the title *Monsieur*, usually reserved for the *chefs de cuisine* of royal households. *Monsù*, as the Neapolitans pronounced the honorific, became a nickname for the city's pizza bakers.

One *monsù* created a classic in 1889, on the occasion of King Umberto I and Queen Margherita's visit to the city. When the queen asked for a pizza, the *pizzaiolo* Raffaele Esposito used green basil, white mozzarella, and red tomatoes, the new state's official colors, to create the first pizza Margherita. An official letter of recognition from the queen's "head of table services" remains on display at Esposito's shop, now the Pizzeria Brandi.

But long after Umberto and Margherita's reign, the "new" Italians continued to eat and speak like the "old" Pisans, Luccans, Sicilians, or Genovese they had always been. The man who almost single-handedly overcame regional divisions to create a truly national cuisine was neither chef nor butcher, but a retired merchant and banker. Pellegrino Artusi (1820–1911), born in Forlimpopoli in Emilia-Romagna, renowned for its opulent cuisine, might never have ventured beyond his staid hometown if not for a dastardly deed that has grown into a local legend.

In the tumultuous mid-1800s, masked brigands swathed in

long black capes terrorized travelers and townspeople throughout Emilia-Romagna. The most infamous was the dastardly Passatore, the Ferryman, nicknamed for his father's occupation. On
January 25, 1851, Forlimpopoli's leading citizens gathered for a
much-anticipated performance at the local theater. In the middle of the show, Passatore's men burst onto the stage and
blocked the exits. Forcing the hostages to surrender their house
keys, they plundered the town.

According to John Dickie's detailed account in *Delizia! The
Epic History of Italians and Their Food*, the bandits pistol-whipped
Artusi, "a shy, shortsighted, hemorrhoidal bachelor of thirty."
Some of his sisters managed to hide; one suffered a knife
wound to the head, and another, Geltrude, was "manhandled
and contaminated," in Artusi's words. The bandits rampaged
the home, stealing money and precious possessions. Geltrude
never recovered from the trauma and lived out her days in the
equivalent of a psychiatric facility. The rest of the family relocated to Florence, where Artusi prospered as a self-styled banker,
trader, voracious scholar, and most of all, as he put it, a passionate seeker "of the good and the beautiful wherever [he
found] them"—particularly in kitchens.

Once he retired at age fifty—*già ricco* (already rich), his biographers note—the lifelong bachelor transformed his kitchen
into a culinary laboratory. A portly man with a bushy white
walrus mustache that extended to his sideburns, Artusi cajoled
recipes from chefs, cooks, friends' wives, and an intriguing assortment of female acquaintances. Over years of tinkering and
testing, his two cooks complained that he drove them crazy
with his experiments. In time Artusi compiled 475 recipes,

along with down-to-earth advice on health and nutrition, into a thick volume worthy of its impressive title, *La scienza in cucina l'arte di mangiar bene* (*Science in the Kitchen and the Art of Eating Well*).

No publisher wanted this homespun cookbook. After a string of contemptuous rejections, Artusi dedicated his book to his two cats and published one thousand copies himself in 1891. It took four years to sell them. But despite this sluggish start, *L'Artusi*, as the book came to be known, became a literary phenomenon and a landmark in Italian culture. The inhabitants of every household, humble or highbrow, wanted their own *L'Artusi*.

When I came across a copy on the bookshelves at L'Ercolana, Artusi won me over with his first sentence, "Cooking is *una bricconcella*—a troublesome sprite," he observed. "Often it may drive you to despair. Yet when you do succeed, or overcome a great difficulty in doing so, you feel the satisfaction of a great triumph."

A prodigious researcher, Artusi reclaimed dishes thought to be French, such as crêpes, which he traced to Tuscan *crespelle*, and bechamel sauce, a derivative of the ancient Roman *colletta*. The chicken Napoleon enjoyed after his victory at Marengo wasn't prepared by his French cook, Artusi reported, but by a peasant woman in Piedmont using local ingredients.

Rather than borrowing French terms, Artusi committed himself to "our beautiful, harmonious language," which, in the newly unified nation, meant the Tuscan tongue of Dante. He included a short guide to Tuscan words, such as *cotoletta*, or cutlet, and *tritacarne*, or mincer, that were not used throughout the peninsula. Translating from other dialects and using a light, engaging style, he also introduced regional recipes, such as *piselli col prosciutto* (peas with ham from Rome) and *strichetti alla bolognese* (noodles from "a young, charming Bolognese woman known as la Rondinella," or "the little swallow"), that many Italians in other places had never tasted.

Describing *pasticcio di maccheroni* (a meat and macaroni casserole), Artusi joked that a *pasticcio*—meaning a hodgepodge, jumble, or mess—"always turns out well no matter how it is prepared." The amateur gastronome created a *pasticcio* of his own, mixing culinary rules, advice, anecdotes, commentaries, and scientific trivia (such as which fish make sounds by expelling air)—all in an avuncular, encouraging tone. "Do not be alarmed if this dessert [strudel] looks like some ugly creature such as a giant leech or a shapeless snake after you cook it," Artusi reassured readers. "You will like the way it tastes."

Italians certainly liked the new tastes he introduced. For the fourteenth edition, bulging with 790 recipes—many contributed by readers—Artusi, who lived to age ninety-one, added a celebratory preface called "The Story of a Book That Is Like the Story of Cinderella," the saga of a scorned manuscript that became a sensation, and laid the foundation for Italian cuisine as we know it.

"The ways of eating and speaking are always what unify a country," Guido Tomassi, an Italian publisher specializing in cookbooks and food history, observes during a breakfast interview in Milan. Writing just a few decades after Italy's unification, he explains, Artusi bolstered "Italians' faith and pride in their cuisine, their new nation, and their new language." The populist cookbook became one of the best-selling literary works of the time, second only to the fairy tale *Pinocchio* (whose name in Tuscan means "pine nut," from the Latin *pinus*, "pine," and the diminutive suffix *occhio*).

My friend Carla Nutti, who has prepared the most delicious meals I've ever eaten, recalls a well-worn *L'Artusi* in the kitchen of the *azienda* (combination ranch and farm, similar to the Spanish hacienda) in Emilia-Romagna where she grew up. When she and I met almost twenty years ago in Rome, I knew a smattering of Italian; Carla spoke—and still speaks—no English. So we combined Italy's two culinary arts: she cooked mouthwatering renditions of such classics as Roman-style gnocchi and artichokes, *tagliatelle* in meat sauce, veal scaloppine, and Neapolitan pastries. And at her *tavola imbandita* (sumptuous table), always set with hand-embroidered linens and heirloom silver and china, I learned to eat like an Italian—not just with my mouth but with my eyes, nose, mind, memory, and, most important, soul.

On our last trip to Rome, Carla outdid herself with a *cenone*, a great holiday dinner (*cena*) that provided a culinary tour of Italy. The feast started with a tribute to Michelangelo—in the form of *bruschettine con lardo di Colonnata*.

"*Lardo?*" I asked, warily thinking of the thick white grease I vaguely remembered from childhood. No, Carla explained, Colonnata's *lardo* (although 100 percent fat) is sliced from the subcutaneous layer of a pig's abdomen—then salted, aromatized, spiced, and aged in marble for six to twelve months.

Melted over hot bread, this high-octane ingredient fueled the stone carvers of Carrara's marble quarries. Michelangelo himself, as Carla put it, *"deliziava il suo palato"* ("delighted his palate") with *lardo di Colonnata* whenever he visited the ever-chilly cav-

erns to select stones. How could I not follow Il Divino's lead?
One bite produced a sensation not entirely remote from the
flush I felt years ago at my first sight of his *David*.

For the first of our *primi* (first courses), *risotto al radicchio di
Chioggia*, Carla chose carnaroli rice, grown in the Po Valley in
northern Italy. Until the 1960s, she told us, young girls called *le
mondine* (from *monda*, for the process of cleaning the rice) came
by the trainloads from all over Italy to plant and weed rice. The
haunting melodies they sang during their backbreaking labor
came to be known as the *canti della risaia* (songs of the rice
fields). A famous neorealist film, *Riso Amaro* (Bitter Rice), made
in 1949, showcased buxom, long-legged migrant workers in a
poignant tale of *una mondina* and two small-time thieves who
plot to steal rice from the storehouses during the celebration of
the harvest's end. To add just a bit of bitterness to our risotto,
Carla chose a crisp *radicchio* from the Veneto that *"si sposa bene con
il riso ma anche con la pasta"* ("marries itself well to rice as well as
pasta").

For the second *primo*, Carla presented a platter of jolly pale
orange handmade pasta called *cappellacci alla zucca*, shaped like
crumpled caps. Stuffed inside was a sweet but tangy mix of
pumpkin, Parmigiano cheese, *amaretti* (almond biscotti), and
*mostarda di Mantova*, which, unlike French mustard, combines
the piquant spice with fruit and sugar. I couldn't resist the
temptation to *fare la scarpetta* (make the little shoe) and soak up
the last of the sauce with a bit of bread.

I had just swallowed a morsel of the tenderest, most delicately flavored lamb I'd ever tasted when Carla told me that it
was *abbacchio*, a suckling no more than a month or so old. I

winced when I learned that the name comes from the Latin *baculum*, the cudgel used to kill lambs, a traditional symbol of innocence and sacrifice, served at Easter dinner. Until a few decades ago, shepherds would lead their flocks into Rome every spring so people could select victims for the annual slaughter. The word *abbacchiato* became slang for someone beaten down physically or mentally.

I can think of nothing more likely to restore such a poor soul's low spirits than Carla's signature dessert: homemade gelato in a circular mold, topped with *zabaione.* This sublime confection could be my downfall. For a dish (preferably two) I would hop on the next plane to Rome.

By the end of Carla's feast, we had not only tasted some of Italy's finest food and wine, but also, thanks to her gastronomic history lessons, ingested bits of its language, history, art, music, movies, and rituals. "To know a territory, you need to eat it," the great Italian writer Italo Calvino once wrote. Keep this in mind the next time you twirl *capellini* around your fork, bite into a piping hot pizza, or savor a dish of steaming risotto. That's not just food you're eating. It's Italy.

# So Many Ways to Say "I Love You"

DURING A CONSULTATION AT A UNIVERSITY HOS-
pital in Italy, an earnest psychiatric resident, a
young woman from Piedmont with long blond
hair and amethyst eyes, presented my husband,
Bob, with a diagnostic dilemma. Italian emer-
gency rooms and clinics, she said, were seeing
an increasing number of agitated young men,
sometimes babbling or crying. Although they
complained of being too restless to sleep and
too distracted to work or study, medical tests
found nothing physically wrong. What could
be the culprit? My husband listed the usual suspects, such as drug abuse and the manic stage
of bipolar disorder.

"In our experience," she commented in a
husky low voice, "it is often love. Do you see

many cases like this in the United States?" Bob and I exchanged quick glances, smiled, and shook our heads no.

Only in Italy can love's *colpo di fulmine* (lightning bolt) set off *spasimi* (spasms) of infatuation of such Richter-scale force that they transform love-struck suitors into *spasimanti, corteggiatori, innamorati, pretendenti,* or, as if almost fatally stricken, *cascamorti* reduced to gazing sheepishly at a beloved. In English a heart breaks just like a dish, but a lovesick Italian soul claims a word of its own—*spezzare*—when it shatters into bits. It's no wonder that the pop singer Tiziano Ferro croons of love making him so *imbranato* (slang for "clumsy" or "awkward") that he's like a "silly little dumpling."

Love, as everyone suspects, truly is lovelier in Italy. "Anywhere else," the nineteenth-century French writer known as Stendhal observed, "it is only a bad copy." Bob and I have spent the most romantic times of our thirty-year marriage there. Yes, we've sipped *vino* and held hands at more candlelit tables than I can count. But Italians always conspire to make even cliched moments special. In Venice, I was pregnant when we glided through the canals, so the gondolier serenaded *la bambina* with some lullabies. At the faded grand hotels on Lake Maggiore and Lake Garda, the orchestra wouldn't stop playing even though we were often the only couple still on the floor.

Once, when our mariner friends Ferruccio and Erasmo docked their boat in Capri on a summer evening, they instructed us to show up at the restaurant they'd chosen at precisely 9:35 p.m. When we arrived at the bustling eatery, they escorted us away from the crowded main dining room to a quiet alcove and insisted that Bob and I take the two chairs looking toward the *faraglioni*, the mammoth rock formations that heave out of the sea like relics of a primeval ruin. Within minutes a spectacular full *luna rossa* (red moon) ascended majestically into the sky, illuminating the towering rocks.

On vacation in 1990 we checked into the most romantic place I'd ever been, Il Pellicano, then a small country inn perched on flower-strewn terraces on a rocky hillside above the Tyrrhenian Sea. Its founders, Michael and Patsy Graham—a dashing British pilot and his glamorous American wife—chose this remote site to build a lovers' hideaway because it reminded them of Pelican Point, California, where they had fallen in love. I said to Bob, "I want you to bring me here every year for the rest of our lives." And he has. The hotel, which opened in 1965, has since developed into one of the most luxurious resorts in Italy. I'm angling for a plaque like the one we came across in a hotel in Ravello commemorating Greta Garbo's romantic interlude there. "I don't believe you're married," Gianni, the maître d', teases me every year. "You laugh too much. You must be lovers." And of course, he says *amanti*, which sounds so much sexier.

Yet despite their romantic reputation, Italians reserve *"ti amo"* ("I love you") only for the loves of their lives. English speakers love everyone and everything with the same profligate word—a lack of precision (and imagination) that confused my friend Francesca when she moved to America from Italy. "People were always telling me they loved my hair, my eyes, my *spaghetti alla carbonara*," she explains. "How could it feel special when a man said he loved me?"

Italian parents, children, even lovers, express affection

with *"Ti voglio bene,"* which translates literally into "I wish you well" but conveys much more: I wish the best for you, I want all good things for you. This phrase echoes in the lyrics of thousands of love songs. Smitten teenagers end their text messages with TVTB for *"Ti voglio tanto bene"* ("I love you so much").

In his monumental *Dizionario de' sinonimi* (Dictionary of Synonyms), published in 1830, the wordsmith Niccolò Tommaseo—described in *The Cambridge History of Italian Literature* as "very bright, proud, touchy, unrefined, unappealing, and oversexed"—dissected the linguistic nuances that differentiate *affetto*, *affezione, amore, amorevolezza, benevolenza, inclinazione, passione, amicizia, amistanza, amistà, carità, tenerezza, cordialità, svisceratezza, ardore,* and *ardenza. L'amore,* he asserted, stands out as a more active, powerful, stirring sentiment that cannot be described with any other name and that can take on both "nobility and depravity."

The latter may have held particular significance for Tommaseo, a religious man who struggled mightily with his uncontrollable libido. In a personal journal, he recorded his daily fights with temptations of the flesh, along with such details as how many mouthfuls of food he ate every day—from fifty to sixty-seven—and how frequently he washed behind his ears and had his toenails cut. This obsessive poet and novelist just as meticulously charted the shades of difference among *voglia* (wish), the first degree of desire; *desiderio,* born of true love; *brama,* a still-stronger craving; and unbridled *appetito, "il primo moto d'amore, e l'ultime furie"* ("the first motion of love, and its final furies").

As Tommaseo definitively showed, Italian qualifies hands down as the language of love. But why does almost all classic

Italian music and writing seem to be about love? When I ask this question of Luciano Chessa, a composer and Petrarchian scholar, his mouth, framed by a thick mustache and beard, breaks into a smile as he responds, "What else is there?" I cannot imagine a citizen of any other nation—certainly no buttoned-down Brit or ambitious American, not even a flirtatious Frenchman or seductive Spaniard—making this statement.

How is it that love, or maybe just the love of love, has embedded itself so deeply in the Italian psyche?

"Solo chi ama conosce." "Only those who love understand," says an Italian proverb. And so I went looking for the answer in Italian love stories.

The Roman Empire itself began with a tale of love—or, more accurately, lust—almost three millennia ago. The libidinous god Mars, smitten by the beauty of a vestal virgin, snuck into her temple in the town of Alba Longa to sleep with her. When the disgraced vestal gave birth to twin boys, remarkable for their size and beauty, the evil tribal king ordered the infants thrown in the Tiber. The cradle containing the babies drifted downstream and washed ashore at the base of the Palatine Hill.

According to legend, a lupa (she-wolf) suckled the twins Romulus and Remus. However, their nursemaid may well have been human. Lupa was slang for "prostitute," and brothels were called lupanaria. In 2007, in an astonishing discovery, archaeologists unearthed the luparcalea, the sacred cave, decorated with seashells and colored marble mosaics, that sheltered the twins and served as a shrine for their worship.

For centuries in this cave, on every February 15, Romans would celebrate a fertility festival called the Lupercalia with the sacrifice of a goat. Priests sliced the goat's hide into strips and dipped them in the sacrificial blood. Boys would run through the streets, gently slapping women with the goatskin strips to enhance their fertility in the coming year. Later in the day, all the young unmarried women in the city would place their names in a large urn. Rome's bachelors each selected a name and became that woman's sexual partner for the year in a sort of trial union that often led to marriage.

As it grew in power, the church abolished this pagan practice but created in its stead the most romantic of saints' days on February 14 to honor a martyred Roman priest named Valentine. Although historical accounts differ, Valentine seems to have served in Rome in the third century A.D., when Emperor Claudius II outlawed marriage for young men because he believed that bachelors made better soldiers. Valentine, sympathetic to young lovers, defied the decree and continued to perform weddings.

Arrested and tortured, the tenderhearted saint developed a friendship with a young girl—perhaps his jailer's daughter—who came to visit him. Some say they fell in love; others claim that he cured her blindness. Before being beheaded, the saint sent her a note that he signed, "From your Valentine." Lovers around the world have been using the same phrase ever since on the holiday Italians call *il giorno della festa degli innamorati* (the day of the feast of the enamored).

Are these mythic stories true? On Palatine Hill, an oasis of shade and birdsong that I like to visit late in the afternoon after the crowds trudge down into the forum, they feel true. This is the oldest part of Rome, named for Pales, goddess of shepherds, and steeped in lore and legends. For centuries emperors and nobles built their houses on this holy site. Visitors to these grand mansions called them *palazzi*—the root of the French *palais*, the Spanish *palla*, and the English *palace*. The Palatine's literary residents left an even grander linquistic legacy: some of the loveliest—and lustiest—love poetry ever written.

Gaius Valerius Catullus (c. 84–c. 54 B.C.) transformed romantic poetry, a Greek invention, by depicting love as a way of life rather than a flicker of lust or fit of madness. He wrote the first extended body of verse describing every phase of a love affair, from the initial quiver of excitement to luxuriant fulfillment to disillusioned bitterness. His inspiration was a beautiful noble, older married woman he called Lesbia (a tribute to the Greek poet Sappho's island of love), who was later accused of poisoning her husband and sleeping with her brother (a not atypical scenario in ancient Rome). One poem begins with a line that could have been the motto of its citizens—*"gaudenti"* (pleasure lovers), as a friend describes them: "Let's live, my Lesbia, let's live and love!"

Utterly besotted, Catullus begged for "a thousand kisses, then a hundred more . . . give me billions and billions of the damn things!" Lost for centuries, a manuscript of more than a hundred of Catullus's poems was found about 1300—stopping up the hole of a wine barrel in his hometown of Verona. His poetic followers served as inspiration for the French troubadours and the Tuscan poets who created the "sweet new style" of writing that Dante popularized.

Publius Ovidius Naso (43 B.C.–A.D. 18), better known as Ovid and nicknamed the Nose, is best known for his collection of classical myths in the *Metamorphoses* and his scandalous *Ars Amatoria* (*The Art of Love*), a primer on flirting and seduction that included advice on how to pick up women at a race or gladiator bout: "Press your thigh against the woman sitting next to you," he suggested. "If by chance a speck of dust falls in the girl's lap, as it may, let it be flicked away by your fingers, and if there's nothing, flick away the nothing: let anything be a reason for you to serve her."

Ovid's advice to women: Arrive late. "Delay enhances charm; delay's a great bard," he noted. "Plain you may be, but at night you'll look fine to the tipsy. Soft lights and shadows will mask your faults." The urbane work, aimed at worldly Romans, was so successful that Ovid wrote a sequel, *Remedia Amoris* (*Remedies for Love*). But the worst of fates, as Ovid saw it, befell him. He was exiled from Rome to a remote village on the Black Sea in the fallout of a scandal involving Emperor Augustus's promiscuous daughter Julia.

Ovid deals with greater tragedy in the story of Pyramus and Thisbe, the doomed lovers who grew up next door to each other in ancient Babylon. Through a chink in the common wall separating their houses, the youngsters, forbidden by their families from seeing each other, would whisper and, as they grew older, try to kiss. Plotting to run away together, they arranged to meet at a mulberry tree, but when Pyramus arrived, he found only a lion's tracks and Thisbe's torn and bloodied cloak (his gift to her).

Assuming she had been killed, Pyramus stabbed himself beneath the tree. Thisbe, however, had only dropped her cloak while fleeing a lion, and the beast had ripped the garment with paws bloody from an earlier kill. When she found the dying Pyramus, she killed herself with his sword (her gift to him) as he opened his eyes to gaze once more upon her. The fruit of the mulberry, once white, turned red with their blood—or so the legend goes. This story, enacted with tragicomical brio in Shakespeare's *A Midsummer Night's Dream* by the artisan actors, also was an archetype for the story of Romeo and Juliet's thwarted love.

We meet another ill-fated couple in the most poignant of Boccaccio's *novelle* in the *Decameron*, Ghismonda, beloved daughter of Tancredi, the Prince of Salerno, and Guiscardo, a young valet "of exceedingly humble birth, but noble in character and bearing." Ghismonda was as beautiful a creature as there ever was—youthful, vivacious, and possessed of "rather more intelligence than a woman needed." After a brief marriage, she returned as a widow to her father's house, but he showed no interest in arranging a second marriage. The eye of the lonely, frustrated young woman fell on Guiscardo, and the two found a way for him to tunnel into the castle and make his way into her room.

When Tancredi discovered the lovers together in his daughter's bed, he thundered at his servant, who did not defend himself but simply said, "Neither you nor I can resist the power of love." Charging Ghismonda with betrayal of him and of her class by choosing "a youth of exceedingly base condition," Tancredi decided to crush her passion by ordering his men to strangle Guiscardo and remove his heart. He had the heart delivered to his daughter in a golden chalice with the message, "To comfort you in the loss of your dearest possession, just as you have comforted me in the loss of mine."

Ghismonda wept over her lover's heart "in a fashion wondrous to behold, her tears gushing forth like water from a fountain." When she finally stopped crying, she poured a vial of poison into the chalice where the heart lay bathed in her own abundant tears and drank the mixture. As her father entered her room, she asked with her dying breath that the two lovers who could not be together in life be buried together forever in death. And so they were.

The world's most famous lovers, Romeo and Juliet, may have actually lived and died in the fourteenth or fifteenth century. The oldest known written version of their fate dates back to 1476, when Masuccio Salernitano (named for his hometown of Salerno) recounted the story of two star-crossed lovers named Mario and Gianozza of Siena in *Il Novellino*. The author swore "heaven to witness, that the whole of them [his *novelle*] are a faithful narrative of events occurring during his own times."

A more stylistically sophisticated writer, Luigi da Porto (1485–1529) renamed the lovers Giulietta and Romeus (later Romeo) in his *Historia novellamente ritrovata di due nobili amanti* (Newly Refound History of Two Noble Lovers), published about 1530. Da Porto relocated the tale to Verona and created the characters of the garrulous nurse, Mercutio, Tybalt, Friar Laurence, and Paris. He insisted that he had heard the story as a soldier in Friuli from one of his archers as they marched along a desolate road.

Da Porto ends his account with a dramatic twist: Romeo, discovering Juliet's seemingly lifeless body, drinks a vial of poison and wraps his arms around her—just as her sleeping potion wears off. In what would have made a hell of a theatrical finale, Juliet, realizing that it is too late to counter the poison he swallowed, beats her breast, tears her hair, throws herself upon Romeo, all but drowns him in tears, and imprints desperate kisses on his lips.

"Must I live a moment after you?" she cries. Romeo, already dead in Shakespeare's script, begs her to live, as does Friar Laurence. Then, in a made-for-the-spotlights moment, Juliet, "feeling the full weight of her irreparable loss in the death of her noble husband, resolute to die, draws in her breath and retaining it for some time, suddenly utters a loud shriek and falls dead by her lover's side."

The British writer Arthur Brooke translated the Italian tales into English verse in 1562; William Painter retold the story in prose in 1582. Shakespeare plucked his plot from these translations when he wrote his play in 1595–96. In all versions, the hatred that had torn the couple's families apart dissolves in the mingled blood of their dead children. But Shakespeare's final lines deserve to be the last word on the tearful tale: "For never was a story of more woe / Than this of Juliet and her Romeo."

The young Romeos who pursued my tall, blond, blue-eyed daughter, Julia, during a college summer in Italy seemed far more interested in living than dying for love. In Florence, the local boys proclaimed that she was their Beatrice and they her doting Dantes. Roses appeared before her at restaurant tables; smitten swains serenaded her with songs. *Ecco!* one young man called out on the street. "It is my heart, which has fallen for you!" After she and her friends hiked (in bikinis and Adidas) the breathtaking Via dell'Amore, the trail of love, in Cinque Terre, Julia dove into the azure bay and surfaced to find, as she describes him, the most beautiful guy she'd ever seen extending a hand from his boat and calling her *"la mia sirena"* ("my mermaid").

Could one expect anything less from the countrymen of Giovanni Giacomo Casanova (1725–1798), whose name has become synonymous with seduction? Curious about the infamous lothario's way with words, I discovered that this romancer's life was full of sex and almost devoid of love.

Casanova's mother, the actress Zanetta Farusi, had a reputation as a beauty who generously shared her charms with princes, noblemen, and wealthy merchants. While she toured Europe with the *Teatro italiano,* her son grew up in Venice in his grandmother's care. By his own account Casanova lost his virginity when he was sixteen to two teen-aged sisters whose aunt he had befriended.

Although his mother wanted him to enter the priesthood, Casanova was expelled from the seminary in Padua after being discovered in bed with a fetching companion. Still wearing the robes of an apprentice priest, he became the secretary of a Spanish cardinal in Rome—only to lose that job after engineering the scandalous abduction of a noble Roman young lady. He enlisted in the Venetian army and seduced women at every garrison. Back in Venice, he tried acting but could only get work playing the violin at theaters and balls.

On his way home one night, Casanova accepted a ride in

the gondola of an elderly gentleman, who within minutes suffered some sort of paralyzing attack. Casanova ran to the home of the nearest doctor, dragged him out of bed to treat his benefactor, and kept vigil at his bedside until he recovered. The wealthy nobleman, convinced that Casanova possessed supernatural powers, installed him in comfort in his palazzo and supported him with a generous allowance.

Casanova's career as a *conquistatore* moved into high gear. His appetite for women was omnivorous, and his effect on women, as the Italian writer and journalist Luigi Barzini described it, was stupefying: "He pleased women at first sight, women of all ages and conditions, and usually succeeded in rendering them helpless and defenseless in front of his pressing entreaties. His physical capacity to satisfy the most exacting mistress by renewing his homages to her a practically unlimited number of times through the night and the following day, with only short *entr'actes*, between the exertions, is not as surprising as the feat of psychological endurance; he admired one woman after another, and slipped into bed at a moment's notice with the fat, the lean, the young, the old, the dirty, the soignée, the lady, the chambermaid, the strumpet, the nun, always admirably animated, till very late in life, by the same schoolboyish eagerness." His estimated lifetime conquests numbered more than two hundred.

Casanova's gambling and whoring tested even Venice's tolerance, and he had to flee the city for France. When he returned a few years later, he was denounced as a Freemason, a spy, and a dabbler in black magic, serious crimes that landed him in the Venetian republic's most dreaded dungeon, I Piombi, the plural of "lead," perhaps for all the chains and bars in the belowground cells. After fifteen months of cunning plotting, he pulled off the impossible and escaped to Paris.

There he found a new patron, the Duchess of Urfe, noble, rich, and gullible, who invested a small fortune in Casanova's experiments in developing a potion to restore her to eternal youth. The clever con man also persuaded the French government to commission him to organize and run a state lottery, based on the Venetian model. This enterprise proved so lucrative that Casanova lived in splendor, with a luxurious house, servants, horses and carriages, and an estimated twenty mistresses whom he kept in twenty different apartments.

A witty conversationalist, Casanova hobnobbed with intellectuals (including Voltaire and the visiting Benjamin Franklin), polished his friend Lorenzo da Ponte's libretto for *Don Giovanni*, launched a silk manufacturing business, skipped around Europe (often in flight from debtors or prison), fought numerous duels, and started calling himself the Chevalier de Seingalt. He came up with the name by drawing cards with letters on them, one after another, at random. A high-stakes gambler, he once reportedly lost the equivalent of a million dollars (in today's numbers) in a single night.

Arrested and jailed repeatedly, Casanova returned to Venice as a broken man. Some biographers blame a teenage prostitute named Marianne de Charpillion, who squandered his money and smashed his spirit. In a feeble stab at revenge, he bought a parrot and taught it to say a single sentence, "Charpillion is a greater whore than her mother!" before reselling it in the market.

For a while Casanova worked as an informer for the Venetian secret police, but a pamphlet he wrote, a vicious satire of Venice's leading citizens, provoked such a scandal that he had to flee again. Wandering through Europe, he dabbled in poetry, theology, mathematics, and philosophy and wrote a history of Poland and a novel called *Icosamero*, one of the first books of science fiction. A charitable friend gave the penniless former philanderer a sinecure as the librarian in his dreary castle in Bohemia, where the servants taunted him with humiliating pranks, such as placing his portrait in the household privy.

In the end, all that Casanova had left were words. He began writing his memoirs in 1790, eight years before his death, and kept revising drafts. "I am writing *My Life* to laugh at myself, and I am succeeding," he said. A biographer described his unfinished autobiography as a virtual substitute for his lonely, unlivable life in exile.

"Aren't there any Italian love stories with happy endings?" I asked my friends after reading of Casanova's dismal denouement. Most puzzled over the question for some minutes before naming the most obvious—*the* great Italian novel. *I promessi sposi* (*The Betrothed*) by Alessandro Manzoni (1785–1873) is the book Italians most love to hate. "School ruins it for us," a friend explains. "We have to read and study it so much that we can't enjoy it."

I couldn't hide behind the same excuse, but I didn't relish tackling the Italian version of one of Victor Hugo's turgid romantic works (especially after my friend added that there's practically no sex). But the introduction to the novel piqued my interest in the author, known in the Milanese dialect as Don

Lizander. His mother, Giulia, was the headstrong daughter of an esteemed penal reformer, Cesare Bonesana, Marchese di Beccaria, whose *On Crimes and Punishment*, published in 1764, ignited a campaign against capital punishment throughout Europe.

At nineteen, Giulia—"a very beautiful, healthy, intelligent girl with a strong character," as Natalia Ginzburg describes her in *The Manzoni Family*—fell in love with a totally unsuitable suitor, the playboy Giovanni Verri, the feckless brother of one of her father's oldest friends. In addition to his reputation as a womanizer, the younger Verri was a Knight of the Cross of Malta and held a quasi-military, quasi-religious rank that forbade marriage at pain of loss of both prestige and income. The families hastily married Giulia off to Don Pietro Manzoni, a forty-six-year-old widower, count, and religious conservative. When Giulia gave birth to Alessandro three years later, gossips whispered about his paternity, but Don Manzoni fully acknowledged him as his son.

That was about the extent of the parental attention the boy received. First shuttled off to a milk nurse, Alessandro was later sent to a long string of boarding schools commencing at age five, each one—in his memory—more wretched than the last. Giulia, who never wrote or visited, moved to Paris to live with a wealthy merchant banker named Carlo Imbonati. Her son, bouncing from school to school, was almost written off as a dunce, until he discovered poetry as a teenager. Then his imagination and scholarship caught fire.

When Manzoni was twenty, his mother's paramour invited him to Paris but died suddenly before his arrival. As his heir, Giulia acquired enough money to assure her and her son's financial well-being. Mother and son formed a tight, affectionate bond and settled happily into a diverting life in the intellectual circles of Paris. Giulia even helped her son find a suitable bride—Enrichetta Blondel, the sixteen-year-old daughter of a Swiss businessman. A Protestant minister married the Calvinist bride and the fiercely anticlerical groom.

However, both began to rethink their religious views. When their first daughter was born, the Manzonis agonized over whether to baptize her as a Catholic or a Protestant. At her father's insistence, she received a Catholic christening. Over the next few years, both her parents converted wholeheartedly to Catholicism. In 1810, a priest remarried the devout Catholics, who eventually took up permanent residence in Milan. After twenty-five years of marriage, Enrichetta, mother of eight surviving children (of twelve births), died. In 1837 Manzoni married Teresa Borri, a count's widow.

Forsaking poetry, Manzoni became intrigued by a seventeenth-century agrarian edict designed to prevent marriages among the lower classes. What better subject for a romantic novel, he thought, than a tale of thwarted love among two poor but pure souls, played out against the background of turbulent political times and culminating with an outbreak of the plague?

This, in an elevator pitch, is the story of I promessi sposi, set in and near Milan in 1628. The lustful village squire, Don Rodrigo, bets his cousin that he will seduce the heroine (Lucia) and forbids the cowardly local priest, Don Abbondio, to marry her and the stalwart Renzo. When the young couple, protected by a good friar (Padre Cristoforo), seek refuge elsewhere, Rodrigo has

Lucia abducted by the powerful Innominato (Unnamed One) and the friar sent to a distant convent. After a religious crisis, Innominato finds God and frees Lucia. Then the plague breaks out, separating the lovers once more before they finally reunite, settle down, and live happily ever after.

Manzoni, who expressed himself best in Milanese and considered French, not Italian, his second language, asked his Italian friends' help with his first draft. After gathering their suggestions into an "untidy heap of paper," he rewrote it from scratch. *I promessi sposi*, published in three volumes between 1825 and 1827, received critical acclaim but didn't attract many readers—largely because its antiquated language bore little resemblance to the way Italians actually spoke.

"I envy the French," Manzoni reportedly lamented. They at least could use a language actually spoken and understood throughout their nation. But this deeply neurotic author, whose agoraphobia (although it wasn't identified as such) prevented him from going outdoors alone, didn't give up. Like so many great Italian writers before him, Manzoni went looking for a language to write a story of love and fell in love with the language of Florence. In mid-1827 he took up residence in Dante's hometown as he revised—page by page, paragraph by paragraph, word by word—his entire novel.

Manzoni's characters' names pop up regularly in contemporary conversations as shorthand for certain Italian types. For a while, I thought all of my friends had the same priest, the pliable Don Abbondio, as their pastor and that unscrupulous politicians happened to be named Rodrigo. No name may better suit a spewer of bureacratic gobbledygook than that of the corrupt lawyer, Azzeccagarbugli, a combination of the words for "guessing" and "confusion." But Manzoni's influence might have gone no deeper if not for an unsung literary heroine.

*"Sempre l'uomo avanti e la donna dietro"* ("Always the man in front and the woman behind"), Cristina, my Italian tutor in Florence, told me as I struggled through the classic. The woman behind Manzoni's masterpiece was not an editor or linguist but Emilia Luti, a Tuscan governess. At Florence's Società Dante Alighieri, Cristina and I turned the pages of a copy of the annotated manuscript of *I promessi sposi*, with Manzoni's questions scribbled in the margins.

"What word should I use for ladder—*scala* or *piolo?*" he asks in a typical query. Time and again, Luti provides the Tuscan preference. When *I promessi sposi* was republished, again in three volumes, from 1840 to 1842, Manzoni presented Luti with a copy, adding a note of thanks for rewashing his "rags"—variously translated as *cenci* or *panni*—in the Arno.

These "rags" provided an entire new wardrobe for Italian. Although its basic plot involves a conventional love story, *I promessi sposi*—in the tradition begun with Dante's *Divina Commedia*—is much more: a passionate, tender, richly textured ode to Italian and, as some saw it, a propaganda vehicle for an Italy that was *"una d'arme, di lingua, d'altare, di memorie, di sangue e di cor"* ("one in arms, language, worship, memories, blood, and heart"). Revered by his contemporaries, Manzoni became a hero of the new nation. He was honored as such at his death in 1873, with a state funeral attended by the royal princes and government chiefs and, a year later, with an even greater tribute, a stirring requiem from a fellow maestro, the composer Giuseppe Verdi.

Verdi himself scandalized his small town of Busseto when he lived openly with his mistress, the soprano Giuseppina Strepponi, for years before they quietly married. Italian, I discovered when I went looking for a term to describe her, has no word comparable to "mistress." While the lady of a house is a *padrona*, the unmarried sexual partner of a man is called only an *amante*, or lover. A friend who had once told me about his father's "other woman" recalls that his family referred to her as *una di quelle* (one of them). "They" were the women who dressed in flashier clothes, sported bigger jewels, ate out alone in elegant restaurants, and always seemed to laugh more loudly than mothers, aunts, sisters, teachers, and other "ladies."

For centuries, Italy, like other Catholic countries, was filled with "them"—some famous as actresses or singers but all gossiped about and scrutinized. In an essay titled "The Italian Mistress," the journalist Luigi Barzini focused on the crucial question about these women: At what moment did a lady—well spoken, well dressed, and well mannered—cease being a lady and become "one of them"?

A lady could have any number of lovers, one after another or all at the same time, he contended, without jeopardizing her social rank, but she would lose this status automatically the moment she accepted a too-precious gift. Anything that could readily be converted into a considerable amount of cash—a villa, jewelry, a thoroughbred horse, a valuable painting—could definitely cost a lady her reputation. So what could she receive with honor? The only acceptable gift, according to common consensus, was a book.

Yet for many years, mistresses were not merely tolerated

but accepted as one of the "arrangements" of Italian marriages. Barzini recounts the story of a Milanese manufacturer whose mistress was almost young enough to be his granddaughter. His wife exploded in outrage on a gala evening at La Scala when she saw her rival, bedecked in ermine and diamonds, in a box. The husband, defending himself, argued that every man in a certain position had a mistress and pointed out his partner's, seated a few boxes beyond his own. The wife peered through her opera glasses, then turned to her husband, and said, "What a choice! Vulgar, dressed in bad taste, loaded with cheap jewelry, and not pretty at all." And she added with pride, "Ours is so much better."

Margherita of the House of Savoy (1851–1926) didn't always share this view. Even before their marriage, the crown prince Umberto, who would rule as Italy's second king, had become enamored with a woman he spotted at a Carnevale ball. She turned out to be Duchess Eugenia Litta, then twenty-five and married to a rich Milanese nobleman. Their affair, which produced a cherished son who died in childhood, continued after his politically crucial marriage to his cousin Margherita. When she came upon La Litta in her husband's bedroom, Margherita flounced off to old King Vittorio Emanuele and threatened to return to her family's home.

"You would leave over such a little thing?" he famously replied. In 1878 Umberto ascended to the throne, Margherita at his side. His relationship with La Litta lasted for thirty-eight years, until an Italian anarchist from Paterson, New Jersey, assassinated the king in Monza on July 29, 1900. Despite her lifelong resentment, Margherita dispatched a courier to invite La

Litta to bid her king and lover a private last farewell. Newspapers of the day praised this concession as a "noble gesture" worthy of a queen—and a touching example of *bella figura*.

Romantic gestures have never gone out of style. In Rome suitors who can't carry a tune hire professional singers to serenade their sweethearts. Accompanied by accordion players, these crooners, dressed in white dinner jackets and cummerbunds, belt out traditional love songs over the roar of street traffic. The love-smitten swains stand at their side, gazing up at the girls who listen from windows and balconies.

A few years ago *Ho voglia di te* (*I Want You*) a bestselling novel that was made into a popular movie, inspired another form of romantic expression. The young hero convinced a potential girlfriend to reenact a fictitious legend: wrapping a *lucchetto* (padlock) with a chain around a lamppost on the Ponte Milvio, a bridge just north of Rome's center, and throwing the key into the Tiber as a gesture of undying love.

So many couples began fastening locks and chains that the posts began to buckle under their weight. In 2007 city officials removed the *lucchetti* and set up designated steel pillars where lovers can now lock in their commitment without damaging the bridge itself. "Lucchettomania" has spread to Florence's famous Ponte Vecchio and dozens of other bridges throughout Italy. If you can't get to an Italian bridge, you can create your own *lucchetto digitale* and read messages (such as "*Ti amissimo*" or "*Ti amooooooo!*") of other couples online at www.lucchettipontemilvio.com.

I began to appreciate the significance of such romantic gestures on my first trip to Italy—through a language lesson of sorts. On my last night in Venice, a full moon, as white as Carrara marble, glided above Santa Maria della Salute. A chilly north wind had blown the tourists back to their hotels. Shrouded gondolas rocked in the lagoon. A gentleman with a white goatee and a jaunty beret stopped where I stood on the quay.

"*Che bella luna!*" I pointed at the moon, proudly unfurling some of the words I'd acquired in my travels.

"*Come Lei—anche Lei è bella!*" ("Like you—also lovely. I pretended not to understand the compliment.")

"*Mi dispiace. Non parlo italiano.*"

"*Signorina, vorrebbe un bicchiere di vino?*" ("Would you like a glass of wine?") he asked, turning to face me.

"*Mi dispiace, signore. Mi dispiace.*"

"Stop telling what is not pleasing to you," he said in a swift change to curt and lightly accented English.

"But I . . ."

"I know, I know. You don't mean to be rude. But I see a beautiful young woman, and I think, 'She should not be waiting alone for the moon to shine on her. She should be telling the moon to make her wishes come true.' Tell me, do you know how to ask for what you want in Italian?"

"*Voglio.*"

"*Beh!* I want! I want! That is for babies. No, you must speak like a lady, like a princess. You must say, 'It would be pleasing to me.' *Mi piacerebbe.*"

"*Mi piacerebbe,*" I replied, rolling the *r* as he had.

"*Sì! Sì! Ma che cosa Le piacerebbe?* What is it you would like, *bella donna della luna*—lovely lady of the moon?"

"I don't know. *Non lo so.*"

"Then you must find out. *La vita vola*: life flies. If you do not know what you want, you will never know where to look to find it."

"I would like—*mi piacerebbe*—to speak Italian, *parlare l'italiano*."

"*Beh.* That's a start."

"And you—*e Lei*? What is your wish?"

"*Io? Sono invecchiato, ma ancora una volta mi piacerebbe baciare una bella donna alla luce della luna.*"

"I don't understand."

He moved very close. "I've become old, but I would like one more time to kiss a beautiful woman in the moonlight."

For several seconds I watched a river of silver moonlight shimmer on the canal. Then I did what it suddenly pleased me to do: I lifted my mouth to make his wish come true.

# Marcello and Me

HE STROLLS WITH HIS HANDS IN HIS POCKETS, A long red scarf tossed loosely around his neck. His hair has turned white, but the familiar hint of a bemused smile plays at the corners of his mouth. The billboard-size image of Marcello Mastroianni, the biggest star in Italian film history, pulls me across Rome's Borghese Gardens to the Casa del Cinema, the chic hub for Italian films and filmmakers. "This is Marcello's place," its publicist tells me, using the phrase *"da Marcello,"* as if it were his personal residence. "We want everyone who loves movies to feel at home here." I certainly do.

The first classic I watch in its elegant auditorium is a 1954 romantic comedy called *Pane, amore e gelosia* (Bread, Love, and Jealousy). *"Capisce?"* ("Do you understand?"), a dapper gent of at least eighty next to me asks as the film begins. I can follow the basic froth of a story about a sexy and spirited girl (Gina Lollobrigida in first bloom), a handsome aging lothario (Vittorio De Sica, the iconic actor and director), and—here's where I start losing the drift—a donkey. Without prompting, the man proceeds to repeat every line—in Italian, only slower and louder than the actors.

Although I didn't realize it at the time, this was once a typical Italian moviegoing experience. When *cinema muto*—silent films—first appeared in the early twentieth century, most Italians spoke in dialect; many were illiterate. *Italiano standard* remained the language of the privileged, the politicians, and the priests.

"After the lights went down, people would call out, 'Who can read Italian?' and someone would shout out the titles," recounts Professor Sergio Raffaelli (also dapper) of the University of Rome, a scholar of language in Italian cinema. "When talking pictures came out in 1930, theaters became schoolhouses. Millions of Italians learned how to speak the national language at the movies."

That's not all they learned. Cinema, with its lifelike immediacy and visceral impact, did for modern Italians what Dante had for his countrymen in the fourteenth century: It created a new way of hearing, speaking, seeing, thinking, and imagining life in this world and beyond. Movies—no less than Italy's great works of literature, art, manners, music, and cuisine—taught Italians how to be Italian.

"In effect, the *Divine Comedy* was a film people played in their imagination centuries before cinema was invented," says

Gianfranco Angelucci, a screenwriter, director, and professor (and the coolest guy I know in Rome), who arrives for lunch at the Casa del Cinema café with a motorcycle helmet in hand and a lissome beauty with curly Botticelli tresses in tow.

His companion remains *muta* until I stumble through a question that requires some tricky Italian tenses. Then she breaks into a Mona Lisa smile that Leonardo, if alive today, would have zoomed in on rather than painted. "Leonardo invented the close-up," says Angelucci. "The vocabulary of all the great Renaissance artists became the visual vocabulary of Italian films."

Like their Renaissance counterparts, Italian filmmakers pioneered a new art form. In the 1890s, the father of Italian cinema, Filoteo Alberini, patented the *cinetografo*—a machine that recorded, developed, and projected films—then opened an ornate movie house (described as a temple of the new art) and a production studio in Rome. A few years later he invented the forerunner of all panoramic projectors.

The golden age of Italian cinema came early: 1909 to 1916, a period when Italian movies, mainly produced in Turin and Rome, captured and dominated the world market. Audiences flocked to see sprawling spectacles, filmed outdoors with huge casts, colossal battle scenes, and ever-more-astonishing special effects. Never again would Italian movies dominate the film industry. Since the end of World War I, the percentage of Italian films distributed within Italy has never risen above one-third of the total.

Early Italian movies both preceded and inspired Hollywood extravaganzas. *Cabiria*, a "sword and sandal" epic released in 1914, greatly influenced the American movie pioneer D. W. Griffith and created the model for spectacular scenes and larger-than-life movie heroes. Shot on location in the Alps, Sicily, and Tunisia, the multimillion-lira film amazed audiences with hand-tinted footage of Mount Etna erupting, the burning of the Roman fleet, and the march of Hannibal and his elephants.

Based very loosely on *Cartagine in fiamme* (Carthage in Flames) by the Italian adventure writer Emilio Salgari and *Salammbô*, a historical novel by Gustave Flaubert, *Cabiria*'s labyrinthine plot—with hyperbolic titles by Italy's most infamous and flamboyant writer, Gabriele D'Annunzio—recounts a tangled blood-and-thunder tale set against the conflict between Rome and Carthage in the third century B.C. During these tumultuous times dastardly pirates kidnap Cabiria, a beautiful Roman maiden, and sell her as a slave to Carthage. Just as the pagan high priest is about to burn her alive in an evil sacrifice, a Roman nobleman and his muscular slave Maciste (think Arnold Schwarzenegger in *Conan the Barbarian*) arrive to save the beauty and the day.

The original Maciste, a barrel-chested stevedore named Bartolomeo Pagano (1878–1947), was working on the docks in Genoa when the moviemakers recruited him to play the fearless giant. The overnight celebrity, who even changed his name to Maciste, starred in some fifteen sequels from 1915 to 1926 before others took over the role.

Mighty Maciste vanquished all comers—vampires, head-hunters, sheiks, cyclops, Zorro, Genghis Khan, and the Mongols. The plots typically featured a dastardly tyrant menacing the life and lovely limbs of a virtuous young woman. Belly dancers often made an appearance. And just in the nick of time, in what would become Hollywood tradition, Maciste employed his superhuman strength to protect the weak, rescue the imperiled, and vanquish the wicked.

If this sounds oddly familiar, it is. "Maciste," according to D'Annunzio, derived from an ancient nickname for Hercules. Others have traced the name back to a combination of Greek and Latin words for "greatest" and "rock." In my mind, this translates into "Rocky" and makes Maciste the great-great-grandfather of the Italian stallion Rocky Balboa—along with every other cinema action hero since.

In Rome I bought a DVD of *Maciste, gladiatore di Sparta* (Maciste, Spartan Gladiator), which may well be the cheesiest movie I've ever seen. But it reminded me of the equally overacted and underplotted films my dad used to take me to on Saturday afternoons. Hercules, Samson, and Sinbad all were Maciste clones, and his cinematic influence lives on in Superman, Hulk Hogan, Rambo, the Terminator, Iron Man, Batman, and the films of Jean-Claude Van Damme.

To Italians, Maciste was more than a celluloid demigod. In the early 1920s he gave them what they hungered for: a hero who could save them from danger and lead them to glory. Mussolini, the swaggering strongman who came to power in 1922 as the head of the black-shirted Fascists, promised to do the same.

Il Duce (the leader) was a film buff who called cinema "Italy's greatest weapon" and started a national film school. The Fascist minister for press and propaganda (Mussolini's son-in-law) encouraged university students to organize film clubs. The glittering Venice Film Festival debuted in 1934 as a showcase for the Italian film industry. In 1937, on April 21, the mythical anniversary of the founding of Rome, Mussolini inaugurated Cinecittà (Cinema City), Rome's equivalent of Hollywood's expansive studio back lots.

For all their enthusiasm for movies, the Fascists themselves produced not a single cinematic triumph. The regime's greatest impact on movies and moviegoers was linguistic. As part of an utterly misguided campaign to purify Italian, Mussolini banned dialects, foreign words, blasphemies, and curses. The makers of silent movies dodged the directives of the language police by emphasizing visual impact over dialogue so viewers could intuit what was going on. Subtitles became increasingly telegraphic, and Italian actresses—film's first *dive* (goddesses)—melodramatically batted their heavy-lidded eyes and sighed, sobbed, swooned, or lifted the back of their hands to their fevered brows. One dared bare her breasts.

*The Jazz Singer*, which opened in Rome in 1929, brought sound to Italian movie theaters. But with the birth of the talkie—*film parlato*—in 1930, the age-old "question of the language" resurfaced. Which tongue should actors use for *recitare* (acting)? *Italiano standard*, precise, pure, and eloquently enunciated, was the government's answer. Diction schools, originally set up to train radio announcers, churned out professional *doppiatori* (dubbers) for both foreign and homegrown films.

In Italian theaters international film stars such as Greta Garbo, Laurel and Hardy, Gary Cooper, and Mickey Mouse talked with "a Tuscan tongue in a Roman mouth"—classic Florentine pronounced with Rome's more melodious accent. Even *Pellerossa* (American Indians—literally "redskins") spoke refined

Italian in deep, low voices. Movie titles also were translated into Italian: *High Noon* became *Mezzogiorno di fuoco* (Midday of Fire) and *Gone with the Wind, Via col vento* (Away with the Wind). In Italy, as everywhere else, Scarlett's (Rossella in Italian) motto, "*Domani è un altro giorno,*" became a catchphrase of the day.

Since Italians still prefer hearing Italian to reading subtitles in foreign films, dubbing has remained a big business—with big stars of its own. When Luke Skywalker battled Darth Vader in the classic *Star Wars* films of the late 1970s, the voice Italians heard was not Mark Hamill's but that of Claudio Capone (1952–2008), then a young, aspiring *doppiatore.* Over the next three decades, Capone supplied the voice for Hollywood actors such as John Travolta, Michael Douglas, John Malkovich, Alan Alda, Bill Murray, and Martin Sheen. On Italian television he dubbed Don Johnson in *Miami Vice* and Ron Moss, who plays heartthrob Ridge Forrester on *The Bold and the Beautiful,* the soap opera called "Beautiful" in Italy. When Moss himself visited Italy several years ago, his fans were crushed that he didn't know the language they heard him "speak" almost every day.

Early scriptwriters (*sceneggiatori*) for Italian films had to struggle to find a level of Italian that most people could understand. "They found the solution in the *fotoromanzi* or picture magazines that covered the new stars of cinema," says Angelucci, who teaches film at the University of Carrara. The writing, geared for the widest possible audience, aimed neither too high nor too low. But government censors restricted what moviegoers could hear in a theater. No actors ever swore, lapsed into dialect, substituted an r for a d (as Neapolitans do), or pronounced a *c* like an *h* (as Tuscans do). And Italian movie directors, then and now, never cried, "Action!" but the ono-matopoeic *"Ciak!"*

The seven hundred movies produced under Fascism included several *filoni*, or genres. Heavy-handed propaganda films exalted Italy's valiant fighting forces. Grand-scale sword-and-sandal epics, called "peplum" films, from the Latin for a Roman robe of state, recreated the glorious conquests of ancient legions. Their writers and directors were derisively called "calligraphers" because they copied themes from history or literature rather than dealing with contemporary issues. Some critics went even further and described the movies as "cadavers."

The people's favorites were bubbly fantasies known as *tele-foni bianchi* (white telephone) films that presented a glamorous fantasy world so rich and rarified that even telephones made a style statement. The smoothest, suavest matinee idol of all was Vittorio De Sica (1902–1974). Born in Naples, the handsome youth worked as an office clerk to support his family, but joined a stage company in his teens and quickly won audiences' hearts. His acting career turned out to be a mere prelude to his later accomplishments as a screenwriter and director.

By the time the grandiose promises of Fascism imploded in 1943, Italians had lost all faith in words, and filmmakers had lost funding, equipment, and studios. But after decades of sup-pression, Italy found its voice. A generation of movie talents burst onto the world stage with such explosive power that they created what Peter Bondanella, author of *Italian Cinema: From Neorealism to the Present*, the first English-language history of Italian film, describes as "the greatest art form of twentieth-century Italy."

I knew nothing about these movies until I started studying Italian. "There are two shortcuts to speaking the language," one of my early teachers told me. "You can take an Italian lover, or you can watch Italian movies." I wisely chose the latter, although the stark black-and-white "neorealistic" films that I viewed week after week turned out to be almost as wrenching as an emotional entanglement.

These movies, produced from 1945 to 1952, were revolutionary, with no heroes, no happy endings, no Hollywood stardust, and often no professional actors. Directors and scriptwriters, *ammucchiati* (heaped together), as they put it, collaborated like artisans in a Renaissance *bottega* (workshop). With unflinching, often excruciating honesty, they recounted the stories Italians were telling one another about their bitter struggles for survival through dictatorship, occupation, war, and devastation.

"If you have any doubt about the power of movies to interact with life and restore the soul, study neorealistic films," the director Martin Scorsese urges in his film tribute to Italian cinema, *My Voyage to Italy*. "They forced the rest of the world to look at Italians and see their humanity. To me, this was the most precious moment in movie history."

Neorealism was "reality transported into the realm of poetry," said De Sica, who won international acclaim for directing raw and powerful dramas. Many consider the movement's true father to be his writing partner Cesare Zavattini (1902–1989), known as Za, a prolific screenwriter who contributed to more than one hundred movies in his long career. So closely did he and De Sica work together that, Za observed, the collaboration resembled a *caffelatte*—a seamless blend.

After studying law and working as a journalist and editor, Za began writing for film and, clandestinely, for the comic strips, including *Topolino* (Mickey Mouse) and *Zorro*, in the 1930s. Finally freed from Fascist cinematic shackles in 1943, Za articulated the fundamental theory behind neorealism: "There must be no gap between life and what is on the screen."

The first neorealistic classic, Roberto Rossellini's *Roma, città aperta* (Rome, Open City), released in 1945, broke down the distinctions between life and art, feature film and documentary. Rossellini (1906–1977) had grown up watching movies every day in Rome's first film theater, which his father built and owned. Rossellini worked as a sound maker and on other technical aspects of filmmaking before directing.

The movie's writers, including the young Federico Fellini (who called Rossellini "the great father, like Adam, who created us all"), drew on their own chilling experiences and actual events, such as the execution of a partisan priest and the savage machine-gunning of a pregnant woman chasing soldiers who had arrested her husband. Its plot focuses on a few dramatic episodes in the lives of several ordinary people: The priest Don Pietro joins with a partisan leader named Manfredi to fight the Nazis. Manfredi's former mistress Marina eventually betrays him to the evil Gestapo officer Major Bergmann. Francesco, a friend of Manfredi's, is engaged to a working-class woman named Nina, who is killed when she runs after the officers taking him away.

In a film seminar at ItaLingua Institute in San Francisco, my daughter, Julia, and I, watching the scene of Nina's brutal, senseless death, held hands and bit our lips to keep from crying. It didn't work, particularly when we heard Don Pietro's words before he faced a firing squad: "It's not hard to die well. It's hard to live well." With *Roma, città aperta*, an American critic observed, Italy regained the nobility it had lost under Mussolini.

Zavattini and De Sica collaborated on twenty-five movies, including several classics of neorealism. With no money to hire professional actors, they plucked men, women, and children from the thousands of destitute refugees camped in makeshift shacks at Cinecittà after the war. De Sica described this practice as "an advantage, not a handicap. The man in the street, particularly if he is directed by someone who is himself an actor, is raw material that can be molded at will."

As screenwriter (with Za) and director of *Ladri di biciclette* (*The Bicycle Thief*) in 1948, De Sica molded the performances of the two nonprofessionals who played the parts of the unemployed father, Antonio Ricci, and his son Bruno, into true cinematic poetry. The Hollywood producer David Selznick had offered to finance the film if De Sica cast Cary Grant in the leading role. De Sica declined. He deliberately made his selections, he explained, because of the expressiveness of the faces of the two unknowns and particular mannerisms in the way they walked.

In the film, Ricci, unemployed for years, finally gets a job posting billboards, but he must use a bicycle to get around Rome. On his first day, a thief steals his bike, and Ricci and Bruno search frantically for it. After consulting a fortune-teller,

Ricci finds the thief but does not succeed in reclaiming his bike. In desperation, Ricci attempts to steal a bicycle from the street but is immediately spotted, chased down, and humiliated by an angry mob in front of his terrified son. The movie ends with the son taking his father's hand as they blend into a crowd.

*Ladri di biciclette*, like De Sica and Za's previous neorealistic masterpiece *Sciuscià* (Shoe-Shine), won a special Academy Award, and the two movies provided the impetus for the creation of an Oscar for Best Foreign Language Film. Critics and film historians, who laud the film as one of the greatest ever made, have mulled over the meaning and profundity of it for decades. Italian critics find parallels to Dante's *Divine Comedy*, since the action takes place between a Friday and Sunday and Ricci travels into an unexpected hell. The brand name of his bicycle, Fides (Latin for Faith), is deliberately ironic, yet the father does find redemption of a sort in his son's love.

I had never been able to view a copy of De Sica and Za's *Umberto D.*, released in 1952, in the United States, even though it too is considered one of the masterpieces of Italian cinema. So I spent a rainy afternoon in Rome watching a DVD on a small screen in a cubicle of the film library at Casa del Cinema. I had read that *Umberto D.* was De Sica's favorite film, dedicated to his father, Umberto, and starring another unknown, Carlo Battisti, a dignified linguistics professor from Florence whom he'd spotted on the street.

In the black-and-white film, a retired government clerk, living in a bleak rented room with his dog, Flik, struggles to survive on his meager pension. The proud, acerbic pensioner panhandles, pleads for more time to pay the rent, searches frantically for his lost beloved pet, and finally, driven to despair, stands on the tracks before an oncoming train. At the last moment, Flik, rescued from the city pound, jumps out of his arms, and Umberto chases after him. The movie ends with an understated but heartbreaking scene of the old man coaxing a wary Flik to play with him.

Church and state officials decried the film's relentlessly grim pessimism, and distribution was limited. Like most of the ninety or so neorealistic films, *Umberto D.*—the last of the genre—did poorly at the Italian box office. "These movies were more popular abroad than at home," says Bondanella, who notes that the most successful, *Roma, città aperta*, caught on first in France and then in the United States before attracting huge Italian audiences.

The neorealistic movies did more than help Italy come to terms with a terrible time in its history; they gave dialects back to Italians. Rossellini's 1946 film, *Paisà*, followed the Allies' advance up the Italian peninusla from Sicily in six episodes, each reflecting a different local dialect. Luchino Visconti's stark *La terra trema* (The Earth Trembles), shot in 1948 with actual Sicilian fishermen speaking and singing in their dialect, was unintelligible on the Italian mainland and had to be given an Italian voice-over.

Some film critics protested what they called "dialect aggression," but the use of regional idioms became a highly effective cinematic flourish. In 1964 the iconoclastic writer and moviemaker Pier Paolo Pasolini fleshed out the characters in *Il Vangelo secondo Matteo* (The Gospel According to Matthew, since the atheist Pasolini was uncomfortable with calling Matthew a saint) by means of accents and dialects. The dialogue is primarily taken directly from the gospel because Pasolini felt that "images could never reach the poetic heights of the text." The disciples speak with a southern Italian accent, the high priest Caiphas talks like a Tuscan, and Salome, the seductress who served up John the Baptist's head on a platter, chirps like a little servant girl from the Veneto. Jesus Christ sounds like the ultimate *doppiatore*, with a polished, nonidentifiable theatrical accent that, as one critic put it, "for Italians, is rather out of this world."

Pasolini soon found that he no longer needed to mix in dialects to make his movies sound real, because something new had happened. *"L'italiano è finalmente nato!"* ("Italian is finally born!") he declared, describing it as the flat speech of postwar technocrats and bureaucrats—thin, bloodless, well suited to what he saw as a squalid capitalist society. "I do not like it," Pasolini declared, although others cheered that for the first time in its history, Italy had a national spoken language, not just a literary idiom used by a minority of its citizens.

Federico Fellini (1920–1993) influenced the vocabulary of both film and Italy. The most famous of Italian directors communicated to the world in a highly personal visual language, but also coined new words in the process. Born in the seaside town of Rimini, this son of a traveling salesman ran away to join the circus at age ten. (His job was caring for a sick zebra.) During World War II, he traveled throughout Italy writing sketches for a touring theater troupe.

After the war Fellini set up a store called the Funny-Face Shop, where he sketched caricatures for American GIs. He also penned gags for comedians, illustrated comic books, and drafted radio plays. Working with Rossellini, he contributed to the scripts for *Roma, città aperta* and *Paisà*. These experiences, Fellini said, taught him that making movies was "the medium of expression most congenial . . . to my laziness, my ignorance, my curiosity about life, my inquisitiveness, my desire to see everything and to be independent, my lack of discipline, and my capacity for real sacrifice."

Fellini, a gifted artist who sketched many of his ideas for scripts, invented words that remain in use today. *I Vitelloni*, the title of one of his first films, literally means "big overgrown calves" but became a derogatory description of layabouts or aimless young men. *Paparazzi*, the plural of the name with which he baptized an aggressive photographer in *La dolce vita* (The Sweet Life), is the universal word for celebrity-chasing photo hounds.

The title of the first Fellini movie I ever saw, *Amarcord*, a semibiographical coming-of-age tale of a year in the life of Rimini, Fellini's hometown, comes from the local dialect word for "I remember." To its natives, *amarcord* conveys a touch of poignancy, as well as the sound of a magical incantation like "abracadabra." One of the women Fellini remembers most fondly is La Gradisca, the town's scandalous beauty, the first to get a permanent wave and wear false eyelashes. She acquired her nickname for the night she spent in the company of a visiting prince of royal blood. Stripping naked before him, she courteously offered her body with the word *"Gradisca!"* ("May it please you!"). I think of her whenever an Italian inquires, *"Gradisce qualcosa?,"* a polite way of asking if I'd like something to eat or drink.

Fellini described himself as *"un bugiardo,"* a liar—but an honest one. Fellini won eight Oscar nominations for screen-writing in addition to a raft of awards for directing. "The script is like the suitcase you carry with you," he once commented, "but you buy a lot of things along the way."

According to his collaborator Angelucci, who contributed to the screenplays for *Amarcord*, *L'Intervista* (The Interview), and *E la nave va* (And the Ship Sails On), an homage to an opera singer and to opera that is my favorite of his films, Fellini "al-ways had great respect for words, but faces were the critical part of the language of his films."

To construct a movie's "human landscape," Fellini consid-ered five to six thousand faces. "They would suggest to me the behavior of my characters, their personalities, and even some narrative sections of the film," he once said, explaining that he wanted "faces which immediately say everything by themselves as soon as they appear on the screen."

For his breakthrough movie of Rome during the 1950s, Fellini searched for the face of an everyman to play Marcello Rubini, a jaded, perpetually horny (*arrapato*, in Roman dialect) gossip reporter chasing scoops—and skirts—on the sultry Via Veneto. The producer, eager for a surefire success, wanted Paul Newman, but Fellini chose a rising but not well known star named Marcello Mastroianni (1924–1996).

"The first thing Fellini said to me was 'I need a face with no personality—like yours,'" Mastroianni later recalled. "That humiliated me, but I asked to see the script anyway." What he got was a batch of blank sheets, except for one, "a drawing of a man in the sea with a prick that reached all the way down to the sea floor. All around his prick, like in an Esther Williams film, were sirens swimming and smiling. I turned red and green and a lot of other colors in my embarrassment. . . . Then I said, 'Okay, it's interesting. I'll do it.' "

The movie—with a working title of "Although Life Is Brutal and Terrible, You Can Always Find a Few Wonderful Moments of Sensuality and Sweetness"—evolved into *La dolce vita*, a vivid panorama of the not-always-sweet life of postwar Rome. Fellini researched it by hanging out with the paparazzi, "getting them to tell me the tricks of their trade . . . waiting in ambush for hours, thrilling escapes, dramatic chases." One evening when he took a group out to dinner, they plied him with ever wilder tales until one of the veterans said, "Stop inventing, you idiots, you're talking to an old hand at the game." Fellini's comment: "I didn't know whether to take it as a compliment or an insult."

The movie was primarily shot in English, with only Mastroianni speaking his lines in Italian. "The words were the least of it," the actor said. "What was important was the language of the film itself." Some critics compared this 165-minute movie, with 104 separate scenes, to Dante's *Inferno*. Like the fourteenth-century pilgrim, the errant journalist wanders through a corrupt world teeming with memorable characters—120 named in the script—to emerge into the light of day. But Fellini's voyager finds neither radiant stars nor any hope of salvation.

Fellini's most controversial and financially successful film, *La dolce vita* enchanted the world with its unforgettable scenes, such as Anita Ekberg's nocturnal dip in the Trevi Fountain, its signature music, and its luscious leading man. The American press crowned Mastroianni the ultimate "Latin lover," and the poor boy from an industrial town south of Rome spent the rest of his career defying this characterization on screen while living up to it off screen. Married for more than four decades to Flora Carabella, mother of his Italian daughter (as he put it), he lived for years with Catherine Deneuve, mother of his French daughter, and carried on often tempestuous affairs with Faye Dunaway and other leading ladies.

Mastroianni insisted that he'd always hated his looks. As a scrawny kid in hand-me-downs so short that his arms hung out from the sleeves, he was teased as "Skinny Paws." Idolizing American actors such as Gary Cooper and Clark Gable, the starstruck fourteen-year-old earned ten *lire* as an extra in a grape-harvesting scene in a film shot at Cinecittà—a fortune to him at the time—plus all the grapes he could eat. Mastroianni badgered a friend of his mother's to introduce him to her brother, the great Vittorio De Sica.

"Study, study, study!" De Sica insisted. "Get your degree, and then we'll see." Years later, after decades of working together, often with Sophia Loren as "the third leg of the triangle," Mastroianni still couldn't bring himself to use the informal *tu* form of "you" with the cinematic titan he considered his professional *zio*, or uncle.

After World War II, Mastroianni got his first big break as a member of Visconti's theatrical company, but he yearned for a movie career. "I couldn't understand what Shakespeare had to do with Gary Cooper," he said. Quite a bit, it turned out.

Nature had endowed the fledgling actor with the bedroom eyes, sensuous lips, dimpled chin, and rueful smile that came to be known as "the Mastroianni look," but his intensive theatrical training produced the Mastroianni sound. When he started acting, he was "a gawky lad who couldn't even say a line," Visconti recalls. In his stage roles, Mastroianni mastered a neutral *italiano standard* with just the faintest resonance of Rome. His voice— initially nasal and reedy—also acquired the timbre, projection, and cadences that gave it the lush quality film critics would describe as "mellifluous."

Bit part by bit part, B movie by B movie, Mastroianni broke into the business. In 1960 *La dolce vita* rocketed him to the heights as the international symbol of Italian film, style, and sexiness. But afterward, he complained, directors mainly wanted him "to slither across the floor after women" in Latin-lover roles. Hollywood, whose offers he resisted for decades, suggested teaming him with Frank Sinatra in a tale of two Latin lovers. Instead, Mastroianni played against type—first as an impotent cuckold in Sicily, then as con man, drunk, lawyer, addict, patriarch, assassin, homosexual, rapist, magician, novelist, police commissioner, director, beekeeper, priest, union organizer, dancer, professor, Russian aristocrat, General Custer (in a French-Italian movie called *Non toccare la donna bianca*, or Don't Touch the White Woman), Henry IV, and film's first pregnant man.

In all, Mastroianni made a staggering 140 motion pictures, starring in about 90 percent of them. "No other actor in Europe or in the United States has worked and talked about his work as much as Marcello Mastroianni," observes biographer Donald Dewey. "He has raged as much as murmured, sung and danced as deftly as [he] crooned sweet nothings, carried off acting awards and won three best actor Oscar nominations."

Mastroianni scoffed at the earnest preparations of American actors and called moviemaking a game. "Acting is a pleasure, like making love," he quipped to a reporter. "Correction: lovemaking can be an ordeal." No one ever saw him studying a script, yet he always knew his lines.

"I read a script the whole thing through maybe twice or three times, then I put it aside," he explained. "This character, this person that I am to become, starts to grow inside me, little by little. He begins to talk to me, and I listen like a *primitif naïf*. If I don't listen, he will die in me. So I'm eating a plate of spaghetti, and I hear him. Then I stop somewhere, say at a traffic light, and there he is in the car next to me. My job is the character, not the lines per se. They always seem to come to me when we get down to shooting."

How Mastroianni, who dubbed his own voice after the filming of his movies, said a line—even a single word—mattered as much as what he said. Take one of his most famous scenes, from the wildly popular *Yesterday, Today, and Tomorrow*, costarring Sophia Loren, directed by the indefatigable De Sica, and written by the neorealist pioneer Zavattini.

Sophia, as a worldly prostitute, lives next door to a seminarian who becomes so infatuated with her that he decides to stop his religious studies. His grandmother accuses Sophia of corrupting him, and she promises God at least temporary chastity if the young man returns to the seminary—as he does. When Marcello, one of her clients, shows up, she performs a titillating striptease that he responds to by howling like a wild beast. Then she remembers her vow and stops abruptly. Marcello squeaks *"Cosa?"* ("What?") with such horrified incredulity that critics raved about his exquisitely droll—and exquisitely delivered—reaction.

Too young to appreciate or even be aware of Mastroianni in his prime, I had no idea that his was one of the most remarkable careers in film history. I've been making up for lost time by watching as many of his movies as I can rent, buy, or borrow. My friend Roberto in Rome offered yet another incentive: "No one speaks Italian more beautifully. Listen to Marcello, and you'll sound more Italian."

And so in the most minor of his many roles, Marcello has become my tutor. While I enjoy the company of his celluloid characters, I prefer Marcello in his own words. In a delightful cinematic autobiography, *Mi ricordo, sì, io mi ricordo* (I Remember, Yes, I Remember), filmed shortly before his death in 1996, by the woman who was his companion for the last decades of his life, Marcello talks of his childhood, his friends, his travels, his movies, his likes and dislikes.

"I believe in nature, in loves, in emotions, in friendships, in this marvelous landscape, in my work, in my companions," he reflects. "I like people. I love life and perhaps for this I have been loved in return [he charmingly says *riamato*, literally "reloved"] by life."

On some nights when Bob isn't home, I pop this DVD into my laptop and take Marcello to bed with me. Every time I listen to his velvety voice, I realize that even this homey experience captures some of the essence of Italian moviegoing: the magic of listening to wonderful stories in the dark.

# Irreverent Italian

"GOOD DAY, MADAME. YOU SEE I SPEAK THE EN-
glish," said the courtly driver who picked
me up at Rome's train station. When he tried
to back out of a postage-stamp-sized parking
space, a matronly Italian woman, dripping
jewelry, behind the wheel of a big Mercedes
was blocking his way.

He rolled down the window and asked in
his accented English. "Please, madame, could
you move?" She stared right through him. He
repeated the request in polite Italian. No response.

"Madame, I'm sure you are a very fine
lady," he said, reverting to English.

Without deigning to look at him, she
replied in a single skewer of a word: "*Vaffanculo!*"

This is how I learned Italian's equivalent of the F-word. The two Romans were just getting started. The driver let loose a volley of invective that practically sizzled in the air. She, color flooding her face, blasted back with equally fiery words, although all I could make out was an occasional *stronzo* (shit) and *cazzo* (prick). The driver spat out dark imprecations I recognized only as *Romanesco*, the local dialect. Turning to me, he explained, "She's a big, fat, stupid idiot!" Then he started the engine and aimed for the Mercedes. Her mouth still moving, the woman backed up.

"*Suina puttana*," he muttered under his breath. "Swine whore." I didn't know whether to blush or applaud.

I probably would feel the same way at the raucous celebrations of V-Day (for *vaffanculo*, not *vittoria*) that have drawn tens of thousands of Italians into city piazzas to protest government corruption and suppression of information. Rather than the classic V sign, the crowds wave their raised middle fingers and shout "*Vaffanculo!*" A generation ago it would have been shocking to hear this word in public; two generations ago under the Fascist regime it would have been a crime.

Yet though V-Day is a recent invention, the use of language, often vulgar, to shock the powerful and awe the masses continues a very old Italian tradition. V-Day's thoroughly modern organizer, Beppe Grillo, a burly, bearded comedian and writer with a mane of unruly gray curls, has positioned himself as the voice of the people through a blog (beppegrillo.it) that ranks among the most widely read in Italy. However, to me he seems the twenty-first-century incarnation of Pietro Aretino, the Renaissance gadfly and "scourge of princes" who harnessed the power of *la parolaccia* (bad language) to grab attention.

Italian's foul words haven't changed much in the five centuries since. Cristina, my history tutor in Florence, shows me a copy of a sign from the 1600s posted by an angry customer on the door of a shop in Milan. It denounces the owners as a *beccone* (big cuckold) and his *puttanissima* (whore of whores) of a wife. These days disreputable expressions—including such downright nasty ones—pepper everyday conversations in parks and piazzas, on television, and in the movies. As we walk on the streets of San Francisco, an Italian friend, incensed at her boyfriend, unlooses a fusillade of epithets—*bastardo, cretino, stronzo, idiota*. When I try to hush her, she points out that no one understands what she's saying. Passersby actually seem charmed by her vivacity.

"Well, you wouldn't use such language on the streets of Rome," I protest.

"Why not?" She shrugs her shoulders. "Everybody in Italy talks dirty these days."

Maybe not everyone, but much of the population, from grade-schoolers to grandparents, seems to have mastered the art of *bestemmiare come un turco* (literally "swearing like a Turk," the equivalent of a "trooper" in English). *Parolacce* have become so common, my Italian friends tell me, that they no longer sound offensive—except when foreigners toss around phrases like *vecchia troia* (old whore, a reference to Helen of Troy) or *rompicoglione* (ballbreaker) and sound like children mouthing words they don't fully understand.

Yet it is *importantissimo* to learn *le parolacce*, one of my first teachers insisted. "You need to know that someone who says 'fica' [fig] isn't necessarily offering you a fruit," she explained.

This slang word for female genitalia stems from the Tree of Good and Evil in the Garden of Eden (which produced figs), a misogynistic way of reinforcing the medieval belief that women are evil temptresses. You certainly wouldn't want to mistake *lo zig-zag* (intercourse) for a dance or *scureggione* (old fart) for a compliment. But don't take it personally if a waiter mutters "*Porca vita*" which sounds vulgar, as he clears the table. He's merely bemoaning his miserable life with this harmless equivalent of "Oh, damn."

The ability to recognize Italian's dirty words has spiced up one of my favorite activities in Italy: eavesdropping. Take *cazzo*, Italy's most popular curse word, generally translated into "prick" or "dick" (as in *testa di cazzo*, or "dickhead"). But the Italian writer Italo Calvino insisted that no precise equivalent exists in any language. He's right. I've heard Italians use it as an expression of surprise (*cazzo!*), praise (*cazzuto*), boredom (*scazzo*), anger (*incazzato*), approximation (*a cazzo*), or plain and simple contempt (*cazzone*). "*Col cazzo che ci vado!*" translates as, "The hell I'll go!"; "*Che cazzo vuoi?*" as "What the f*** do you want?"

The same versatility applies to other Italian vulgarities. Though a shit remains ever so in English, a group of charming young Italian women once explained that in Italian a guy can be a big disgusting shit (*stronzone*), a small charming one (*stronzino* or *stronzettino*), a shit with something going for him (*stronzetto*), a disagreeable shit (*stronzaccio*), or a bad but irresistible shit (*stronzuccio*). A filthy place, in case you ever find yourself in one in Italy, is a *stronzaio*.

In addition to butt, bottom, or ass, *culo* can refer to surrendering the last bastion of dignity (*dare anche il culo*); the final or bottom part of something, such as a sack or glass (*cul di sacco, culo di bicchiere*); being as close to someone as a shirt on skin (*essere culo e camicia*); badly made (*fatto col culo*); deceiving someone (*mettere nel culo*); pulling one's leg (*prendere per il culo*); not being able to move (because of a *culo di pietra*, or "ass of stone"); and having good luck (*avere culo*). The expression *restare col culo per terra*, which means to lose everything and be left with nothing, comes from medieval Lombardy, where prisoners had to lower their *pantaloni* and rest their bare buttocks on the grass to discourage escape attempts.

One insult that never seems to change is *cornuto*, the ancient term for cuckold, sometimes symbolized by a raised index and little finger. (If you're from Texas, resist any temptation to flaunt this Longhorn hand cheer.) The word may have come from the masculine form of "goat" (*capro* or *becco*). *Essere becco* means the same as *essere cornuto*, from *corno*, for "horn of a goat," a fickle animal that changes sex partners frequently.

*Le bocche sporche* (the dirty mouths) aren't the only Italians who relish *parolacce*. A trattoria in Trastevere, originally called Osteria da Cencio for its owner Vincenzo (Cencio) De Santis, was rechristened La Parolaccia in 1951 because of its reputation as a place to hear *stornelli sboccati*—popular bawdy verses. An actor showed up one night with a group of friends dressed in black tie. The waiters called them penguins; they teased back. Soon other stars, such as Anna Magnani and Alberto Sordi, started dropping in to join the fun. Tourists are still doing the same.

La Parolaccia gained a national reputation in 1958 when *la principessa triste*, the sad princess Soraya, divorced by the shah of

Persia because she couldn't have children, came with a local prince (and a contingent of paparazzi) to pass a carefree evening. Newspaper headlines read *"Soraya in un locale malfamato"* (an infamous place). The name, if not the cheeky attitude, has traveled as far as Long Beach, California, where the local La Parolaccia advertises good food and wine in the sort of place where you don't have to watch what you say.

Wondering what Vito Tartamella, the man who wrote the book on bad words, *Parolacce*, would have to say about language, I arranged to meet him in Milan at the offices of the magazine *Focus*, where he is a staff editor. The earnest young journalist struck me immediately as a freedom-fighter of sorts, with a shock of thick black curls, the combination of goatee and mustache that Italians call a *pezzino* (a little piece of hair), and a Garibaldi-red shirt.

The first word he teaches me sounds anything but dirty: *turpiloquio*, the formal term for foul language. "Civilization couldn't exist without it," Tartamella observes. "Obscenities were among the oldest, if not the oldest, words in human history. Instead of throwing rocks at each other, men learned to hurl insults and vulgarities." In his meticulously documented book, Tartamella identifies 301 such *parolacce*. The *Dizionario storico del lessico erotico italiano* (Historic Dictionary of the Erotic Italian Lexicon), which includes antiquated and dialect terms, lists ten times as many—3,500 impudent entries.

"Do Italians curse more than other people?" I ask.

"They curse differently," says Tartamella, noting that, unlike French, German, or English speakers, Italians express powerful emotions such as anger, disgust, surprise, and horror with sexual obscenities rather than scatalogical ones. They certainly have more of these expressions at their command. In the course of his scholarly research, Tartamella identified dozens of euphemisms for the sex organs.

Italians refer to male genitals as objects (tool, handle, mallet, hammer, club, telescope), weapons (cannon, pistol, nightstick), musical instruments (flute or fife), structures (bell tower or column), animals (fish, eel, bird), and foods (carrot, celery, asparagus, biscotto, salami, sausage, and *leccalecca*, "lick-lick," for lollipop).

The lascivious lexicon for female genitals includes words for containers (bread box, stove, oven, trap), weapons (sheath or shield), musical instruments (guitar, bagpipe, castanet), places (nest, woods, bush, valley—and *paradiso*), animals (cat, sparrow, mouse, clam), plants and fruits (fig, flower bud, lily, rose, strawberry, prune), jewel, treasure, "her," and sister. Multiplying all of these at least tenfold are dialect words, most from foods.

*Le parolacce* have served Italians well in war as well as love, Tartamella tells me, because Italian's gruffer vulgarities pack a verbal punch. Their linguistic ingredients—the twinned *zz* in *cazzo*, the forceful double *ff* in *vaffanculo*, the triple consonants in *stronzo*—cause these words to explode out of the mouth. Their phonetic force actually helped the ancient Romans conquer the world.

According to historical accounts, before a battle, Roman legions would line up just a few yards away from their enemies and unleash a verbal artillery barrage, screaming vile insults and bloodcurdling threats. Intimidated by these savage cries, the enemy soldiers in the rear would often panic and flee. Soon enough the front line would do the same.

Unlike the anything-goes Greeks, the Romans felt a need to set some linguistic limits and invented censorship in the fifth century B.C. Originally *censori* (censors) had been charged with ascertaining the wealth of the citizenry, a crucial reckoning because different social and economic classes had different rights and obligations. In 443 B.C. these magistrates took on the extra duty of assuring the respect of public morals, although they objected less to foul language than to offensive satires.

Censors didn't seem to inhibit writers such as Catullus (84–54 B.C.), who trilled of passion in ecstatic odes to his beloved Lesbia. He also wrote the following blistering diatribe, translated by Peter D'Epiro, co-author of *Sprezzatura: 50 Ways Italian Genius Shaped the World*, when she betrayed him.

> Hey, all you regulars of that pickup joint
> nine pillars down from the Temple of the Twins.
> Do you actually think you're the only guys with
>    pricks,
> with some sort of license to screw all the girls
> while the rest of us schmucks have b.o.?

In the following century, *The Satyricon* by Gaius Petronius (A.D. 27–66) lived up to the double implications of its name: a satire, from *satura* for medley and satyr for a mythical creature with male human traits and animal ears and tail. The narrator's name, Encolpius, means "in the fold," or more explicitly "in the crotch." He fights with his friend Ascyltos (Unwearied) over the affections of a boy named Giton (Neighbor) in language that ranges from extremely elegant to equally vulgar.

Vernacular Italian, taking wing in the Middle Ages, retained Latin vulgarities such as *culo* (ass) and *merda* (shit) but added new insults or *spregiativi*. The crusaders contributed *pagano* for "pagan" and *infedele* for "infidel"; city dwellers derided those who lived in the country as *villani* (peasants whose crude houses were considered inferior to urban *palazzi*). Religious phrases, such as for *la croce, i piedi, il cuore, la vita,* or *la passione di Dio* ("the cross," "feet," "heart," "life," or "passion of God"), turned profane in the mouths of blasphemers. "When a gambler loses his money and nerve," a monk of the time observed, "he calms himself by chopping up Christ piece by piece."

Vulgarity gained new status—higher or lower is a matter of debate—when the church deemed it a mortal sin. The most renowned prelate of his time, St. Thomas Aquinas (1225–1274), hailed as "the titan of theology," declared that *la bestemmia* was graver than homicide because it sprang from the intention to attack the goodness and generosity (*bontà*) of God himself, whereas insults took from a man the honor due him and the respect that meant as much as house and home.

Dante didn't reserve a spot in hell for the foulmouthed, but a famous *puttana*, Thais, appears—"filthy, with tangled hair"— among the flatterers, while he rails against corrupt popes for *puttaneggiar*, whoring it up, with earthly kings. A milder profanity intrudes into the *Purgatorio* when Dante, lamenting Italy's fate, calls his native land "no queen of provinces but of bordellos."

The second of Italian's three crowns, Boccaccio, whose

very name serves as a synonym for bawdiness, sometimes seemed inspired by the devil himself. In the first story of the third day in his *Decameron*, he introduces Masetto, a fine lad "of remarkably handsome physique and agreeable features." This studly youth pretends to be a deaf-mute to persuade the abbess at a convent with eight lovely young nuns to take pity and hire him as a gardener. As the muscular hunk labors, the nuns, thinking he can't hear, tease him with the foulest language imaginable.

One day one of the nuns confides to another—within earshot of Masetto—that the dimwitted, deaf, and dumb gardener might be the perfect person to help them find out if it is true that other pleasures pale compare to being with a man. Masetto responds to their overtures with big imbecilic grins and gladly satisfies their curiosity—and then their enthusiastic appetites. As the other young nuns catch on, all demand shares of "the dumb fellow's riding ability." After she comes across Masetto lying in the sun one day, his clothes "undone from recent exertions," the aroused abbess enlists him into her service.

Finally Masetto, unable to cope with the constant sexual demands, breaks his silence and says to the abbess, "Whereas a single cock is quite sufficient for ten hens, ten men are hard put to satisfy one woman, and yet here am I with nine of them on my plate." The abbess is doubly shocked that Masetto can speak and that he is having sex with all her young charges. Rather than send him away to spread stories, she arranges for him to become steward and to divide his natural talents among the not-so-good sisters "in such a way that he could do them all justice." After fathering a brood of "nunlets" and "monklets," Masetto retires as an elderly and prosperous father "spared the bother of feeding his children and the expense of their upbringing."

Boccaccio, at least in his lusty youth, would have fit right in with the humanist writers of the succeeding centuries. "The Italian man of the Renaissance," as one contemporary historian put it, "reasons more with his phallus than his spirit." The humanists brought their delight in sensual expression to the language, transforming their joy in life and love into verse and prose, some quite smutty.

The Renaissance was *"il secolo d'oro della parolaccia"* ("the golden century of bad language"), says Tartamella. It was certainly the most phallocentric of times. Although I'd visited and revisited the famous nudes in Florence's museums many times, it wasn't until my college-age daughter accompanied me last summer that I realized that we were always looking up or straight at the male member. (Much to my embarrassment, I learned in a conversation class that *il membro* is not always used interchangeably, like its English counterpart, for someone in a social group [*socio*]. A fellow student further informed me that the diminutive *membrolino* is the surest way to shrink an Italian man's ego, not to mention other body parts, whereas *membroso* elicits the opposite effect.)

The penis unquestionably inspired Florence's entire roster of artists and artisans. The archives of L'Accademia della Crusca, the bastion of the Italian language, contain verses from the *canti carnascialeschi*, the bawdy ditties the Florentines sang in the streets at Carnevale and during the two-month celebration of San Giovanni, their patron saint. Many of the tunes—*canti priapei* (priapic songs)—praise their composers' *strumenti sessuali*. As they paraded through the streets, the different guilds touted the praises of their "merchandise" with words from the jargon of their trades, such as "brush," "spinner," "wood," "iron," and "club."

The same enthusiastic appreciation inspired Pacifico Massimo, governor of Ascoli, a declared bisexual, and infamous libertine, to pen an essay called *"Sul suo cazzo,"* "On His Dick." His narrator laments, *"Misero me.* My dick is so big and of such heavy weight that among people I would pass for having three legs." On the other hand, he also exults, *"Io godo contemplando la mia mastodontica colonna"* ("I enjoy contemplating my mastodon of a column").

That master of all arts, Leonardo da Vinci, shared his contemplations in a more scientific essay called "About the Penis":

> This confers with the human intelligence and
> sometimes has intelligence of itself, and although the
> will of the man desires to stimulate it, it remains
> obstinate and takes its own course, and moving
> sometimes of itself without license or thought by
> the man, whether he is sleeping or waking, it does
> what it desires. Often the man is asleep and it is
> awake, and many times the man is awake and it is
> asleep. Many times the man wishes it to practice
> and it does not wish to, many times it wishes to
> and the man forbids it. It seems, therefore, that this
> creature has often life and intelligence separate from
> man, and it would appear that the man is in the
> wrong in being ashamed to give it a name or exhibit
> it, seeking rather constantly to cover and conceal

what he ought to adorn and display with ceremony
as one deserves.

Pietro Aretino, father of modern pornography, would certainly have agreed. In the first erotic book written in any Western vernacular, a world-weary old courtesan named Nanna
declaims at considerable length on the obscene things women
do in their three roles: as nuns, wives, and prostitutes (who
come off best). Although the tales are Boccaccian in nature, they
are far coarser, featuring dildos made of Murano glass, group
sex, and obscene murals. All the men crave sex only for physical release; women, only for money or greed.

The Aretine age ended abruptly in 1557 when the Inquisition published the Index of Prohibited Books, a list of books
(including his) judged dangerous because they were immoral,
obscene, or contained heresy, errors of theology, or vulgarity.
Anyone who owned a prohibited book at home risked excommunication. Its thirty-second (and last) edition, published in
1948, contained four thousand titles, including authors such as
Balzac, Sartre, Casanova, Sade, Hugo, and Flaubert. The Index
itself was abolished only in 1966.

I always wondered what happened to these forbidden volumes. Were they burned or destroyed? "No," Tartamella tells
me. "The Inquisition actually ended up protecting and preserving the very books it banned." The volumes, including priceless
manuscripts dating back to the fourteenth century, remain to
this day in *la biblioteca dei censori*, the library of the censors, one
of the most important collections of the Vatican Library. Scholars refer to it as *L'Inferno*.

In the centuries of foreign rule, the Italians cultivated their skill at *dire pepe*, or "talking pepper" by lacing a conversation with sarcasm, puns, vulgarities, and scabrous allusions. This form of entertainment, still popular today, also served as the sole safe outlet for emotions too dangerous to release in other ways.

After unification, in the almost puritanical atmosphere of the late nineteenth century, purely pornographic literature blossomed. These crude books and magazines were mainly anonymous tales, written without style and often combined with obscene illustrations. Titles such as *Il trionfo del culo* (The Triumph of the Ass) capture the level of the writing. Gone were the erudition, wit, and humor that had accompanied licentious literature in the past. However, these grace notes survived in Italy's long tradition of oral word duels, well laced with *bestemmie* and *parolacce*.

One of the best of the young verbal jousters of his day was none other than Benito Mussolini (1883–1945), who prided himself on his skill in *sbandierare le bestemmie* (clever and ostentatious swearing) and his audacity in challenging the religious establishment. In his book *Mussolini com'era* (Mussolini as He Was), Cesare Rossi recounts a blasphemous confrontation between the future *duce* and a priest in Switzerland in 1902.

"If God exists," Mussolini declared, "I give him five minutes to strike with a lightning bolt the enemy who speaks of him." Looking at his watch, Mussolini counted down the seconds and said, "See? I am still living. Therefore, God does not exist." Mussolini changed his mind and his language when he came to power. Under the Italian Codice Rocco of 1930, vulgarity and blasphemy became crimes.

Of course, Italians didn't stop swearing; they just found new ways to do so. Many adopted *fregarsene* (literally "to give oneself a rub"), coined by the writer Gabriele D'Annunzio. *Me ne frego*—ubiquitous today—stood in for "I don't give a damn" (or a stronger expletive).

Others made clever word substitutes, such as *per Diana!* instead of *per Dio* and *porca vacca!* (damn cow) instead of *porca puttana* (damn whore). A son of a bitch (*figlio di puttana*) became the son of a good woman (*figlio di buona donna*). Instead of *vaffanculo*, an angry Italian told someone to go lay an egg (*va affa' l'ovo!*) or go to that country (*va a quel paese*), meaning hell.

With Fascism's fall, Italians unleashed decades of pent-up *parolacce*. Friends recall hearing saintly grandmothers and dignified teachers spewing vulgar phrases in public and private. But despite free speech in the streets, the influence of the church and government preserved media censorship for decades. The director Vittorio De Sica dared to insert a vulgarity into his neo-realistic classic *Umberto D.* in 1952. *"Siamo tra uomini, dica pure, dica pure, puttane,"* says the impoverished protagonist, commenting that since they are among men, he and his friends can use the word "whores." Not at the time. Such words were snipped from Italian movies until 1988.

The regulations that best exemplify the absurd extremism of Italy's language police were the *Norme di autodisciplina per le trasmissioni televisive* (Rules of Self-Discipline for Televised Transmissions), guidelines developed with Vatican input for state television. As Menico Caroli recounts in the book *Proibitissimo*, words such as *alcova* (alcove), *sudore* (sweat), *vizio* (vice), and *verginità* (virginity) could not be spoken. Thigh (*la coscia*) was allowed, but only in reference to a part of a chicken. *Divorzio*, prohibited as a vulgarity, was paraphrased as *scioglimento del vincolo coniugale* (dissolution of the conjugal bond).

Even words that sounded somewhat like *parolacce* were banned, such as *cazzotto* (punch) for its root (*cazzo*, or "prick") and *magnifica* (magnificent) for its ending (*fica*, or "fig"—slang for "vagina"). *Cornea*, the part of the eye, could not be spoken because the very sound might conjure up the vulgar horns of a betrayed *cornuto*. Times have certainly changed. These days a single episode of *Il Grande Fratello* (Italy's *Big Brother*) averages fifty *parolacce*.

Meanwhile politicians have made one *parolaccia—coglione* (literally "testicle," but generally translated as "loser" or "fool")—into a household and headline word. It started in 1986 when a journalist in an interview told the former prime minister Bettino Craxi that the socialists wanted to *autoaffondare* (self-sabotage) their own government coalition. "Whoever says that is a *coglione*," Craxi commented. When the reporter noted that his source was Renato Altissimo, head of the liberal party, Craxi punned that then he was an *"altissimo coglione"* (highest-level idiot). In 1992 Umberto Bossi charged that a political enemy "would like to hold me by the balls [*coglioni*], like he has Berlusconi by his testicles. But mine don't stay in his hand." *"Le mie non gli stanno in mano"*—presumably because they are too big.

In 2007 Silvio Berlusconi, campaigning for reelection, described Italians in an opposing party as *coglioni*. With the expletive as their national slogan, Berlusconi bashers created a blog called sonouncoglione.com and showed up at rallies with signs and T-shirts declaring *"Siamo coglioni!"* With the controversy raging, a dictionary publisher made a heartfelt public plea: *"Basta volgarità e parolacce! Impariamo ad insultare con garbo!"* "Stop vulgarity and bad words. Let's learn to insult with grace and style."

I agree. But nonetheless, I felt I should find an all-purpose, nonoffensive, not-really-smutty *parolaccia* to keep in my linguistic quiver, just in case. I couldn't just look for this one-size-fits-all expletive, of course; I had to listen for it. And so I did—in coffee bars, on bus lines, in shops, on trains, in banks, on television, in the mouths of everyone from magistrates to maids. The word I found—*cafone*, the three syllables of which are pronounced' caw-fo-nay—traditionally meant a peasant or bumpkin.

My etymological dictionary traces its history back to Cafo or Cafonis, a centurion of Mark Antony, mentioned several times by Cicero, although it adds the more plebian (and probable) root of *cavare*, for someone who *cava*, or works the land. Its linguistic pedigree includes a debut in Italian literature in 1861, the very year of Italian unification, in a publication called *La perseveranza* (Perseverance). Best of all, *cafone* can mutate into the son of an ignorant bumpkin (*figlio d'un cafone*), a crude slob (*cafone rozzo*), a tasteless boob (*cafone sciocco*), an ill-mannered fool (*cafone maleducato*), an officious ass (*cafone impertinente*), a tasteless jerk (*cafone senza gusto*), or a disgusting boor (*cafone ripugnante*).

Confronted by any of these loathsome varieties, you might ask, *"Ma Lei cafone ci è nato, o ci è diventato?"* ("Were you born a *cafone* or did you become one?")

I have used my chosen pseudo *parolaccia* exactly once. I had gone to a free concert commemorating April 21, Rome's official birthday, at the city's opera house. The mainly elderly Romans, dressed smartly (as their generation always does), were already seated when a pudgy foreigner in cargo shorts and short-sleeved shirt squeezed into our row to take the empty seat next to mine.

"Please don't let him be American," I prayed, but as soon as I heard his string of "Excuse me's," I knew he was. Just as he sat down, he erupted into a volcanic sneeze. Obviously lacking a handkerchief, he blotted his nose with the back of one hand and then wiped it dry on his hairy thigh.

The appalled woman on my other side and I locked eyes and almost simultaneously mouthed the same words, *"Che cafone!"*

# Mother Tongue

THE EARLIEST ROMANS, LEGEND TELLS US, FOUND a human skull on one of the hills of their new settlement. They took it as a sign that Rome would one day become the *Caput Mundi* ("head of the world" in Latin). From *caput* came the hill's Latin name *Capitolium* and the Italian *Capitolino*, roots of the English word "capitol." No other piece of Roman real estate remains more sacred or more steeped in history. The temple of Jupiter, god of light and sky and protector of the state, built in 509 B.C. and almost as large as the Parthenon in Athens, hallowed this site. The Temple of Juno Moneta (Juno the Admonisher) housed the Roman mint, and *moneta* became synonymous with "money." The kings of Rome honored their family gods here—and hurled traitors to their death from its heights.

To placate his deities, Julius Caesar once ascended this hill on his knees.

After the sack of Rome in 1527, the muddy, devastated Capitoline became known as "goat hill." To restore its former glory, Michelangelo designed the Piazza del Campidoglio, one of the most graceful urban spaces in the world, for the seat of Rome's government. Atop his monumental staircase a bronze statue of Marcus Aurelius on horseback surveys the city. As long as this figure of the Roman emperor stands, an old saying goes, Rome will endure. Its citizens shrug at such superstitious nonsense, but when the ancient equestrian started showing signs of erosion, they substituted a copy and whisked the original inside the Capitoline Museum.

On a misty September morning I stand on the Campidoglio and contemplate the glory that was Rome. In *The Tongues of Italy*, the linguist Ernst Pulgram observes that the Romans and their descendants "thrice ruled the Western world in three different domains of human endeavor: once in government and law, once in religion, and once in art." To this trio of triumphs, he added a fourth—in language.

I have come to an event that both honors and testifies to this conquest: the biannual conference of the Società Dante Alighieri, founded at the Campidoglio in 1890 by the poet Giosuè Carducci (1835–1907), the first Italian to win the Nobel Prize in Literature. La Dante, as the society is called, teaches Italian to more than 200,000 students in more than seventy-five countries around the globe.

"It is only fitting that we are here in the most important place in Greco-Roman civilization," says Ambassador Bruno

Bottai, president of La Dante, as he welcomes hundreds of the society's members, instructors, and students. Each holds a scroll printed with La Dante's original mission statement, a rallying cry to every Italian, "whatever his religious faith is, whatever his political opinions are": *"tutelare e diffondere la lingua e la cultura italiane nel mondo...alimentando tra gli stranieri l'amore e il culto per la civiltà italiana"*—"to teach and defend the Italian language and culture in the world . . . nourishing among foreigners love and respect for Italian civilization."

At the time of La Dante's formation, Italy itself was barely clinging together. The provinces of Trentino-Alto Adige and Friuli-Venezia Giulia remained under Austrian rule (they joined the Italian state after World War I). The new nation, beset by ineradicable poverty, was hemorrhaging citizens; more than ten million Italians emigrated between 1870 and 1920. La Dante's first objective was to use language to maintain their ties to their homeland; its ongoing mission is to create a global community of *innamorati della lingua*, lovers of the language.

La Dante has succeeded to an extent its literary founders could never have imagined. I wonder how many mother tongues are represented in the assemblage of Italianophiles from Europe, Africa, Asia, the Americas, and Oceania. As I chat amiably with attendees from various continents a rather astounding realization hits me: We all, regardless of nationality or ethnicity, are communicating with each other in what is essentially the fourteenth-century Tuscan dialect that Dante, peering down from a pedestal in the grand Sala della Protomoteca del Campidoglio, also would have understood.

When the morning's speakers laud the merits of Italian as

the ideal international language, the notion doesn't strike me—as it might have at one time—as preposterous. No other tongue expresses human feelings and emotions more powerfully. No other language offers so many *sfumature* (subtle shadings) that can sidestep conflict and foster understanding and cooperation. Sure, other idioms may be better suited to commerce, technology, science, or finance, but Italian embodies something far greater and more universal: civilization itself. As I sit in the very heart of Rome, on a hill sanctified as a seat of power, law, and government for almost three millennia, within steps of some of the world's greatest art treasures, I wholeheartedly agree that Italian is indeed the language of humanity—and therefore everyone's mother tongue.

Later, in a conversation with Alessandro Masi, La Dante's *Segretario Generale*, I trip over my tenses and apologize for my imperfect Italian. *"Non fa niente,"* he assures me. "You speak better Italian than most Italians." At first, I simply accept the compliment. But on my way back to my apartment, I stop at a *supermercato* for a few items and inadvertently draw the ire of the harried cashier for not having any small coins. Incapable of retrieving a single word to counter her tongue-lashing, I meekly grab my *sacchetto* and dash out the door. Mother tongue, indeed!

Once again I have slipped headlong into the gap between the two parallel forms of the national language: *italiano scritto* (written Italian), the formal, literature-based language taught in schools, and *italiano parlato* (spoken or vernacular Italian), the feisty modern *vernacular* that no one masters in a classroom. Thanks to obligatory education and the mass media, the two have become more similar than ever before, but at times my formal Italian makes me feel like Petrarch in a pizzeria. Just as it has for the last five hundred years, *la questione della lingua*—the question of the language, of which form is better, purer, more important, more Italian—rages on.

"We are still asking what language to write in because we still do not write in the language we speak," observes Raffaele Simone, director of the Department of Linguistics at Università Roma Tre. "Every Italian's Italian is different. This makes the language as rich in flavors and varieties as Italian cooking, but it makes foreigners crazy." The phrase *fare impazzire* perfectly describes how I feel on Italy's streets.

One friend describes the Italian of many of his countrymen as a *macedonia*, a mix of all kinds of verbiage casually tossed together. I learned this use of the word from Lina, the cook at Monte Vibiano Vecchio, who once asked me (I thought) if I liked the war-torn little nation, a former province of the Roman Empire. It turns out that Italians call a fresh fruit salad a *macedonia*, perhaps—Lina speculates—because it's been chopped up into little pieces so often.

Italian too has been diced and spliced, purged and purified by linguistic law enforcers, none more zealous than the Fascists, who took their name from the bundles of sticks, called *fasces*, that symbolized power in ancient Rome. In 1923 Mussolini's government levied a tax on foreign words used in shop signs. At the beginning of the Second World War, a law banned them altogether. Posters blazed, *"Italiani, boicottate le parole straniere!"* ("Italians, boycott foreign words!") No one pointed out that *boicottate* was itself foreign, derived from the name of Captain

Charles C. Boycott, the first victim of this treatment in Ireland. "Boycott" had passed from English, to French, to Italian.

Under Fascism an Italian *chauffeur* became an *autista*; soccer turned into *calcio*; a bar was rechristened *qui si beve* (here one drinks). Shakespeare's name, like other foreign appellations, had to be pronounced as if it were Italian: Shah-kay-spay-ah-ray. In 1933 the journalist Paolo Monelli published *Barbarian Domination: Five Hundred Foreign Expressions Examined, Attacked, and Banished from the Language with Old and New Argument, with the History and Etymology of the Words and with Anecdotes to Entertain the Reader.* By the second edition in 1943, the list had grown to 650. In the preface, the author explained that he was campaigning for "pride and dignity."

A strong people "do not pick up foreign rubbish," Monelli declared. "The pollution of language is usually the work of people who are ignorant, presumptuous, slavish." A Fascist law prohibiting the "slavish" practice of giving foreign Christian names to Italian children stayed on the books until 1966. My Italian-born friend Narriman's parents, who named her for an Egyptian queen, were told that no Christian name ends with an *n*. Hers went down in the municipal records as Narrima, although the young priest who baptized her (at his first christening) used Narriman for the church register.

Fascism also tried to exterminate *la malerba dialettale* (the dialect weeds) that it saw as sullying the purity of the national language. In effect the restrictions on dialect silenced generations of Italians of all social and educational levels, including nobles, who spoke mainly in the language they heard in their homes and villages. "For my parents, speaking dialect was like using your right hand," a friend explains. "Following the rules of *italiano standard*, even if you had a university degree, was like using your left."

Today, according to Italy's national statistics bureau, 55 percent of Italians still use dialect some or most of the time when they are with family and friends. A quarter use dialect even when speaking to strangers. Almost all Italians, including those whose parents forbade them to speak dialect when growing up, know at least a few words. *Ragazzo* may be the proper Italian word for child, but a "kid" remains a *bimbo* in Florence, a *cittino* in Siena, a *puteo* in Venice, a *figgeu* in Savona (Liguria), a *burdel* or *burdlin* in Romagna, a *frut* in Friuli, and a *quatraro* in some southern dialects (Dante mentions this word in his treatise on language, *De Vulgari Eloquentia* [Vernacular Eloquence]).

A far greater threat to contemporary Italian are verbal immigrants, say some purists and politicians (who set up an Allarme Lingua commission after the European Union snubbed Italian to select English, French, and German as its principal languages). To protest such linguistic discrimination, Prime Minister Berlusconi has advised his ministers to walk out of European Union meetings in which they are forced to speak another language and to boycott those that provide no documentation in Italian.

According to Cristina, my Florence language history tutor, foreign words make up about 10 percent of the Italian vocabulary, but only .3 percent have entered the language without change or adaptation. I learned a German acquisition in a restaurant when I was fiddling with a turn-tilt window with a hinge on the lower edge. A waiter volunteered to help me with the thingamajig, which he called a *vasistas*, from the query *"Was ist das?"* A friend taught me a Russian import when she accused me of being a *stacanovista* (workaholic), from Stachanov, a Russian miner who introduced new techniques to increase productivity.

American English has been infiltrating the Italian language ever since the Allies invaded the peninsula during World War II. (Italians still call chewing gum *gomma americana*.) Linguists estimate that several thousand English terms have shouldered their way into Italian, including "computer," "software," "bestseller," "killer," "manager," "boyfriend," "cowboy," "popcorn," "massmedia" (one word), "playboy," "coffee break," "stress," "babysitter," "flirt," and "weekend." But Italian ingenuity has cast some English words in somewhat different roles. A *golf* refers to a pullover; a *mister*, a coach of a soccer team; a *smoking*, a tuxedo; a *spot*, a commercial; and a *fiction*, a film for TV. From American politics journalists took "ticket" for a party's presidential and vice presidential candidates and created *tricket* for three contenders in an Italian election.

At times I find Italian's "English" words more confounding than its homegrown ones. Instead of going for a jog, for instance, I must *fare il footing*, a term that may have entered Italian from a nineteenth-century Spanish word for hiking. Even Italians get confused by what some call the "Englishing" of their language. When a beauty salon dubbed itself "Top one," Italians read the name as *topone*, or big rat, and didn't venture inside.

Some words that sound English actually have Italian roots. "Snob" may date back to Renaissance Florence, when the burgeoning middle class sought acceptance in the upper strata of local society. To distinguish between the true noble families and the nouveau riche, census-takers wrote *s.nob* (*senza nobiltà*, for "without nobility") next to the names of social climbers (known in contemporary Italian as *arrampicatori sociali*). Seemingly all-American "jeans" started off as *blu di Genova* for the color of the denim used by its sailors on their boats. According to the *Oxford English Dictionary*, the term migrated into French as *bleu de Genes* before its global reincarnation as jeans.

Despite the ubiquity of nonsense English words ("Meating," for a restaurant; "Boomerang" for a trucking company, "Shopping U" for a store), slightly more than half of Italian's linguistic base—its 10,000 most-used words—dates back to the 1300s and 1400s. I heard firsthand evidence of this recently when trash piled up on the streets of Naples and precipitated a national crisis. Listening to reports on the Italian nightly news (also broadcast in the United States), I kept hearing one of the first words I learned in Italian echoing through the outraged protests of citizens, the alarmed warnings of health experts, and the ranting of the politicians: *spazzatura*.

Years ago at a class at the ItaLingua Institute in San Francisco, I entered the room with an empty paper coffee cup in hand.

"*Spazzatura?*" the cheery young teacher asked.

"*Sì,*" I responded, certain that I wanted whatever this spray of sibilant syllables offered. Then I tracked her outstretched arm, pointing to the wastebasket in the corner.

"Trash," she said in English.

After class I used the school's massive etymological dictionary to trace the word back to its root: *spazzare* ("sweep" or, in some contexts, "wipe out"), which appeared in Boccaccio's works. Over time it sprouted offshoots such as *spazzamento*, a good sweeping; *spazzatina*, a dusting; *spazzola*, a brush; and *spazzolino da denti*, a toothbrush.

Other Italian words have remained in the vocabulary but completely changed their meanings. As an example, Professor Giuseppe Patota cites *le veline*, the scantily clad young women who traipse about on Italian television shows. Originally *velina* referred to very light, soft paper, he tells me, and later the tissue-thin sheets of onion paper used for carbon copies of typewritten pages. During the Fascist regime, government censors issued directives specifying what newspapers could or could not report. Thin-sheeted copies (*veline*) went to editors; the originals remained in state archives. After the war various ministries continued to send lightweight *veline* not just to newspapers but to RAI, the government-sponsored television network.

In the 1980s a program on Silvio Berlusconi's private Canale 5 that satirized RAI news shows featured sexy dancers in flimsy outfits who carried *veline* to the announcers. They became known as *veline*, a name now used for all the leggy girls (and there are many) who appear regularly on Italian television. Two variations on *velina*—*velinesco* (slim and coy) and *velinismo* (behavior typical of a *velina*)—appear in a recent edition of *Parole nuove: un dizionario di neologismi dai giornali* (New Words: A Dictionary of Neologisms from Newspapers).

This compendium of linguistic inventions provides fascinating insights into the ever-evolving Italian vernacular. Some English words, such as "Bluetooth," "crossover," "e-payment," and "podcasting," look, sound, and mean the same in Italian. Italians give others a top spin. A blogger becomes a *bloggista. Hollywoodità* captures the glitz and glamour of movie stardom. Another invention—*marilynizzarsi*—describes someone who imitates the eternal star Marilyn Monroe. *Minidollaro* all too accurately summarizes the state of the weakened American dollar. Other entries recycle traditional Italian words to describe thoroughly modern things, such as *lampadarsi* (from *lampada* for lamp, a fifteenth-century word the fanatical friar Savonarola used) for tanning under an ultraviolet light.

I've become a regular user of one particular neologism: *messaggiata*, referring to the sending of a text or SMS (the abbreviation used worldwide, including Italy, for Short Message Service) greeting. The very first one I received consisted of just four symbols: "dv 6?" I had to call Cristina so she could explain that she was asking, *"Dove sei?"* "Where are you?" (Italian messagers use the numeral six, which also translates as *sei*, for "you.") My SMS vocabulary now includes ke (*che*—what), ki (*chi*—who), km (*come*—how), and *smpr* (*sempre*—always). However, the longest message I've ever sent was "Dm c sent" for *"Domani ci sentiamo,"* "We'll talk tomorrow."

I've had a much harder time struggling to understand the *paroloni* (big words) spun by politicians and bureaucrats. Time and again I have pondered an official notice, such as an explanation of why the post office is once again closed in the middle of a workday. *"Non è italiano,"* said an older woman puzzling over the words with me in Assisi, *"è ostrogoto"*—a reference to the unintelligible language of the Ostrogoth barbarians who captured Rome in the fifth century.

The government itself has declared war on arcane, overly ornate phraseology and launched Progetto Chiaro (Project Clear) to eliminate bureaucratese. I see no evidence of progress, however. Beppe Severgnini, Italy's national wit, has cataloged some of the verbal monstrosities spawned by Italy's recent political woes. His *"vocabolario della crisi"* (vocabulary of the crisis) includes a neologism, *parlamentarizzazione*, the act of carrying the crisis into parliament, that he deems so horrible that he recommends *infanticidio. Termovalorizzatore*, a word substituted for the politically charged *inceneritori* (garbage incinerators or people who operate them), strikes him as *"il pudore verbale italiano"* (Italian verbal prudery).

Despite such egregious excesses, I have no fears for the fate of a language that has survived invasions, ruthless inquisitors, foreign tyrants, strutting dictators, corrupt politicians, the European Union, ubiquitous English, and tourist hordes from around the world. Italian was born of an insatiable hunger to express, communicate, and connect. Nothing and no one can quench this urge.

Italian also has new linguistic heroes, latter-day versions of Lorenzo de' Medici and Leon Battista Alberti. Professors Valeria della Valle and Giuseppe Patota have been championing the cause of keeping Italian *bello* through a series of books with titles—*Il salvalingua, Il salvastile, Il salvaitaliano, Il nuovo salvalingu*—that are plays on the the word "save" or *salva*, as in *salvagente* for a life preserver. Their academic colleagues initially responded to their efforts to improve common speech with what della Valle describes, flicking her nose upward with a finger, as *"molto snobismo"* and complaints about *divulgazione* (vulgarization) of the language. Yet their lively practical guides have been selling as briskly as gelato in the summer.

"Italians do care about their language, and they want to speak it well," says della Valle, "but even for Italians, Italian is very old, complex, and difficult." *I dubbi* (doubts) about the best or correct way of using the language are the stuff of heated dinner conversations as well as popular television programs. I turned to her to clarify one *dubbio* that Bob and I have debated with Italians for years: at what hour of the day do you stop saying *"Buongiorno"* (Good day) and start using *"Buonasera"* (Good evening) or *"Buonanotte"* (Good night)?

In Tuscany, if we said *"Buongiorno"* a minute after noon, people would often respond with *"Buonasera."* In Rome we kept hearing *"Buongiorno"* well into the afternoon. La Professoressa's rule of thumb: *il buongiorno* until lunchtime (likely to be later in Rome), *la buonasera* afterward, and *la buonanotte* only before going to bed. But if an Italian injects a *buonasera* in the middle of a conversation, don't get up to leave. It's also an ironic way of signaling the end of a task or discussion—or of the impossibility of ever sorting out a thorny problem.

Della Valle found herself in a thorny dilemma in the 1970s when she got her first job after graduation preparing entries for a grand new dictionary, *Il vocabolario della lingua italiana*. (At our first meeting, she led me into her book-lined den to show me its massive four volumes.) Her boss, who had dedicated his life to organizing and cataloging Italian, explained her tasks with

ever-growing uneasiness. When she reached the words beginning with *ca* (the initial letters of some of Italian's oldest scato-
logical terms), he said, reddening and coughing, she would have
to pass the material to him because the contents *"non era adatto a
una donna"* (were not suitable for a woman).

Della Valle never forgot how angry and embarrassed these
*brutte parole* made her feel. "It was the first time I realized that
Italian, until very recently, has always been a man's language
and conveyed a completely masculine vision of reality. Ever
since I have been trying to change things, at the very least to
make sure that *la donna* [woman] is no longer defined as *fem-
mina dell'uomo* [feminine of man]."

In 2008 Nicoletta Maraschio, a professor of the history of
the Italian language at the University of Florence, shattered the
glass ceiling of Italian letters by becoming *la prima donna Presidente*,
"the first woman president," of L'Accademia della Crusca. Caterina Franceschi Ferrucci, a nineteenth-century writer, poet, and
political activist, had become the first female member 137 years
previously. On the occasion of this honor, Ferrucci wrote *Della
necessità di conservare alla nostra lingua e alla nostra letteratura l'indole schi-
ettamente italiana* (Of the necessity of preserving in our language
and our literature the true Italian character).

On a sunny September Saturday in Rome, Bob and I confronted the full range of the Italian character. He wanted to see
the two-thousand-year-old Ara Pacis Augustae, the altar of imperial peace to honor the long Pax Augusta that had allowed
Roman civilization to flourish. I wanted to go to an exhibit on
Valentino's forty-five years in fashion. Both were housed under
the same roof—the Ara Pacis Museum, designed by the Ameri-

can architect Richard Meier and generally derided by Romans as resembling a mammoth gas station.

But just like English words in Italian conversations, the building faded into the background, our eyes dazzled by visions of dresses, displayed as we'd never seen them before: on sleek, long-necked, faceless mannequins with their arms upraised, arranged into pyramids of red, mountains of white, and long chic rows of black. A bridal train cascaded down a sky-high pedestal like a waterfall. A jewel-toned harlequin design, surrounded by mirrors, shimmered like a kaleidoscope. The showstopping dresses worn by Oscar winners such as Julia Roberts and Sophia Loren appeared next to videos of their red carpet moments. In the middle of this finery stood the ancient altar, destroyed in the Dark Ages, partially excavated in the Renaissance, and painstakingly reconstructed over more than half a century. Its walls contain the most exquisite relief carvings in the world, portraying ancient Romans so vividly that you can't help but smile at a child tugging at his father's toga for attention.

Dazed by the double delights of ancient glory and modern style, Bob and I were strolling along the Tiber when a car pulled up and an Italian man asked directions. (This alone should have made us suspicious, since we don't look like natives.) I could tell from his accent that he wasn't a *Romano*. (Alarm bells should have been going off, because friends are always warning us that street-smart con men would snatch a bite from your pizza when you're not looking.) He proceeded to tell us an entertaining, somewhat plausible tale of being in town for a trade show but having to get on the road to Padua for a family wedding.

"Take these as a gift," he said, proffering samples of his

firm's jackets. Then it came: the ever-so-embarrassed confession that he'd run out of cash and needed money for gas. "Look!" he entreated. We could see for ourselves that his tank was empty. Bob and I glanced at each other. The chances were that we were being played. We knew it. He knew we knew it. But we took the jackets, which we gave to children in our apartment building, and gave him some gas money. Our friends were horrified that we had let ourselves *fare i fessi*, or play the fools. Well, yes. But we'd appreciated his outrageous *furbizia* (trickery)—and, I admit, I'm a sucker for anything anyone tells me in Italian.

I'm not alone. Has any other language ever inspired a love song? In *"La nostra lingua italiana"* (Our Italian Language), written in 1993 and featured on YouTube, the songwriter Riccardo Cocciante celebrates Italian as serene, sweet, welcoming, universal, generous, and sensual, the language of the ancient marble of cathedrals, of boats and serenades at sea, of looks and smiles from afar, of palaces and fountains, of opera and the grand Italian cinema, the language always looking for *un po' d'amore* (a little love).

*L'amore*, according to a recent Società Dante Alighieri poll, is the favorite word of Italians living in other countries; *mamma* comes in second. With so many beguiling possibilities to choose from, I could never select just one. But I do have a favorite phrase: *Mi sento a mio agio*. Although it doesn't quite translate into English, it more or less means "I feel at home," or "I'm at ease," and it resonates at a deep level with Italians. The first time I said this to our hosts at Monte Vibiano Vecchio, we all got a little teary.

Over the last quarter-century, I've come to feel at home in

Italy and in Italian. Yet, even after spending three months in Italy last year, I returned to San Francisco feeling I was still missing out on something, still not quite comprehending *le cose italiane* (Italian things). Italian may be the mother of all tongues, but at times I still feel like a stepchild.

"*Certo,*" Alessandra said when I described this sense of an Italy and an Italian I had not yet explored. "That's the difference between learning Italian and living Italian."

"Does that mean it can't be learned?" I asked.

"Not at all," she said, "but you have to learn differently."

The next week she showed up with a deck of playing cards for a game called *scopa*, a CD of Milanese cabaret songs, a comic book about a Batman-like figure called Diabolik, an *ex-voto* (a small heart-shaped painting of the Madonna bought to express gratitude to God for a favor granted), and *La smorfia*, a book for interpreting dreams by associating them with numbers and then betting the numbers in the Italian lottery.

"*Cominciamo!*" Alessandra said with a smile. "Let's get started."

# Glossary

## A

*abbacare*  v. to daydream

*abbacchiato*  slang for someone beaten down physically or mentally

*abbacchio*  n.m. baby lamb that has been nourished only by its mother's milk

*abbaiare*  v. to bark

*abboffarsi* or *abbuffarsi*  v. to stuff oneself to the bursting point

*abbondante*  adj. abundant, plentiful

*a cazzo*  (an approximation) poorly executed

*acqua*  n.f. water

*addio*  n.m. farewell

*affetto*  n.m. affection

*affezione*  n.f. affection, attachment

*agio*  n.m. a sense of comfort and ease

*aiutino*  n.m. a little bit of help

*albergo*  n.m. hotel

*alla burchia*  in a hurry, piled up at random, higgledy-piggledy

*alla frutta*  literally "in the fruit," slang for being fed up

*allegro*  adj. quick, lively

*altissimo*  adj. very high (*altissimo coglione*  a highest-level idiot)

*altro*  n.m. other

*allievo*  n.m. pupil

*al verde*  in the green, out of money

*amabile*  adj. lovable, adorable

*amami*  love me

*amante*  n.m.f. lover

*amaretto*  n.m. almond biscotto

*amato*  adj. beloved

*amatore* (n.m.), *amatrice* (n.f.)  a lover of something, such as wine, music, or the fine things in life

*amicizia*  n.f. friendship

*ammucchiato*  adj. heaped together

*amore*  n.m. love

*amoroso*  adv. amorous

*anche*  adv. also

*anguria*  n.f. watermelon (used more in the north of Italy)

*anima*  n.f. soul

*animato*  adj. spirited

*ano*  n.m. anus

*anno*  n.m. year

*aperto*  adj. open

*appetito* n.m. appetite; used also to reference an unbridled romantic passion

*approfondire* v. to go deeper

*ardore* n.m. ardor

*argento* n.m. silver

*arrapato* adj. horny

*arrugginito* adj. rusty

*arte* n.f. Florentine dialect for a guild

*artigiano* n.m. artisan

*asciugamano* n.m. towel

*aspettare* v. to wait

*assaporare* v. to taste, savor, enjoy

*attimino* n.m. tiny little moment

*audace* adj. bold, audacious

*autista* n.m. chauffeur

*autoaffondare* v. to self-sabotage

*autoveicolo* n.m. motor vehicle

*avaro* n.m./adj. miser; stingy, tight

*avvocatuccio* n.m. small-time lawyer

*azienda* n.f. business, company

*Azzurri* n.m. Blues, the national Italian team

*azzurro-azzurro* adj. intensely blue, sky blue

## B

*babbo* n.m. daddy

*baccalà* n.m. dried cod, slang for someone who is uptight

*bacino* n.m. tiny little kiss

*bacio* n.m. kiss

*bambino* n.m. baby

*bancho* n.m. counter, origin of "bank"

*barcollare* v. to sway or move like a boat

*barzelletta* n.f. funny story

*basso* adj. low

*bastardo* n.m. a bastard

*battesimo* n.m. baptism

*battibecco* n.m. bickering, a noisy argument over something trivial

*becchino* n.m. gravedigger

*beccone* n.m. a big cuckold

*beffa* n.f. prank

*bel canto* operatic singing

*belli di natura* natural beauties

*bellino* n.m. little beauty

*bello* adj. (m.), *bella* (f.) beautiful, nice

*beltà* n.f. beauty

*benestanti* adj. well-off

*bestemmiare* v. to swear

*bestia* n.f. beast

*bicchiere* n.m. glass

*bimbo* n. (m.), *bimba* (f.) a child

*birboncello* n.m. rogue

*bistecca* n.f. steak

*bloggista* n.m. blogger

*boccaccesco* adj. spicy, racy, dirty, lewd

*bollente* adj. boiling hot

*bontà* n.f. goodness

*bottega* n.f. shop

*brache* n.f. (pl.) breeches, trousers, slacks, and their makers

*braghettoni* slang for big underpants makers (used for the painters who covered Michelangelo's nude figures)

*brama* n.f. romantic craving, longing

*bricconcella* n.m. a troublesome sprite

*briccone* n.m. rascal

*brigata dei crusconi* n.f. literally "brigade of crusty ones" (became the Accademia della Crusca)

*brindisi* n.m. toast

*bronzo ignivomo* fire-vomiting bronze (cannons in opera lyrics)

*bugiardino* n.m. little liar; the term doctors use for the patient information insert for a prescription drug

*bugiardo* n.m. liar

*buona forchetta* hearty eater

*buonanotte* n.f. good night

*buonasera* n.f. good evening

*buongiorno* n.m. good day, good morning

*buongustaio* n.m. food lover

*busta* n.f. envelope

*bustarella* n.f. bribe, envelope with money inside

## C

*caballo* n.m. vernacular for nag, morphed into *cavallo,* for horse

*cacio sui maccheroni* cheese on macaroni

*cafone* n.m. an ignorant bumpkin (*cafone impertinente* an officious ass; *cafone maleducato* an ill-mannered fool; *cafone ripugnante* a disgusting boor; *cafone rozzo* a crude slob; *cafone sciocco* a tasteless boob; *cafone senza gusto* a tasteless jerk)

*calcio* n.m. soccer

*caldo* adj. hot

*calduccio* adj. nice and warm

*calzini, calzette, calze, calzettoni, calzettini* n.f. (pl.) socks in various dialects

*calzoncicchi di Gesù Bambino* pillows of stuffed pasta fried and then sprinkled with sugar and cinnamon; served at Christmastime

*cambusa* n.f. galley on a boat

*cambusiere* n.f. person who prepares food on a boat

*camera* n.f. room

*camerata* n.f. salon, club, association; also a dormitory or big bedroom shared by several people

*canti carnascialeschi* n.m. (pl.) carnival-related festivities

*canti della risaia* n.m. (pl.) songs of the rice field

*canzoniere* n.m. songbook

*caotica* adj. chaotic

*capire* v. to understand (*ho capito* I've understood)

*capo* n.m. head, boss

*capomastro* n.m. master builder

*caponi* n.m. (pl.) big heads

*cappellacci alla zucca* squash pasta shaped like crumpled caps

*caput mundi* head of the world

*carità* n. charity

*cartellate* n.f. sweets named for the cloths that cradled the baby Jesus, served at Christmastime

*casa* n.f. house, home

*castello* n.m. a castle

*castrato* n.m. a singer castrated before puberty to preserve his high voice

*cavalier servente* or *cicisbeo* n.m. an Italian man who flagrantly courted married women

*cavallo* n.m. horse

*cazzo* n.m. vulgar slang for penis

*cazzone* n.m. a prick, prat, fool

*cazzotto* n.m. punch

*cenci* n.m. rags

*Cenerentola* Cinderella

*cenone* n.f. a great holiday dinner

*censore* n.m. censors

*centro* n.m. the heart of the city

*c'era una volta* once upon a time

*certo* adv. certainly

*cervellone* n.m. big brain

*chiacchierare* v. to chat

*chiarissimo* adj. most clear

*chiaroscuro* n.m. the contrast of darkness and light

*chiesa* n.f. church

*chiocciola* n.f. snail; @ key of computer keyboard (*scala a chiocciola* spiral staircase)

*ciambellone* n.f. ring cake

*ciao* informal way of saying "hi" or "bye"

*cielo* n.m. heaven, sky

*cinema muto* n.m. silent films

*cinetografo* n.m. a machine that recorded, developed, and projected films

*Cinquecento* n.m. 1500s

*città* n.f. city

*civetta* n.f. literally, an owl; also a flirt (*civettino* a precocious boy

flattering a pretty woman;
*civettone* a boorish lout flattering
a pretty woman; *civettina* an
innocent coquette; *civettuola* a
brazen hussy)

*coccolona* adj. cuddly

*cocomero* n.m. watermelon (used
more in south of Italy)

*coglione* n.m. literally "testicle";
more generally, loser or fool

*colpo della strega* n.m. strike of a
witch, term for a back spasm

*colpo di fulmine* n.m. stroke of
lightning; love at first sight

*colombeggiare* v. to kiss like doves,
bill and coo

*colti* adj. educated

*cominciamo* v. (first-person plural of
*cominciare*) let's get started

*commosso* adj. moved, touched

*commovente* adj. moving, touching

*complimenti* n.m. compliments,
regards

*conciossiacosachè* conj. a pretentious
literary term for "since"

*conquistatore* n.m. ladies' man

*contrappasso* n.m. punishment
perfectly suited to the crime or
sin; most famously used by
Dante in his *Divine Comedy*

*copia* n.f. abundance (used in
literature and poetry)

*cornice* n.f. picture frame

*corona* n.f. crown (*tre corone* the
three crowns of Italian literature:
Dante, Boccaccio, Petrarca)

*cosa* n.f. what, thing (*cose dell'arte*
the things of art or artistic
matters; *cose italiane* Italian things)

*coscia* n.f. thigh

*cotoletta* n.f. cutlet

*cotto* adj. literally, "cooked"; slang
for having a crush on someone

*croce e delizia* n.f. torment and
delight (from Verdi's *La Traviata*)

*crusca* n.f. chaff or bran

*cucina* n.f. cooking, kitchen (*una
cucina italiana* an Italian kitchen;
*cucina del ritorno* homecoming
cooking; *cucina principesca*
princely cooking)

*culo* n.m. coarse term for buttocks
(*culetto* sweet little baby bottom;
*culoni* big butts, nickname for
Americans)

# D

*da asporto* to carry away

*damerino* n.m. dandy

*Dantista* n.m. Dante scholar

*darci del tu* to use with each other
the informal "you"

*denaro* n.m. money

*desiderio* n.m. desire, longing

*deus ex machina* "god from a
machine" (Latin)

*difficultà* (*difficoltà* in contemporary
Italian) n.f. the technical and
aesthetic challenges of creating
works of beauty

*dire* v. to tell, to say (*dimmi* tell
me, informal; *mi dica* tell me,
formal; *dire pepe* tell pepper or
use "salty" language)

*disinvolto* adj. spontaneous, free
and easy

*dito* n. finger (*dita degli apostoli*
"fingers of the apostles," crêpes
filled with sweetened ricotta)

*diva* n.f. goddess, movie star

*dizionario* n.m. dictionary

*dolce* adj. sweet

*dolcezza* n.f. sweetness

*domani mattina* tomorrow morning

*domenica* n.f. Sunday

*donna* n.f. woman (*donnaccia* ugly
woman)

*doppiatore* n.m. film dubber

*dove* adv. where

*dubbio* n.m. doubt

E

*ecci* the sound of a sneeze

*ecco* here

*emozionante* adj. exciting

*emozionata* adj. excited, moved

*essere* v. to be

*estremità* n.f. extremity; poetic word for foot

*etichetta* n.f. etiquette; label

F

*faccia* n.f. face

*facoltà* n. faculty

*falsificatore* n.m. forger, counterfeiter

*fare* v. to make or do (*fare una bella* or *brutta una figura* behave in a way that gives either a good or an ugly impression; *fare respirare i morti* making the dead breathe; *fare alla romana* go dutch; *fare le fusa* purr; *fare il fesso* make or act the fool)

*farfalla* n.f. butterfly

*fazzoletto* n.m. handkerchief

*fegato* n.m. liver; slang for courage

*fettuccine* n.f.pl. golden eggy noodles

*fico* n.m. fig; slang for "vagina"

*fiction* n. film for TV

*figlio di buona donna* son of a good woman, alternative to the vulgar *figlio di puttana* (son of a whore)

*fiore di zucchine* n.m. fried zucchini flower

*film parlato* n.m. talking film

*filone* n.m. genre

*fischiare* v. to whistle (*fischiettare* whistle with joy)

*fotoromanzo* n.m. picture magazine

*fregarsene* v. literally to "give oneself a rub" (*me ne frego* "I don't give a damn")

*fritta e rifritta* adj. fried and refried; slang for a story that's been told over and over again

*frullone* n.m. a sievelike device that separated wheat from chaff to produce flour

*fuoco* fire

*furbo* n.m. cunning enough to pull off a clever deception (*furbacchione* or *furbacchiotto* trickster)

*furtivo* adj. hidden, secretive

G

*galeotto* n.m. a seductive ploy or whatever brings two lovers together

*gamba* n.f. leg (*in gamba* on top of one's game)

*garbo* n.m. pitch-perfect combination of style and grace

*garbuglio* n.m. muddle

*gaudente* n.m. pleasure-lover, -seeker

*gelosia* n.f. jealousy

*giada* n.f. jade

*giallo* adj. yellow

*giudizio dell'occhio* n.m. judgment of the eye

*gola* n.f. throat

*golf* n.m. a pullover

*goloso* adj. greedy (for food)

*gomma Americana* n.f. chewing gum

*gradisca* v. (from *gradire*) may it please you

*grammatica* n.f. grammar

*gramo* adj. wretched, miserable

*(i) grandi* n.m.pl. Italy's greatest artists and authors

*grazia* n.f. grace, gracefulness

*grillo* n.m. cricket

*grotta* n.f. cave

*grottesca* adj. grotesque, artistic style based on drawings from Roman excavations

*guerra* n.f. war

I

*idiota* n.m./adj. idiot

*ignorante* adj. ignorant

*imbranato* adj. slang for clumsy or awkward

*imparadisato* adj. lifted into heaven

*importantissimo* adj. of great importance

*incazzato* adj. angered, pissed-off

*inferno* n.m. hell

*ingarbugliarsi* v. get oneself into a muddle

*innamorati della lingua* lovers of the language

*innamorato* adj. enamored

*intermezzo* n.m. intermission

*invecchiare* v. to become old

*involto* adj. rolled, wrapped up; parcel, bundle

*inzuppato* adj. soaked, drenched

*italianissimo* adj. very, very Italian

*italianità* n.f. the essence of being Italian

## L

*lacrima* n.f. tear (*lacrime d'amore* tears of love; a type of candy)

*ladro* n.m. thief

*lardo* n.m. fatty tissue sliced from the subcutaneous layer of a pig's abdomen

*lattuga* n.f. lettuce

*lecca lecca* n.f. literally "lick-lick"; a lollipop

*leggiadria* n.f. gracefulness

*leone* n.m. lion

*lettura* n.f. reading

*libretto* n.m. little book; opera lyrics

*lieta brigata* n.f. a particularly amiable conversation group, from Boccaccio's Decameron

*lieto fine* n.m. happy ending

*lingua* n.f. language; tongue

*lingue di suocera* n.f. (pl.) pasta named for twisted mother-in-law tongues

*lirica* n.f. Italian word for opera; lyrics

*litigioso* adj. quarrelsome

*loggione* n.m. compressed gallery of cheaper seats in an opera house

*luna rossa* n.f. red moon

*lupa* n.f. she-wolf; historically used as slang for prostitute

*lupanare* n.m. brothel

## M

*macchina* n.f. car

*macedonia* n.f. a mess; fruit salad

*macinato* adj. milled into flour

*maestro* n.m. title for conductor, instructor

*magnifico* adj. magnificent

*mago* n.m. magician

*malavita* n.f. bad life, criminal life

*maleducato* adj. ill-bred or rude

*malocchio* n.m. evil eye

*mangiamaccheroni* n.m. (pl.) macaroni eaters

*mangiapreti* n.m. literally "priest-eater"; anti-cleric

*mano* n.f. hand

*medico* n.m. doctor

*melodramma* n.m. a generic term for any story set to music

*melomania* n.f. a mania for music

*membro* n.m. limb; slang for penis

*meno male* thank goodness

*meravellosamente* (obsolete)/ *meravigliosamente* (current) adv. marvelously

*meraviglia* n.f. marvel or an extraordinary delight

*merda* n.f. vulgar slang for excrement

*merenda* n.f. snack

*mezzogiorno* n.m. the midday sun; term for southern Italy

*minestra* n.f. soup

*minestra riscaldata* n.f. old reheated fare

*minestrone* n.f. a big, hearty soup

*mi piacerebbe* I would like, it would please me

*moglie* n.f. wife

*mozzo*  n.m. ship's boy
*muscolo*  n.m. muscle

## N

*naso*  n.m. nose
*nasone*  n.m. big nose
*nastrino*  n.m. ribbon
*nave*  n.f. ship
*nebbiolo*  n. the Piedmont wine
  whose name (little fog) describes
  the region's typical weather
*neutrino*  n.m. particle even smaller
  than the neutron, coined by
  Enrico Fermi
*ninna-nanna*  n.f. children's song
*nodi degli innamorati*  n.m. lovers'
  knots (type of cookie)
*nonna*  n.f. grandmother
*notaio*  n.m. professional scribes
*novella*  n.f. news or novelty
*nube*  n.f. cloud

## O

*occhi di Santa Lucia*  n.m. (pl.)
  literally "eyes of Santa Lucia,"
  circles of durum bread
*opera*  n.f. work
*opera amorosa*  n.f. labor of love
*opera buffa*  n.f. comic opera
*opera seria*  n.f. serious opera
*osteria*  n.f. originally a tavern;
  casual restaurant

## P

*padrone*  n.m. master of the house,
  owner
*pala*  n.f. shovel-like paddle that
  bakers used to slide loaves of
  bread from an oven
*palco*  n.m. ornate boxes of an
  opera house
*palla*  n.f. ball
*pancia*  n.f. belly
*pane*  n.m. bread
*panforte*  n.m. strong bread; a
  Sienese specialty
*panino*  n.m. a sandwich

*panni*  n.m.pl. rags
*pantaloni*  n.m.pl. pants
*paracadutista*  n.m. parachute
  jumper
*paradiso*  n.m. heaven, paradise
*parlare*  v. to speak
*parola*  n.f. word
*parolaccia*  n.f. dirty or bad language
*parolone*  n.f. big meaningless word
*parterre*  n.f. the open area in front
  of the stage
*pasticcio*  n.m. a hodgepodge,
  jumble, or mess; a common
  name for pie
*pasticcio di maccheroni*  n.m. meat
  and macaroni pie
*pazzo*  adj. crazy
*pellerossa*  n. American Indian;
  literally redskin
*pesce*  n.m. fish
*petrarchino*  n.m. small book
  popular in Renaissance
*petroliere texano*  n.m. Texas oilman
*pezzo*  n.m. piece
*piagnoni*  n.m.pl. snivelers and
  whiners; term for followers of
  the friar Savaranola in fifteenth-
  century Florence
*piazza*  n.f. a town square
*pici*  n.m.pl. rolled pasta, specialty
  of Umbria
*piede*  n.m. foot
*pietra dura*  m.f. hard stone
*pioggia*  n.f. rain
*piolo*  n.m. ladder's step, rung (*scala
  a pioli*  stepladder)
*pizzo, pizzetto*  n.m. little piece of
  hair; goatee and mustache
*poetucolo*  n.m. untalented poet
*polentoni*  n.m.pl. big eaters of
  polenta; slang for northern
  Italians
*polpettone*  n.m. a large meatball;
  slang for a worthless or banal
  movie
*popolo magro*  n.m. the skinny or
  poor people

*porca miseria*   the equivalent of "oh, damn"

*porca vacca*   damn cow; often substituted for *porca putana* (damn whore)

*pranzo*   n.m. lunch

*precipitazione*   n.f. rain

*prezzemolo*   n.m. parsley; slang for a busybody

*primavera*   n.f. spring; also the title of Botticelli's iconic painting

*primo*   n.m. first course of a meal

*principe*   n.m. prince

*problema*   n.m. problem (*problemino* small problem)

*prodigo*   n.m. spendthrift

*pronto*   adj. ready

*prosecco*   n.m. a sparkling Italian wine

*psichiatra*   n.m. psychiatrist

*pugno*   n.m. fist

*punto affettuoso*   n.m. an affectionate period; Renaissance term for the exclamation point

*purgatorio*   n.m. purgatory

*puttana*   n.f. a whore

*puttanesca*   n.f. savory sauce named for Italy's ladies of the evening

## Q

*qualcosa*   n.f. something

## R

*raccolta*   n.f. collection

*rammentare*   v. to remember (with the brain), for facts

*rassettatura*   n.f. a reordering

*riamato*   adj. reloved

*ricco*   n.m. rich

*ricordare*   v. to remember (with the 7

*rimembrare*   v. to remember (with the body), for physical sensations

*rinascita*   n.m. rebirth (root of "Renaissance")

*risorgimento*   n.m. resurgence (*Il*

*Risorgimento* was the campaign for the unification of Italy in the 1800s)

*Romanesco*   n.m. local Roman dialect

*rosolare*   v. to make golden, roast brown

*russare*   v. to snore

*ruvidezza*   n.f. roughness, used to describe Verdi's powerful music

## S

*sacchetto*   n.m. small sack

*saggio*   n.m. wise man

*salame*   n.m. salami; slang for a silly fool

*salvagente*   n.f. lifesaver

*salvare*   v. to save

*saper vedere*   to know how to see, a mantra from Leonardo da Vinci

*sapienza*   n.f. wisdom

*sbaffo*   n.m. smudge

*sbriciolare*   v. to crumble

*scala*   n.f. ladder, stairs

*scalco*   n.m. carver, steward

*scapigliati*   n.m.pl. loose, messy hair; members of Scapigliatura (an artistic movement founded in Lombardia in the late nineteenth century)

*scarpetta*   n.f. little shoe; reference to soaking up the last of pasta sauce with a bit of bread

*sceneggiatore*   n.m. scriptwriters

*scherno*   n.m. scorn, derision

*scherzare*   v. to joke

*schiavo*   n.m. slave

*sciacquare*   v. to rinse

*scilinguare*   v. to babble

*scilinguagnolo sciolto*   loquacity, gift of the gab, chattiness

*scimmia*   n.f. monkey

*scolatura*   n.f. the very last drop from a bottle of wine, dregs

*scopa*   n.m. a popular card game, from word for "sweep"

*scureggione*   n.m. an old fart

*secondo me*   according to me

*sedia, seggiola,* or *seggia*   n.f. chair, seat

*sempre libera*   always free, from Verdi's *La Traviata*

*seno*   n.m. breast or, more precisely, the delicate spot between a woman's breasts

*settimana*   n.f. week

*sfumatura*   n.f. nuance, subtle shading

*signora*   n.f. lady

*sistemarsi*   v. to organize one's life

*smacco*   n.m. defeat, failure, humiliation, shame

*smeraldo*   n.m. emerald

*smoking*   n.m. tuxedo

*società*   n.f. society

*socio*   n.m. member of a group

*sonetto*   n.m. little poem

*sorella, suora, sorore, serocchia, sirocchia, sorocchia, suoro*   n.f. sister, in various dialects

*sorridere*   v. to smile

*sostenitore*   n.m. supporter

*sovramagnificentissimamente*   adv. in a very, very, very magnificent way, a word coined by Dante

*spasimanti*   n.m.pl. literally "sufferers of spasms of love"

*spasimo*   n.m. spasms

*spazzare*   v. to sweep (*spazzamento* a good sweeping; *spazzatina* a dusting)

*spazzatura*   n.f. trash

*spazzola*   n.f. a brush (*spazzolino da denti* a toothbrush)

*spezzare*   v. to snap, to break (*un cuore spezzato* a broken heart)

*spiriti*   n.m. spirits

*spiritoso ignorante*   clever ignoramus

*sporcaccione*   n.m. dirty old man

*sporche*   adj. dirty

*spot*   n.m. commercial

*squillo*   n.m. telephone ring

*stalla*   n.f. horse stall or pigsty

*stella*   n.f. star

*stile gonfiato*   n.m. inflated style (of opera lyrics)

*storia*   n.f. history; story

*strada*   n.f. road

*stradaccia*   n.f. bad road

*stronzo*   n.m. vulgar word for excrement; turd

*strozzapreti*   n.m. priest-stranglers; type of rich pasta

*stupire*   v. to amaze, surprise, astonish

*stuzzicadenti*   n.m. toothpick

*suina*   n.f. swine

T

*tacchino*   n.m. turkey

*tavola imbandita*   n.f. an elegant table

*telefoni bianchi*   n.m. (pl.) white telephones; comic movies popular in Italy in the 1930s

*telefono azzurro*   n.m. twenty-four-hour hotline for abused children

*tempio*   n.m. temple

*tenerezza*   n.f. tenderness

*terra*   n.f. land

*terribilità*   n.f. terribleness, the word most associated with the forceful work and fierce temperament of Michelangelo

*terroni*   n.m.pl. peasants who work the land

*terzina*   n.f. type of rhyme

*testa*   n.f. head

*ti amo*   I love you (used only for the loves of one's life)

*tic-tac*   sound of clocks

*tiramisù*   n.m. literally "pick me up," popular layered Italian dessert

*ti voglio bene*   expression of love and affection that means "I wish you well"; conveys "I want all good things for you"

*tradizionale*   adj. traditional

*tremare*   v. to tremble

*tremendo*   adj. terrible

*triste*   adj. sad

*turpiloquio* n.m. the formal term for foul language

## U

*uffizio* n.m. office (now in use: *uffico*)

*università* n.f. first defined as a corporation, then as a body of students

## V

*valigia* n.f. suitcase

*vangelo* n.m. gospel

*vecchio* n.m. old

*velina* n.f. showgirl, scantily clad woman on television (*velinesco* slim and coy)

*venticello* n.m. nice little breeze

*vento* n.m. wind

*ventre* n.m. abdomen

*vermicelli* n.m.pl. little worms, type of thin pasta

*vincerò* v. "I will win," from Puccini's *Aida*

*viola* adj. violet

*VIP* n.m. very important person, pronounced "veep"

*viso* n.m. face, used more in written than in spoken Italian

*vizio* n.m. vice

*voglia* n.f. a wish, the first degree of desire

*voglio* v. (from *volero*) I want

*volgare* n.m. vernacular; now vulgar, gross

*volto* n.m. visage

## Z

*zanna* n.f. animal's fang

*zappa* n.f. farmer, hoe

*zerbinetto* n.m. lady killer

*zerbino* n.m. doormat, person so passive he is treated as a doormat

*zia* n.f. aunt

*zio* n.m. uncle

*zuccotto* n.m. sponge bombe filled with ice cream

*zuppa* n.f. soup

# Bibliography

GENERAL REFERENCES

Barzini, Luigi. *The Italians*. New York: Simon & Schuster, 1964.

Brand, Peter, and Lino Pertile, editors. *The Cambridge History of Italian Literature*. Cambridge: Cambridge University Press, 1996.

della Valle, Valeria, and Giuseppe Patota. *L'italiano: Biografia di una lingua*. Milan: Sperling & Kupfer Editori, 2006.

D'Epiro, Peter, and Mary Desmond Pinkowish. *Sprezzatura: 50 Ways Italian Genius Shaped the World*. New York: Anchor Books, 2001.

italian.about.com.

Kay, George R., editor. *The Penguin Book of Italian Verse*. New York: Penguin Books, 1958.

Migliorini, Bruno. *The Italian Language*. Abridged and recast by T. Gwynfor Griffith. London: Faber and Faber, 1966.

Nelsen, Elisabetta Properzi, and Christopher Concolino. *Literary Florence*. Siena: Nuova Immagine, 2006.

## Introduction: My Italian Brain and How It Grew

Lesser, Wendy, editor. *The Genius of Language*. New York: Pantheon Books, 2004.

Nadeau, Jean-Benoit, and Julie Barrow. *Sixty Million Frenchmen Can't Be Wrong*. New York: Sourcebooks, 2003.

## Confessions of an *Innamorata*

Brockmann, Stephen. "A Defense of European Languages." In *Inside Higher Education*. insidehighered.com., May 15, 2008.

Calabresi, Mario. *"Usa, la rivincita dell'italiano: è boom di corsi all'università."* *La Repubblica*, April 23, 2007: 17.

Duggan, Christopher. *A Concise History of Italy*. Cambridge: Cambridge University Press, 1984.

Esposito, Russell R. *The Golden Milestone*. New York: The New York Learning Library, 2003.

Falcone, Linda. *Italian Voices*. Illustrations by Leo Cardini. Florence: Florentine Press, 2007.

Hofmann, Paul. *That Fine Italian Hand*. New York: Henry Holt and Company, 1990.

Lepschy, Anna Laura, and Giulio Lepschy. *The Italian Language Today*. New York: Hutchinson, 1977.

Lepschy, Giulio. *Mother Tongues and Other Reflections on the Italian Language*. Toronto: University of Toronto Press, 2002.

Mondadori, Oscar. *Motti e proverbi dialettali delle regioni italiane*. Milan: A. Mondadori, 1977.

Tommaseo, Niccolò. *Dizionario dei sinonimi*. Milan: Vallardi, 1905.

## The Unlikely Rise of a Vulgar Tongue

Cattani, Alessandra. *L'italiano e i dialetti*. San Francisco: Centro Studi Italiani, 1993.

Consoli, Joseph. *The Novellino or One Hundred Ancient Tales: An Edition and Translation based on the 1525 Gualteruzzi editio princeps.* Routledge; 1 edition. 1997.

Lewis, R. W. B. *The City of Florence.* New York: Farrar, Straus and Giroux, 1995.

Maiden, Martin. *A Linguistic History of Italian.* London: Longman, 1995.

Menen, Aubrey. *Speaking the Language Like a Native.* New York: McGraw-Hill Book Company, Inc., 1962.

Migliorini, Bruno. *Storia della lingua italiana*, vols. 1 and 2. Florence: Sansoni Editore, 1988.

Montanelli, Indro. *Romans Without Laurels.* New York: Pantheon, 1959.

Pulgram, Ernst. *The Tongues of Italy.* Cambridge, MA: Harvard University Press, 1958.

Roberts, Mark. *Street-Names of Florence.* Florence: Coppini Tipografi Editori, 2001.

Spadolini, Giovanni. *A Short History of Florence.* Florence: Le Monnier, 1977.

Tartamella, Vito. *Parolacce.* Milan: BUR, 2006.

Usher, Jonathan. "Origins and Duecento." In *The Cambridge History of Italian Literature.* Peter Brand and Lino Pertile, editors. Cambridge: Cambridge University Press, 1996.

## To Hell and Back with Dante Alighieri

Alighieri, Dante. *The Divine Comedy.* Translated by John Ciardi. New York: New American Library, 1954.

———. *Inferno.* Translated by Robin Kirkpatrick. New York: Penguin Classics, 2006.

———. *Purgatorio.* Translated by Allen Mandelbaum. Drawings by Barry Moser. New York: Bantam, 1984.

Fei, Silvano. *Casa di Dante.* Florence: Museo Casa di Dante, 2007.

Gallagher, Joseph. *A Modern Reader's Guide to Dante's "The Divine Comedy."* Liguori, MO: Liguori/Triumph, 1999.

Lewis, R. W. B. *Dante.* New York: Viking Penguin, 2001.

Montanelli, Indro. *Dante e il suo secolo.* Milan: Rizzoli Editore, 1974.

Web edition, Dante's *Divine Comedy,* http://www.italianstudies.org/ comedy/index.htm. Center for Italian Studies, State University of New York at Stony Brook.

## ITALIAN'S LITERARY LIONS

Bargellini, Piero. "The Ladies in the Life of Lorenzo de' Medici." In *The Medici Women.* Florence: Arnaud, 2003.

Boccaccio, Giovanni. *The Decameron.* Edited and translated by G. H. McWilliam. New York: Penguin, 1972.

Brinton, Selwyn. *The Golden Age of the Medici.* London: Methuen & Company, 1925.

Burckhardt, Jacob. *The Civilization of the Renaissance in Italy.* New York: Modern Library, 2002.

Cesati, Franco. *The Medici.* Florence: Mandragora, 1999.

*"Chi vuol esser lieto, sia."* Florence: Accademia della Crusca, 2006.

Grafton, Anthony. *Leon Battista Alberti.* New York: Hill and Wang, 2000.

Hibbert, Christopher. *The Rise and Fall of the House of Medici.* New York: Penguin, 1974.

Montanelli, Indro, and Roberto Gervaso. *Italy in the Golden Centuries.* Translated by Mihaly Csikszentmihaly. Chicago: Henry Regnery Company, 1967.

Patota, Giuseppe. *Lingua e linguistica in Leon Battista Alberti.* Rome: Bulzoni, 1999.

Plumb, J. H. *The Italian Renaissance.* Boston: Houghton Mifflin, 1989.

Severgnini, Beppe. *L'italiano: Lezioni semiserie.* Milan: Rizzoli, 2007.

Winspeare, Massimo. *The Medici: The Golden Age of Collecting.* Florence: Sillabe, 2000.


THE BAKING OF A MASTERPIECE

Accademia della Crusca, www.accademiadellacrusca.it.

Aretino, Pietro. *Aretino's Dialogues.* Edited by Margaret Rosenthal. Translated by Raymond Rosenthal. New York: Marsilio, 1994.

Bondanella, Julia Conaway, and Mark Musa, editors. *The Italian Renaissance Reader.* New York: Penguin, 1987.

Harris, Joel, and Andrew Lang. *The World's Wit and Humor,* vol. 13, *Italian-Spanish.* New York: Review of Reviews Company, 1912.

Manacorda, Giuliano. *Storia della letteratura italiana.* Rome: Newton & Compton, 2004.

Norwich, John Julius. *The Italians: History, Art, and the Genius of a People.* New York: Portland House, 1983.


HOW ITALIAN CIVILIZED THE WEST

Bondanella, Peter, and Mark Musa, editors and translators. *The Portable Machiavelli.* New York: Viking Penguin, 1979.

Carollo, Sabrina. *Galateo per tutte le occasioni.* Florence: Giunti Demetra, 2006.

Castiglione, Baldesar. *The Book of the Courtier.* Edited by Daniel Javitch. Translated by Charles S. Singleton. New York: W. W. Norton, 2002.

della Casa, Giovanni. *Galateo.* Translated by Konrad Eisenbichler and Kenneth Bartlett. Toronto: University of Toronto Press, 1986.

McCarthy, Mary. *The Stones of Florence.* San Diego: Harcourt, 1963.

Roeder, Ralph. *The Man of the Renaissance.* New York: Viking Press, 1933.

Severgnini, Beppe. *L'italiano: Lezioni semiserie.* Milan: Rizzoli, 2007.

La Storia dell'Arte

Besdine, Matthew. *The Unknown Michelangelo.* Garden City, NY: Adelphi University Press, 1964.

Boase, T. S. R. *Giorgio Vasari: The Man and the Book.* Princeton, NJ: Princeton University Press, 1979.

Bronowski, J. "Leonardo da Vinci." In *The Italian Renaissance*, edited by J. H. Plumb. Boston: Houghton Mifflin, 1989.

Bull, George. *Michelangelo: A Biography.* New York: St. Martin's Griffin, 1998.

Buonarroti, Michelangelo. *Poems and Letters.* Translated by Anthony Mortimer. New York: Penguin Classics, 2007.

Clark, Kenneth. "The Young Michelangelo." In *The Italian Renaissance*, edited by J. H. Plumb. Boston: Houghton Mifflin, 1989.

Cole, Michael. *Sixteenth-Century Italian Art.* Malden, MA.: Blackwell, 2006.

Condivi, Ascanio. *The Life of Michelangelo.* Edited by Hellmut Wohl. Translated by Alice Sedgwick Wohl. University Park: Pennsylvania State University Press, 1976.

de Tolnay, Charles. "Michelangelo and Vittoria Colonna." In *Sixteenth-Century Italian Art*, edited by Michael Cole. Malden, MA.: Blackwell, 2006.

Hale, J. R., editor. *The Thames & Hudson Dictionary of the Italian Renaissance.* London: Thames & Hudson, 2006.

Hartt, Frederick, and David Wilkins. *History of Italian Renaissance Art*, 4th ed. Upper Saddle River, NJ: Prentice Hall and Harry N. Abrams, 1994.

King, Ross. *Brunelleschi's Dome.* New York: Penguin, 2000.

Langdon, Helen. *Caravaggio: A Life.* London: Chatto & Windus, 1998.

Nicholl, Charles. *Leonardo da Vinci: Flights of Mind.* New York: Penguin, 2004.

Nuland, Sherwin. *Leonardo da Vinci.* New York: Lipper/Penguin, 2000.

Puglisi, Catherine. *Caravaggio.* London: Phaidon Press, 1998.

Roscoe, Mrs. Henry. *Victoria Colonna: Her Life and Poems*. London: MacMillan & Company, 1868.

Sebregondi, Ludovica. *Giotto a Santa Croce*. Florence: Opera di Santa Croce, 2006.

Summers, David. *Michelangelo and the Language of Art*. Princeton, NJ: Princeton University Press, 1981.

van Loon, Hendrik Willem. *The Arts*. New York: Simon and Schuster, 1937.

Vasari, Giorgio. *The Lives of the Artists*. Translated by Julia Conaway Bondanella and Peter Bondanella. London: Oxford University Press, 1991.


## On Golden Wings

Berger, William. *Puccini Without Excuses*. New York: Vintage, 2005.

———. *Verdi with a Vengeance*. New York: Vintage, 2000.

Bleiler, Ellen, editor and translator. *Famous Italian Opera Arias*. Mineola, NY: Dover, 1996.

Bolt, Rodney. *The Librettist of Venice*. New York: Bloomsbury, 2006.

Carresi, Serena, et al. *L'italiano all'opera*. Rome: Bonacci, 1998.

Conrad, Peter. *A Song of Love and Death*. St. Paul, MN: Graywolf Press, 1987.

Dallapiccola, Luigi. *Dallapiccola on Opera*. Translated and edited by Rudy Shackelford. Milan: Toccata Press, 1987.

Da Ponte, Lorenzo. *Memoirs*. Translated by Elisabeth Abbott. New York: New York Review Books, 2000.

Duchartre, Pierre Louis. *The Italian Comedy*. New York: Dover Publications, 1966.

Gossett, Philip. *Divas and Scholars: Performing Italian Opera*. Chicago: University of Chicago Press, 1996.

Kimbell, David. *Italian Opera*. Cambridge: Cambridge University Press, 1995.

Noè, Daniela, and Frances A. Boyd. *L'italiano con l'opera.* New Haven, CT: Yale University Press, 2003.

Plotkin, Fred. *Opera 101.* New York: Hyperion, 1994.

Rosselli, John. *The Life of Verdi.* Cambridge: Cambridge University Press, 2000.

———. *Singers of Italian Opera.* Cambridge: Cambridge University Press, 1992.

Smith, Patrick. *The Tenth Muse: A Historical Study of the Opera Libretto.* New York: Schirmer, 1970.

Verdi, Giuseppe. *Verdi: The Man in His Letters.* Edited by Franz Werfel and Paul Stefan. Translated by Edward O. D. Downes. New York: Vienna House, 1970.

## EATING ITALIAN

Artusi, Pellegrino. *Science in the Kitchen and the Art of Eating Well.* Translated by Murtha Baca and Stephen Sartarelli. Toronto: University of Toronto Press, 2006.

Capatti, Alberto, and Massimo Montanari. *Italian Cuisine: A Cultural History.* Translated by Aine O'Healy. New York: Columbia University Press, 2003.

de' Medici, Lorenza. *Italy the Beautiful Cookbook.* Los Angeles: Knapp Press, 1988.

Dickie, John. *Delizia! The Epic History of Italians and Their Food.* New York: Free Press, 2008.

Ehlert, Trude. *Cucina medioevale.* Milan: Guido Tommasi Editore, 1995.

Field, Carol. *Celebrating Italy.* New York: Harper Perennial, 2007.

———. *In Nonna's Kitchen.* New York: HarperCollins, 1997.

Martino, Maestro. *The Art of Cooking: The First Modern Cookery Book.* Edited by Luigi Ballerini. Translated by Jeremy Parzen. Berkeley: University of California Press, 2005.

———. *Libro de art coquinaria.* Milan: Guido Tommasi Editore, 2001.

Nestor, Brook. *The Kitchenary: Dictionary and Philosophy of Italian Cooking.* New York: iUniverse, 2003.

Peschke, Hans-Peter von, and Werner Feldmann. *La cucina dell'antica Roma.* Milan: Guido Tommasi Editore, 1997.

———. *La cucina del rinascimento.* Milan: Guido Tommasi Editore, 1997.

Piras, Claudia, and Eugenio Medagliani, editors. *Culinaria Italy.* Cologne: Konemann, 2000.

Plotkin, Fred. *The Authentic Pasta Book.* New York: Fireside, 1985.


## So Many Ways to Say "I Love You"

*Amore e amicizia.* Milan: Baldini Castoldi Dalai, 2003.

Barzini, Luigi. *From Caesar to the Mafia.* New York: Library Press, 1971.

Casanova, Giacomo. *The Many Loves of Casanova.* Los Angeles: Holloway House, 2006.

Ginzburg, Natalia. *The Manzoni Family.* Translated by Marie Evans. London: Paladin Grafton Books, 1989.

Manzoni, Alessandro. *The Betrothed.* Translated by Bruce Penman. New York: Penguin, 1972.

Tommaseo, Niccolò. *Dizionario dei sinonimi.* Milan: Vallardi, 1905.

———. *D'amor parlando.* Palermo: Sellerio, 1992.


## Marcello and Me

Aprà, Adriano, and Patrizia Pistagnesi, editors. *The Fabulous Thirties: Italian Cinema 1929–1944.* Rome: Electa International Publishing Group, 1979.

Biagi, Enzo. *La bella vita: Marcello Mastroianni racconta.* Rome: Rizzoli, 1996.

Bondanella, Peter. *The Cinema of Federico Fellini.* Princeton, NJ: Princeton University Press, 1992.

———. *Italian Cinema: From Neorealism to the Present.* New York: Continuum, 2004.

Brunnetta, Gian Pietro. *Guida alla storia del cinema italiano 1905–2003*. Turin: Piccola Biblioteca Einaudi, 2003.

Comand, Mariapia. *Sulla carta: Storia e storie della sceneggiatura in Italia*. Turin: Lindau, 2006.

Dewey, Donald. *Marcello Mastroianni*. New York: Birch Lane Press, 1993.

Fellini, Federico. *Fellini on Fellini*. Translated by Isabel Quigley. New York: Da Capo Press, 1996.

Hochkofler, Matilde. *Marcello Mastroianni: The Fun of Cinema*. Edited by Patricia Fogarty. Rome: Gremese, 2001.

Iannucci, Amilcare, editor. *Dante, Cinema, and Television*. Toronto: University of Toronto Press, 2004.

Kezich, Tullio. *Federico: Fellini, la vita e i film*. Milan: Feltrinelli, 1990.

———. *Primavera a Cinecittà*. Rome: Bulzoni, 1999.

Maddoli, Cristina. *L'italiano al cinema*. Perugia: Guerra Edizioni, 2004.

Malerba, Luigi, and Carmine Siniscalco, editors. *Fifty Years of Italian Cinema*. Rome: Carlo Bestetti, 1959.

Mastroianni, Marcello. *Mi ricordo, sì, io mi ricordo*. Milan: Baldini & Castoli, 1997.

Reich, Jacqueline. *Beyond the Latin Lover: Marcello Mastroianni, Masculinity, and Italian Cinema*. Bloomington: Indiana University Press, 2004.

Rondi, Gian Luigi. *Italian Cinema Today, 1952–1965*. New York: Hill and Wang, 1966.

Scorsese, Martin. *My Voyage to Italy*. DVD. Cappa Production, 2001.

Sorlin, Pierre. *Italian National Cinema, 1896–1996*. London: Routledge, 1996.

Wood, Mary. *Italian Cinema*. New York: Berg, 2005.

## IRREVERENT ITALIAN

Caroli, Menico. *Proibitissimo*. Milan: Garzanti, 2003.

Delicio, Roland. *Merda!* Illustrations by Kim Wilson Eversz. New York: Plume, 1993.

Mueller, Tom. "Beppe's Inferno." In *The New Yorker*, February 4, 2008. www.newyorker.com/reporting/2008/02/04/080204fa_fact_mueller.

*Pronto? L'Italia censurata delle telefonate da Radio Radicale.* Milan: Mondadori, 1986.

Tartamella, Vito. *Parolacce.* Milan: BUR, 2006.

MOTHER TONGUE

Adamo, Giovanni, and Valeria della Valle. *Parole nuove 2006.* Milan: Sperling & Kupfer Editore, 2007.

della Valle, Valeria, and Giuseppe Patota. *Il nuovo salvalingua.* Milan: Sperling & Kupfer Editore, 2007.

———. *Le parole giuste.* Milan: Sperling & Kupfer Editore, 2004.

De Mauro, Tullio. *Storia linguistica dell'Italia unita.* Rome: Editori Laterza, 2005.

Lepschy, Anna Laura, and Giulio Lepschy. *The Italian Language Today.* New York: Hutchinson, 1977.

Lepschy, Giulio. *Mother Tongues and Other Reflections on the Italian Language.* Toronto: University of Toronto Press, 2002.

Murray, William. *City of the Soul: A Walk in Rome.* New York: Crown Journeys, 2003.

Pulgram, Ernst. *The Tongues of Italy.* Cambridge, MA: Harvard University Press, 1958.

Sabatini, Francesco. *La lingua e il nostro mondo.* Turin: Loescher Editore, 1978.

Severgnini, Beppe. *La testa degli italiani.* Milan: Rizzoli, 2005.

*Reader's Guide*

1. The subtitle of this book is *My Love Affair with Italian, the World's Most Enchanting Language*. In what ways does Dianne Hales's relationship with Italian qualify as a romantic one? What does her use of this term imply about her feelings for Italy's language and culture?

2. In the first chapter, Hales describes how she looked for *Domani Mattina* to help retrieve her lost suitcase in Milan. Her quest for "Mr. Tomorrow Morning" motivated her to start studying Italian. Have you had similar linguistic stumbles in your travels? What kind of experiences did they lead to?

3. Hales traces Italian's history back thousands of years to the *volgare*, the street Latin of ancient Rome, which gave rise to all the Romance languages. In other countries, the dialect of the most powerful city evolved into the national language. Why didn't that happen in Italy? What were the consequences?

4. On pages 20 to 27 Hales gives examples of the wit, vitality, and versatility of Italian words. Do you have any favorites? What does the playfulness of Italian terms tell you about the language?

5. Hales says she resisted reading Dante's *Divine Comedy*. Can you understand why? Did her comparison of this epic poem to the *Harry Potter* series or to a Hollywood movie change the way you think of it? Why does Dante mean so much to Italians?

6. L'Accademia della Crusca (the Academy of the Bran), described on pages 113–121, is certainly not a conventional linguistic society. What does its creation say about Italians' views of food and of language? Can you understand why Hales was so moved to visit La Crusca and to see a first edition of *Il Vocabolario*?

7. *Bella figura* is one of the most complex aspects of Italian life. Hales came to appreciate it fully when she visited a dying professor. Did her chapter on "How Italian Civilized the West" provide any new insights as to why appearance and social grace matter so much to Italians?

8. Most people associate the great Renaissance masters Leonardo da Vinci and Michelangelo only with works of art. Did learning about their writing and their love of words add to your appreciation of these artists?

9. Hales contends that opera could not have emerged in any country other than Italy. What do you think are the Italian qualities that contributed to this musical genre? Were you aware of the role Verdi's operas played in the campaign to unify the Italian nation? Why do you think his music had such an impact?

10. Italian food and language, Hales says, "meld together as smoothly as *cacio sui maccheroni* (cheese on macaroni)." Discuss the colorful ways that Italians use gastronomic terms in everyday conversation. What did learning the history of such universal favorites as pasta and pizza add to your appreciation of these dishes?

11. In "So Many Ways to Say I Love You," Hales searches for the reasons for Italians' love of *amore* in their stories. Were you surprised

to find that many Italian love stories end tragically—including the true story of Casanova's life? Why do you think this is so? Hales comes to share the Italian appreciation for romantic gestures. Do you think this explains her behavior with the older gentleman in Venice?

12. "Movies," Hales says, "taught Italians how to be Italian." Why does she make this assertion? Do you agree? Were you aware of the use of dubbing in movies shown in Italy? Why do you think dubbing is much less popular in the United States?

13. Some of the oldest and most colorful Italian terms are *le parolacce* (bad or naughty words). How do they differ from obscenities in other languages? Do you agree with the author of the book *Parolacce* that civilizations couldn't exist without vulgarities and curses? In your opinion, have Italians elevated swearing to an unconventional art form?

14. The Romans and their descendants, a linguist observed, thrice conquered the world: once in government, once in religion, and once in art. To this trio of triumphs, he added a fourth: language. By the end of her book, Hales comes to agree. Do you understand why she "wholeheartedly agrees that Italian is indeed the language of humanity—and therefore everyone's mother tongue"?

15. Despite her many years studying the language, Hales still finds herself struggling to understand everyday Italian. Her tutor tells her that's the difference between "learning Italian and living Italian." What do you think she means? Is it possible to "live" a second language? What would it require?

16. Although it ranks nineteenth as a spoken language (in numbers of speakers), Italian has become the fourth most studied language in the world. After reading *La Bella Lingua*, can you understand its appeal?